ADVANCE PRAISE FOR # Uplifting a People

"*Uplifting a People* is an important contribution to the ongoing study of African American philanthropy. The book documents how both individual African Americans and their institutions have given their time, talent, and money to create opportunities, often where none existed. It is essential reading for anyone interested in learning more about African American philanthropy."

Emmett D. Carson, President and CEO, The Minneapolis Foundation and Author of A Hand Up: Black Philanthropy and Self Help in America

"These essays not only educate but challenge older perceptions of philanthropy. Informed by fresh research and disciplined analysis, they offer valuable new insights on key aspects of an important and often neglected topic. As a whole, they illuminate the many ways in which various expressions of African American philanthropy have been a form of agency that addressed the needs of a disadvantaged group; frequently influenced the giving and thinking of those who exercised power through their ability to bestow gifts of money, time, and ideas; and profoundly shaped social policy and social thought in the United States."

Alfred A. Moss, Jr., Associate Professor of History, University of Maryland, College Park and Co-author of From Slavery to Freedom: A History of African Americans

Uplifting
a People

PETER LANG
New York • Washington, D.C./Baltimore • Bern
Frankfurt am Main • Berlin • Brussels • Vienna • Oxford

Uplifting a People

African American Philanthropy and Education

EDITED BY

Marybeth Gasman and
Katherine V. Sedgwick

PETER LANG
New York • Washington, D.C./Baltimore • Bern
Frankfurt am Main • Berlin • Brussels • Vienna • Oxford

Library of Congress Cataloging-in-Publication Data

Uplifting a people: African American philanthropy and education /
edited by Marybeth Gasman, Katherine V. Sedgwick.
p. cm.
Includes bibliographical references and index.
1. African Americans—Charities. 2. African Americans—Charitable contributions. 3. African
American philanthropists. 4. Endowments—United States. I. Gasman, Marybeth.
II. Sedgwick, Katherine, V.
HV3181.U64 361.7′4′08996073—dc22 2004020882
ISBN 0-8204-7475-4 (hardcover)
ISBN 0-8204-7474-6 (paperback)

Bibliographic information published by **Die Deutsche Bibliothek**.
Die Deutsche Bibliothek lists this publication in the "Deutsche
Nationalbibliografie"; detailed bibliographic data is available
on the Internet at http://dnb.ddb.de/.

Cover design by Lisa Barfield

The paper in this book meets the guidelines for permanence and durability
of the Committee on Production Guidelines for Book Longevity
of the Council of Library Resources.

© 2005 Peter Lang Publishing, Inc., New York
275 Seventh Avenue, 28th Floor, New York, NY 10001
www.peterlangusa.com

Printed in the United States of America

Table of Contents

Acknowledgments

Over the past ten years, I have concentrated my research efforts on issues related to African American higher education. In doing so, I've explored the contributions of wealthy White industrialists to the Black community. I've also tried to understand the complex relationships that existed between these industrial philanthropists and the African American recipients. Although there is merit in exploring these types of issues, I began to notice the dearth of scholarship on African Americans, both well-known and unknown, who have contributed philanthropically to Black persons and causes throughout history. As a result, I asked a group of U.S. scholars to submit essays that illuminate the lives and actions of such African Americans. *Uplifting a People* is, in part, the result of my curiosity and the response of other scholars interested in African American philanthropy.

I am grateful to several people for their support during the writing and editing of this book. First and foremost, my colleague and co-editor, Kate Sedgwick, helped enormously—editing, proofing, and helping to make sometimes difficult decisions about the direction of the book. I thank all of the authors who contributed to this book. They worked diligently and sometimes quickly to produce a comprehensive group of essays. I am also indebted to my colleague Matt Hartley at the University of Pennsylvania. His upbeat personality and enjoyment of life are a welcome pleasure in the academic environment. As with most projects with which I am involved, I am grateful to those who have mentored me throughout my academic career, including Andrea Walton, Wayne J. Urban, Asa G. Hilliard, Anthony E. Hargrove, B. Edward McClellan, and John Thelin.

On a more personal note, I offer thanks to my husband, Edward M. Epstein. Edward not only contributed a chapter to this volume of essays but provided support and motivation to me throughout the editing process. Lastly, I am thankful to my daughter, Chloe Sarah Epstein. She provides amazing joy during times of stress!

Marybeth Gasman

First and foremost, I would like to thank my mentor and colleague, Marybeth Gasman, for inviting me to join her on this project. It has been a privilege working with and learning from her, and I daily realize how truly fortunate I am to have her as an advisor and model. I am also indebted to the authors of these chapters, who have worked hard and often quickly, responding to two rather opinionated editors.

The University of Pennsylvania has been a wonderful place to be a graduate student, and I am grateful for the support and flexibility I have received from my department as I have pursued my studies. My professors—particularly Marvin Lazerson, Matt Hartley, and Sarah Igo—have provided much-needed intellectual stimulation and inspiration, and my colleague Ann Tiao has been a fantastic office mate and fellow-learner, often helping me to look at ideas from new angles.

Lastly, I would like to thank my family, who from the beginning raised me to believe in the power and importance of education, and my dad, who did not balk at his 16-year-old daughter going 3,000 miles away to finish high school. This has made all the difference. My dear friend and roommate, Melanie Brown—computer fixer extraordinaire, wonderful cook, and encourager—has kept me sane, taken over my chores when I was too busy, and reminded me that it's ok to play occasionally.

Kate Sedgwick

The editors, as well as the chapter authors, are grateful to the many people affiliated with archives and manuscript collections who assisted us with acquiring information for this book. The following collections were used:

The United Negro College Fund Papers, The Robert Woodruff Library, The Atlanta University Center, Atlanta, Georgia

The C. Eric Lincoln Papers, The Robert Woodruff Library, The Atlanta University Center, Atlanta, Georgia

Special Collections, Skillman Library, Lafayette College, Easton, Pennsylvania

The General Education Board Papers, Rockefeller Archive Center, Sleepy Hollow, New York

The United Negro College Fund Oral History Collection, Columbia University, New York, New York.

Schomburg Center for Electronic Text and Images, University of Pennsylvania, Philadelphia, Pennsylvania

Maryland State Archives, Baltimore, Maryland

Urban Archives Center, University Library, California State University

Howard Thurman Collection, Mugar Memorial Library, Boston University, Boston, Massachusetts

Alabama Moments in History, Alabama Department of Archives and History, Birmingham, Alabama

Special Collections, Tuskegee University, Tuskegee, Alabama

The Library of Congress, Washington, D.C.

Introduction

MARYBETH GASMAN AND KATHERINE V. SEDGWICK

According to a report issued by the 1999 Council on Foundations,

> The term "philanthropy" in America has long been associated with a relatively small number of White families and individuals who enjoyed access to education, owned major businesses, held leadership positions in government, dominated the professions and inherited wealth.[1]

Because much of African American giving falls outside of this narrow scope, those who study philanthropy have often overlooked it. African Americans are typically looked upon as recipients of philanthropic efforts, but scholars rarely examine the contributions made by members of this group.[2] For example, scholarship on the history of historically Black colleges and universities has tended to focus on the problematic role of White industrial philanthropists in building institutional curricula. While this is an important topic, it is also essential to consider the role of Blacks in shaping their own institutions and communities—their agency and its impact. This concept of agency—"the assumed ability of individuals to shape the conditions of their lives"—is the core of the conceptual framework for this volume of essays.[3] We view African Americans as active participants in philanthropic and fundraising processes.

The origins of Black giving and the organizations around which it is focused are rooted in efforts to overcome oppression. The communalism and social solidarity that mark the African American experience trace back to ancestral roots in Africa. A strong network of mutual aid and community support was critical to surviving slavery. Black churches, the first Black-owned and operated institutions, played a central role in early social services and education, and they continue to be a focal point for Black philanthropy. The history of Black philanthropy shows that Blacks are motivated by those who are close to them and inspired to join efforts that make a difference in the daily lives of other African Americans. As mentioned, in many cases Black philanthropy has been a response to discrimination—in the past, slavery and segregation; today, inequality in education and the workplace.

The chapters in this edited volume focus on the philanthropic efforts of African American individuals and groups. Examining a wide variety of philanthropic endeavors and placing a special emphasis on education, these essays explore three related questions. First, how did African Americans shape society through philanthropic contributions and service? Second, what has been the role of African American philanthropists in defining the future of the African American population as a whole? Third, how have African American philanthropists supported the education of the Black population, other racial and ethnic minorities, and the White population? In exploring these issues, the essays draw upon a broad spectrum of research methods, including historical inquiry, case study, visual communications, and biography.

Education and philanthropy have been defined differently at various times by different audiences. For this reason, we provide working definitions to guide the essays included in this book. We define education broadly to include both formal and informal education.[4] We explore the impact of African American philanthropists on diverse educational institutions such as schools, colleges and universities, community centers, clubs, churches, the courts, and society as a whole.

Likewise, we use a wide-reaching definition of philanthropy. Originating from the Greek word meaning "love to mankind," the meaning of philanthropy is contextual and is continually evolving.[5] Until the late 1800s, scholars and practitioners defined philanthropy as both financial giving and volunteering time and services. At times, particularly after World War II, the prevailing understanding of philanthropy narrowed and became tantamount to financial support from wealthy individuals and foundations.[6] More recent scholars of philanthropy, however, have sought to re-explore philanthropic traditions in an effort to provide a more multifaceted view of philanthropic action and motivations and to be more reflective of philanthropic efforts in communities of color. Drawing upon the current literature, the definition of philanthropy for this group of essays embraces financial giving, the giving of time through volunteerism, and the commitment of self to a cause. This broader definition is critical for considering the depth and variety of African American contributions, including the many forms and examples of philanthropy that are not recorded by majority organizations and mainstream research.

Philanthropy is based on social relationships that are meaningful for both the benefactors and beneficiaries.[7] In addition to identifying the financial contributions of African Americans to educational activities, we will focus on "relationships of power, exchange of information, and the process of education between giver and receiver."[8] As the essays in this book demonstrate, the history of philanthropy and African American education is more complex than a story of unselfish giving versus manipulation. Together, the introduction, essays, and bibliography reflect the historical roots of African American philanthropy and the changing nature of African American philanthropy.

In chapter one, "Nineteenth-Century Traditions of Benevolence and Education: Toward a Conceptual Framework of Black Philanthropy," Jayne Beilke discusses the origins of African American philanthropy, specifically its response to slavery, Jim Crow, and segregation. Beilke complicates our understanding of self-help as it relates to the Black community and shows us the diversity among philanthropic actions. Her work explores churches, education, and mutual aid societies, making current connections to past struggles and accomplishments. Throughout her exploration of nineteenth-century philanthropy, Beilke reminds us that African American giving places an emphasis on one's connectedness to a larger community—especially one's obligation to that community.

Jeff Mullins' "Standing on Their Own: African American Engagements with Educational Philanthropy in Antebellum America" raises the question—"Is any act of philanthropy ever truly selfless?" In telling the story of two slaves and their different paths to freedom, Mullins examines the motives behind the philanthropy of White benefactors, some of whom were also slave owners. The philanthropy of many of these men was aimed at getting Blacks out of America by resettling freed slaves in the new African colony of Liberia, created for this purpose. Yet more importantly, Mullins shows us how the recipients of this philanthropy—in this case slaves—craftily interacted with their so-called benefactors in order to garner and maintain their support and how they ultimately used it to further their own interests and the lives of other African Americans.

In chapter three, "Booker T. Washington: Philanthropy and Aesthetics," Michael Bieze takes on a giant in the field of history of education—James D. Anderson. Although Bieze acknowledges the validity of Anderson's arguments related to industrial philanthropists and philanthropy—that the core ideology of industrial philanthropy was to squelch civil rights and to enforce Black subordination—he urges us to take a more nuanced look at Booker T. Washington, often criticized as a mere pawn in the games of White men. Bieze shows us a Washington who was a skilled fundraiser—as evidenced, for example, by subtle differences in tone and message when he addressed northern White audiences versus southern Black audiences—who served his own agenda and not that of the industrialist philanthropists. Bieze delves deep into Washington's life, showing us how the "Wizard of Tuskegee" exploited art and culture to make himself and his initiatives attractive to donors.

In chapter four, "Creating an Image for Black College Fundraising: An Illustrated Examination of the United Negro College Fund's Publicity, 1944–1960," Marybeth Gasman and Edward M. Epstein explore the use of visual images in fundraising efforts by the United Negro College Fund (UNCF). Using a visual communication lens, Gasman and Epstein capture the evolving image of Black colleges in the mid-twentieth century and the UNCF's ability to mold its fundraising campaigns to fit any audience. The authors juxtapose the operations of the UNCF with issues of the Cold War, thus revealing a calculated strategy for raising funds for the education of Blacks.

Noah D. Drezner, in "Thurgood Marshall: A Study of Philanthropy through Racial Uplift," asks us to take a fresh look at Thurgood Marshall, the Supreme Court Justice and NAACP attorney renowned for his years of dedicated pursuit of legal equality for all. Marshall's crucial role in the Civil Rights Movement has been well documented; by using an emerging definition of philanthropy, Drezner shows us that Marshall's work should also be understood as the truest philanthropy. Although Marshall's philanthropic work was also his profession—for which he was of course remunerated—Drezner provides a convincing argument that Marshall's role extended beyond the confines of a regular job to become a philanthropic cause. His dedication to fighting injustice and segregation was a profound contribution to racial uplift.

In chapter six, "The Links, Incorporated: Advocacy, Education, and Service in the African American Community," Kijua Sanders-McMurtry and Nia Woods Haydel offer a poignant example—in the elite women's social group of The Links—of wealthy and privileged African Americans acting as philanthropists. Although at first glance this may appear to be the story of check-writing women from the upper class aiding the poor and downtrodden, Sanders-McMurtry and Haydel show us that The Links is an effective combination of traditional philanthropy (monetary giving) and African American philanthropy (giving of oneself and of one's time). In exploring this influential group of women, the authors call into question ideas of elitism and exclusion within the African American community and juxtapose these notions with the benefits of philanthropy.

Fred H. Downs, in his chapter "A. G. Gaston: A Story of Philosophy, Perseverance, and Philanthropy," examines the life of a destitute boy turned capitalist, then turned philanthropist. Downs shows us a complex man whose life and ideas brought together the progressive (upon retirement Gaston sold his company to his employees at a fraction of its worth), the stereotypical "Uncle Tom" (Gaston refused to speak out in favor of Civil Rights leaders), and the paradoxical (he later bailed out those same leaders when they went to jail). Downs crafts a story that details the growth of Gaston's economic empire, the influence of Booker T. Washington on Gaston's personal philosophy, and lastly Gaston's philanthropic endeavors aimed at redistributing wealth for the uplift of Blacks.

In chapter eight, "Not in Vain: The Philanthropic Endeavors of C. Eric Lincoln," Darryl Holloman shows us the life of a scholar—C. Eric Lincoln—who benefited from White philanthropy and, in turn, used these funds to shape an area of research and encourage junior scholars to pursue the study of African American history. Holloman argues that looking at Lincoln as merely a recipient without agency dehumanizes him and fails to see the ways in which African Americans worked with White philanthropists, and sometimes manipulated them, to uplift the race.

In "Howard Thurman: A Life Journey for Service, Religion, and Philanthropy," Mark Giles examines the life and actions of Howard Thurman, one of the most influential ministers of his time. Much like Noah Drezner does with Thurgood Marshall, Giles asks us to consider the life of this minister as philanthropic. Thurman, according to Giles, held more than a job; his profession became a profession of himself and his beliefs. In looking at the life of Thurman, Giles also explores the pivotal role of the Black church during a time when Blacks were turned away from White churches, organizations, and cemeteries.

In chapter ten, "Quiet Grace, Clothed Spirit: Oseola McCarty and the Benevolence of a Gift," Marci Middleton introduces us to a simple Mississippi laundress, Oseola McCarty, who exemplified the "everyman" of philanthropy. Her own educational ambitions thwarted due to poverty and tragic family circumstances, McCarty saved her meager earnings for seven decades and eventually built a small fortune that she used to provide educational opportunities for African American students. Part of what is so remarkable about McCarty's story, according to Middleton, is how unremarkable she herself thought it was. With a firm belief in religion and frugality and a desire to help others and uplift her race, McCarty made her donation without fanfare and was somewhat bewildered by the commotion it caused. By sharing McCarty's actions and her response to the reaction of others, Middleton shows us the essence of the ethic of giving in the Black community.

The final chapter, "A Gift of Art: Jacob Lawrence as Philanthropist" by Edward M. Epstein, examines the life and art of painter Jacob Lawrence, asking us to consider Lawrence's art and activism as philanthropic. Although Lawrence started a foundation to help young Black artists, Epstein urges us to look beyond this obvious philanthropic act to see Lawrence's work—which provided a window into society and culture and thereby offered to us a way to see ourselves—as itself a philanthropic gift. By urging us to consider if and how professional work, political activism, and philanthropy may intersect, Epstein shows that these distinctions are quite blurry and expands the margins of what is typically considered philanthropic.

In addition to the overarching themes of this collection articulated at the beginning of the introduction, each of these chapters connects to others in interesting—and sometimes surprising—ways. While all are about philanthropy and education, other imbricated themes emerge. For example, the chapters by Bieze, Epstein, and Gasman and Epstein all deal with art as it relates to philanthropy, yet Bieze's chapter also resonates with Fred H. Downs' exploration of a man influenced by Booker T. Washington and with Jeffrey Mullins' analysis of two slaves' seeming acquiescence to White demands in order to achieve their own ends. Edward M. Epstein's chapter, which argues that a man's professional work can also be seen as philanthropic, makes a claim similar to that articulated by Noah D. Drezner's work on Thurgood Marshall and Mark Giles's chapter on Howard Thurman. The chapter on the fundraising techniques of the UNCF by Marybeth Gasman and Edward M. Epstein shares with Kijua Sanders-McMurtry's and Nia Woods Haydel's chapter a focus on a philanthropic organization rather than an individual person. Other themes—such as religion, the role of fundraisers, the notion of self-help, the Civil Rights Movement, and legalized segregation—emerge throughout. This list is incomplete, but we will leave other themes, and the ways they connect across and within chapters, to the reader to discern.

Lastly, we have included a bibliography of pertinent works related to African American philanthropy. In some cases these references are directly from the individual chapters, however, most refer to supplemental works that may further your understanding of the subject.

Because this is an edited book, we left several items up to the individual authors. For example, the authors have chosen to define philanthropy as it relates to their individual chapter subjects. In addition, individual authors were given the liberty to use either African American or Black in discussing their subject matter, and the choice of whether or not they felt words such as Black and White should be capitalized.

Marybeth Gasman
Kate Sedgwick
University of Pennsylvania
Philadelphia, Pennsylvania

NOTES

1. Council on Foundations, "Cultures of Caring: Philanthropy in Diverse American Communities," Washington, D.C. 1999, 7.

2. Cheryl Hall Russell and Robert H. Kasberg, *African American Traditions of Giving and Serving: A Midwest Perspective* (Indianapolis: Indiana Center on Philanthropy, 1997).

3. Meredith D. Gall, Walter R. Borg, and Joyce P. Gall, *Educational Research* (New York: Longman, 1996), 610.

4. Informal does not imply less important.

5. *Oxford English Dictionary*, accessed on-line, 13 October 2002.

6. Andrea Walton, ed., *Women, Philanthropy, and Education* (Bloomington: Indiana University Press, 2003).

7. Susan Ostrander and Paul G. Schervish, "Giving and Getting: Philanthropy as a Social Relation," in Jon Van Til and Associates, *Critical Issues in American Philanthropy: Strengthening Theory and Practice* (San Francisco: Jossey-Bass, 1990).

8. Walton, ed., *Women, Philanthropy, and Education*, 6.

CHAPTER ONE

Nineteenth-Century Traditions of Benevolence and Education

Toward a Conceptual Framework of Black Philanthropy

JAYNE R. BEILKE

In Toni Morrison's acclaimed novel *Beloved*, the character Denver goes to the home of Lady Jones, her former teacher, and asks to work in exchange for food. Lady Jones tells her that no one she knows could afford to pay someone to do work they could do for themselves. But if it is food that Denver needs, she has only to ask. She goes on to mention her church's committee, "invented so nobody had to go hungry."[1] Afterwards, offerings of food appear on the property where Denver lives with her mother, a haunted former slave. Eventually, Denver decides to stop relying on the charity of neighbors and chooses to "hire herself out somewhere."[2] In so doing, she takes the first steps toward independence and her own salvation.

Morrison's vignette personifies the spirit and nature of African American philanthropy as it emerged during the nineteenth century. The traditions of Black philanthropy emphasize the importance of one's connection to the larger community and the primacy of the church as an institutional form of charity.[3] Denver's decision to "hire herself out" as a domestic servant is also consistent with an early and persistent emphasis on self-help. But although the self-help philosophy has drawn much attention from historians (due in large part to its association with Black leader Booker T. Washington),[4] self-help is only one aspect of African American philanthropy. Representative of a wide range of traditions and patterns, African American philanthropy is a complex blend of charitable impulse and political, social, and economic activism. It is also distinguished by a persistent emphasis on education, both formal and non-formal, and ranging from basic literacy to advanced professional education.

Derived from Greek and Latin words meaning "the love of mankind," the term "philanthropy" has been associated positively with charity, civic spirit, and humanitarianism as well as social control of the poor since the seventeenth century. Coming of age in the United States with the rise of industrial philanthropy during the twentieth century, the term currently refers to private, voluntary financial giving, individually and collectively, for the good of others.[5] For reasons of race and class however, African American philanthropy has not been well established in the scholarship on philanthropy.[6] Instead, the field of philanthropic studies has focused largely upon the actions of powerful White donors who amassed large fortunes during the Gilded Age, such as Andrew Carnegie, Julius Rosenwald, John D. Rockefeller, and others. Studies of nineteenth-century educational philanthropy have concentrated on northern philanthropists such as industrialist John F. Slater and Philadelphia Quaker Anna T. Jeanes, who contributed money in support of Black literacy and industrial training during the Reconstruction period. In addition to focusing on White benevolence to Blacks, the philanthropic literature has often cast southern Blacks, in particular, as passive recipients of northern charity. Since the historical narratives of this philanthropy have largely been the products of the funds themselves, this characterization is not surprising.[7]

According to historians Eric Anderson and Alfred A. Moss, Jr., "both celebrators and critics of philanthropy have sometimes treated blacks as more or less helpless victims or mostly passive objects of charity."[8] Revisionist scholars, most notably educational historian James D. Anderson, have begun to balance our understanding of African Americans' role in philanthropy, and the full measure of Black benevolence has emerged. This newer scholarship provides needed nuance to the picture of African Americans and philanthropy in the nineteenth century, showing the many ways in which Blacks themselves were philanthropists in and for their communities, and demonstrating their active participation in the philanthropy of others even when on the so-called receiving end.

Self-help, charity, voluntarism, and the more formalized expressions of philanthropy have a long history in the African American community.[9] Viewed against the backdrop of slavery, emancipation, and the development of southern public education, the nineteenth century emerges as a formative period in the history of African American philanthropy. This chapter explores the nineteenth-century origins and characteristics of African American philanthropy within the framework of its imbrications with education and social uplift. African American philanthropy developed differently than White benevolence due to Black Americans' experience as an enslaved and oppressed group. But if slavery was the crucible within which an African American identity was forged, it was also the condition that tempered all aspects of African American culture and tradition, before and after emancipation. Black philanthropy is both a response to and an outgrowth of the institution of slavery. As a condition of the African American experience in the United States, slavery and racism, its descendant, give shape and substance to Black institutions. By examining several models of Black benevolence, distinct patterns and impulses of African American philanthropy can be discerned.

To a great degree, African American philanthropy is the formalization of spontaneous acts of Black benevolence. Although its roots can be found in the eighteenth century, the traditions of African American philanthropy come to fruition in the nineteenth century as the result of emancipation. This chapter examines the integral connection between benevolence and education, the formalization of Black philanthropy, the motivations of early Black philanthropists, and the use of Black philanthropy as an instrument of social activism. The evolution of Black philanthropy during the nineteenth century necessarily reveals much about White philanthropy during this period as well, particularly the skillful manipulation of White philanthropy by Blacks who used it to further Black self-determination.

As it developed in the United States, Black philanthropy ranged from singular, spontaneous acts of charity (such as that exemplified in Morrison's *Beloved*) to philanthropy organized in and channeled through institutions. Institutionally, the development of Black welfare services was intimately connected to Black churches and schools. Within both free and enslaved communities, the church evolved as one of the few institutions controlled and operated primarily by Black people. The church therefore developed a powerful role in the Black community, was the source of a clerical leadership class, and served as a means of diffusing the church's message of mutual concern and support for church members throughout the larger Black community. According to historian Ira Berlin, the antebellum church "expressed the community's social conscience by aiding the poor, supporting missionary activities, and helping other free Negro communities establish like institutions."[10] Although some religious historians credit the Judeo-Christian tradition for the charitable nature of the church, sociologist and historian W. E. B. Du Bois credited the Black church's African roots: " . . . the African clan life of blood relatives became the clan life of the plantation; religious leader became the head of the religious activity of slaves, and of whatever group was left." Du Bois continued that, with emancipation, "the minister added political and economic functions to his religious duties."[11] Sociologist E. Franklin Frazier regarded the Black church as the basis of social cohesion in the Black community, whose functions included social control, the development of economic cooperation, and the provision of refuge in a hostile White world.[12] After Reconstruction, the church was the main source of the development of clubs and organizations founded to benefit the Black community and its members.[13]

Second in importance only to churches, Blacks saw schools as integral to achieving racial uplift and self-advancement. For southern African Americans in particular, literacy was seen as a means to liberation as well as a functional skill. Barred from learning to read by restrictive "Black Codes" passed by southern and border states prior to Emancipation, literacy—and education in general—emerged as a priority for freed Blacks and an object of Black philanthropy.[14]

As for southern education, there was no system of universal schooling in the south until after the Civil War. While some free Blacks attended private schools in the south, enslaved Blacks were forbidden to attend schools. This situation did not change until Emancipation, when northern benevolent societies and church organizations sent men and women to the south as teachers. The Bureau of Refugees, Freedmen and Abandoned Lands, which was attached to the Union army, was responsible for sponsoring thousands of teachers and building hundreds of schools during the period 1866–1870. It was also during this period that the first historically Black institutions of higher education began as little more than elementary schools. As direct products of philanthropy, the teachers and schools sponsored by benevolent organizations and churches led directly to the development of a system of public education in the south. The Black churches and schools were often closely associated, as churches sponsored private education for Blacks, who were excluded from White schools. Generally, the Black community established only Sabbath and primary schools, although there are some examples of secondary schools that were sponsored by larger congregations.[15]

Northern Blacks in the antebellum period, barred from good educational opportunities, also worked together to provide for their children that which society was denying them. For example, before 1822 there were no publicly funded schools for Black children in Philadelphia. Private academies invariably refused to admit Black pupils, and the charity schools for Blacks generally offered only a basic or vocational education for poor children. While Black parents could teach their children literacy and numeracy at home, middle-class families, in particular, desired a classical-liberal education for their children rather than a rudimentary or vocational curriculum. Two families whose concern for their own children had extended to a concern for the wider community of color pooled their resources in 1819 to start their own elementary school. They hired a White male teacher by the name of Britton E. Chamberlain, who helped the school grow in numbers and reputation for academic excellence. The second teacher of the school was the daughter of one of the founding families, who went on to establish a female academy for Black girls. After the Civil War she continued to train teachers, not only for Black schools in the north but also for Black schools in the south.[16]

Fanny Jackson Coppin and Mary Jane Patterson, the first Black American women to obtain four-year college degrees (from Oberlin College), served as educational philanthropists in an even more direct way. In 1852, Orthodox Quakers chartered the Institute for Colored Youth, the only private school in Philadelphia that offered secondary course work for African Americans and prepared graduates for teaching careers. Originally meant to be a trade school, the Institute's Board of Managers was persuaded by Black men to establish instead a school with classical higher learning for women as well as men. Coppin and Patterson were appointed as Principal and Assistant Principal, respectively, of the school. They combined strenuous classical education with the concepts of race obligation and self-help. Coppin paid the tuition for many students, and when the Board of Managers decided against her request to build a dormitory next to the school, Coppin rented a house nearby for boarding pupils from southern regions. Under their leadership, the Institute became one of the most prestigious academic institutions for African Americans in the nation.[17]

Two other well-known models of education for Blacks were promulgated later by W.E.B. Du Bois and Booker T. Washington. In a fund-raising address to a White audience in 1910, Du Bois stated:

> What the Negro needs, therefore, of the world and civilization, he must largely teach himself; what he learns of social organization and efficiency, he must learn from his own people. His conception of social uplift and philanthropy must come from within his own ranks, and he must above all make and set and follow his own ideals of life and character.[18]

Entitled "The College Bred Negro," the appeal was made on behalf of historically Black Atlanta University, where Du Bois was in the final year of a thirteen-year teaching career. Du Bois was well aware of the fact that the African-American experience influenced all aspects of Black life—political, social, and economic. The first African American to earn a doctoral degree from Harvard University, Du Bois firmly believed that the formation of a "Talented Tenth," a college-educated Black intelligentsia, was essential to the survival of African American culture in the United States. Fundamentally, Du Bois saw education as a political act—a radical process that held the potential to transform society. Preferring self-determination to the self-help philosophy of Booker T. Washington, Du Bois viewed the acquisition of a classical-liberal education as imperative to changing the social order.

Booker T. Washington, on the other hand, maintained that Black separatism was necessary for economic development because it would foster race pride and achievement through self-help. Accused by Du Bois of accommodating White interests, Washington believed that Blacks would progress by remaining in the south and contributing to the economic rebuilding of the region. By assuring White donors that Blacks would not press for social equality and downplaying any threat of racial "amalgamation," Washington gained the support of philanthropic funds that eventually created the "Tuskegee machine." A skillful fundraiser, Washington's endorsement of a vocational-industrial curriculum for southern Blacks made sense to northerners who subscribed to views of racial inferiority.

In addition to churches, mutual aid societies emerged during the early nineteenth century as an organized form of Black philanthropy. Like churches, mutual aid societies incorporated education into their often wide-ranging array of services to the Black community. As early as 1790, free Blacks in urban areas banded together to provide education for their children, charity for the needy, sick dues for those who could not work, and burial plots for the dead. Known by such names as the Brotherly Association, the Friendly Union and the Friendly Moralist, these fraternal organizations were charged with the care of the disabled, orphans, elderly, widows and children. Assuming the responsibility for wide-ranging social services, they provided comfort and aid in the face of loss, disability, and racial discrimination.[19] In many ways these mutual aid societies epitomize the character of Black philanthropy, which combined a strong emphasis on self-help with a broad concern for "the race" as a whole. The aid societies raised money for their work primarily through required membership dues, a practical manifestation of the ethic of individuals taking responsibility for themselves. At the same time, those unable to afford full membership dues were not simply left to fend for themselves. Wealthy Blacks who supported many charitable associations often subsidized these benevolent societies, enabling poorer Blacks to reap their benefits despite their inability to contribute.

Black mutual aid societies joined Black churches in stressing moral development. As secular organizations, however, mutual aid societies went beyond moral development to act as relief-bringing agencies, to provide a forum for information exchange, and to foster Black leadership. As historian John Rury argues, they also "helped develop a distinct black identity in the face of popular prejudice and genteel paternalism," thereby cultivating Black self-respect.[20]

As such, Black mutual aid societies developed a distinctly African American character despite the fact that some may have been modeled on White societies. Among other similarities, both White and Black nineteenth-century aid societies developed a political dimension. White aid societies like the Manumission Society vacillated between paternalistic "protection" of Blacks and social control. Black aid societies, on the other hand, had to contend with the equation by Whites of "benevolence" with "political activism," particularly with respect to fugitive slaves. Free Blacks who felt compelled to aid fugitives put themselves at considerable risk. Within the context of the nineteenth-century segregated system, the penalties for assisting runaway slaves—even in northern states—could be severe.[21]

Organized institutions—such as churches, schools and benevolent societies— were central locations of African American philanthropy and the mediums through which it flowed in the nineteenth century. Yet in addition to these collective efforts there are also early examples of individual Black philanthropists. By the eighteenth century, many wealthy Blacks in America participated in educational philanthropic endeavors. Some of these patrons derived their wealth from inventions, while others owned businesses and plantations or made a comfortable living as professional artists, artisans, or members of the Black intelligentsia. Although their contributions could not match the conspicuous contribution of White millionaires, middle-class, highly literate professional members of the Black community such as doctors, lawyers, and teachers contributed knowledge and expertise as well as money to needy individuals, churches, and associations. Blacks who had experienced success in business joined them. Their philanthropic efforts were early examples of race obligation, or the imperative to "give back" to the Black community.

James Forten (1766–1842), the wealthiest Black in early nineteenth-century America, began his career as an errand boy on the Philadelphia docks before amassing a personal fortune as a sail maker. A radical abolitionist, Forten contributed to a variety of causes including purchasing the freedom of slaves and financing the escape of others. He and his wife were also two of the co-founders of the elementary school established for Black children in 1819.[22]

Thomy LaFon (1810–1893) is often described as the first "Negro philanthropist." Deserted by his French father early in his childhood, he supported himself and his Haitian mother by doing odd jobs, eventually getting an education and becoming a schoolteacher. In 1850, at the age of forty, he opened a small dry-goods store in New Orleans and began to invest in real estate. He became one of New Orleans' richest men, Black or White. A cosmopolitan city with a well-established Black upper class, New Orleans produced a number of Black philanthropists, but LaFon's contributions to the development of New Orleans were extraordinary. His gifts helped build benevolent associations, churches, and schools that served to knit the Black community together, create a leadership class, and promote the general welfare. LaFon also made large contributions to the abolitionist movement, the American Anti-Slavery Society, and the Underground Railroad in addition to promoting the general welfare of free Blacks. He made direct contributions to New Orleans University and Straight University, which sixty-one years later would merge under the name of Dillard University.[23] Both Forten and Lafon exemplify the principles of connectedness to their community and race obligation. According to Jean E. Fairfax, race obligation—or "giving back" is "an expression of gratitude for what has been received (and it may not be a material benefit), often from unknown benefactors."[24] By using their wealth to help escaping slaves and contribute to Black causes and community development, Forten and Lafon demonstrated a belief in a kind of eternal gratitude by making gifts to unknown recipients with no expectation of reciprocity.

As a marginalized population in the United States, African Americans who lived in free communities (north and south) incorporated benevolence into community-building itself through aid societies, churches, and schools. While some forms of mutual aid were modeled after that of Whites, Black culture, history and tradition also determined the shape and course of Black philanthropy. Whether free or enslaved, the goals of survival, liberation and self-determination were at the forefront of Black mutual aid, and education played an instrumental role in the achievement of those goals. Philanthropic deeds, however, are not apolitical; by its very definition, private giving for the good of others mandates a relationship between more and less powerful parties. As an historically oppressed racial group, benevolent African Americans have linked philanthropy with Black political, economic, and social concerns. This is particularly evident in the nineteenth century when examining the role of philanthropy in the anti-slavery movement.

During the nineteenth century, abolitionism and the activities of the Underground Railroad (UGRR) were frequent outlets for Black philanthropy. The UGRR was a systematic effort by Blacks and Whites to aid slaves in their escape to Canada. The most well-traveled of the railroad's routes were a northeastern corridor route from Maryland's eastern shore through Delaware and Pennsylvania and several Midwestern routes through border states such as Indiana and Ohio that terminated in Canada.[25] The UGRR relied on Black charitable giving and voluntarism for much of its success. The many acts of benevolence included the sponsorship of national and international fundraising campaigns, service as volunteers, use of the homes of supporters as railroad stations, and the provision of food, clothing, shelter, new identity papers, and money to fugitive slaves. Many of the Black mutual aid societies and fraternal organizations were actively (but clandestinely) involved in supporting all aspects of the railroad's operation, while Quakers and other groups raised money, provided safe houses, and guided fugitives to the next station.

Harriet Tubman (1822?-1913) was an active participant in the eastern route of the UGRR. After her own escape from slavery, she made numerous trips back to the south to extricate enslaved Blacks and shepherd them to Canada. But she also used her domestic talents to aid freed slaves. For example, she financed the building of a laundry house in order to train local African American women to become laundresses.[26] After the Civil War ended, she provided a home not only for members of her family but also those who had been abandoned or needed shelter.[27] She was constantly soliciting funds for the needy. She collected money for freedpersons' schools and hospitals. She attended to the needs of the aged and indigent. In 1873, the Auburn, New York, newspaper referred to its resident as "the celebrated colored philanthropist" despite the fact that she had barely enough money on which to survive.[28] Eventually, the Harriet Tubman Home became "the only charity outside New York City dedicated to the shelter and care of African Americans in the State."[29]

African American philanthropy in the nineteenth century was varied and robust. It found expression institutionally, individually, spontaneously, and politically. It included elements of a strong self-help ethic and a deep community concern. Black philanthropy emerged in this era as a responsibility of every individual, regardless of their wealth. These patterns have endured through time and may still be discerned in the Black community today. In order to gain a full understanding of the development of a uniquely African American model of philanthropy, however, we must also understand the role played by White philanthropists during this time. Scholarly literature has tended to depict African Americans as mere beneficiaries of White benevolence; this chapter and the other essays in this book show that this depiction is inadequate. Yet many northern Whites did give a great deal of money to causes purporting to help Blacks. Although much of this White philanthropy to Blacks was motivated by a genuine desire to help, it was also tempered by a less-altruistic goal of keeping Blacks "in their place." Examining examples of White philanthropy to Blacks in the nineteenth century reveals this troubling aspect of philanthropy as well as demonstrates that African Americans were always participants in their own uplift.

Just prior to the issuance of the Emancipation Proclamation in 1863 and the advent of Reconstruction, relief efforts for recently freed southern Blacks became crucial. Left to fend for themselves, thousands of hungry and destitute former slaves were in need of food, shelter, and medical care. At the least, former slaves were disoriented by the sudden demise of the plantation system. Many were too old, too young, or too disabled to care for themselves, and nearly all of the former slaves were illiterate. Recognizing the scope of the emergency, General Sherman of the Union Army called for immediate action on the part of Whites, to whom he referred as "a highly favored and philanthropic people." Benevolent societies answered the call, sending clothing, food, money, religious leaders, and teachers southward. Added to these were the efforts of the Quakers and the Bureau of Refugees, Freedmen, and Abandoned Lands (commonly called the Freedmen's Bureau), which was located within the war department. But as historian Henry A. Bullock points out, the freed-persons themselves also shouldered the burden by contributing $672,989 in taxes and tuition through the Freedmen's Bureau and donating approximately $500,000 through Black church organizations. Significantly, this foreshadowed a practice that would be formalized by White industrial philanthropic foundations such as the Rosenwald Fund during the early twentieth century; namely, that Blacks were required to match funds donated by Whites for Black schools.[30]

According to Bullock, records from 1867 show that despite poverty and dislocation, freed people of Louisiana, Tennessee, and Virginia had sustained forty-six schools entirely, contributed to the support of forty-two others, and purchased thirty-three buildings, all through their own resources.[31] There were undoubtedly hundreds of these local efforts, which contributed to building a system of mass education in the south. Furthermore, Blacks were a major source of financial support for the schools sponsored by the northern societies. In Maryland, for example, the freedpeople raised over $23,000 for their education in 1867 and built sixty schoolhouses. They also paid taxes that went exclusively to White schools. In addition to tuition and subscriptions, freedpersons directly aided the societies in other ways. According to historian Ronald E. Butchart, "buildings and land, board and room, an occasional teacherage, fuel, light, books, teachers' salaries in whole or part, and other expenses were assumed by, and later imposed on, the community."[32] Foreshadowing the practice of matching funds, Butchart's statement is not only a testament to Black self-determination, but also a reminder of the "cost" to Blacks of White philanthropy.

Historian James D. Anderson has provided a scholarly revision of the Julius Rosenwald Fund which carried out philanthropic educational work among southern Blacks half a century after Emancipation. Begun in 1917 by Julius Rosenwald, the president of Sears, Roebuck, and Company, the Rosenwald Fund had a philanthropic agenda that included race relations, education, health and educational scholarships and fellowships. An admirer of Booker T. Washington's philosophy of self-help, Rosenwald directed the bulk of the Fund's largesse southward. The Fund is best-known for the Rural Schoolbuilding Program that eventually took credit for the construction of 4,977 public schoolhouses, 163 vocational shops, and 217 teachers' homes for Blacks throughout the south before the program ended in 1932. But despite the fact that the buildings were often referred to as "Rosenwald Schools," Anderson found that the fund's contribution to the cost of a schoolhouse generally amounted to only about one-sixth of the total cost of the building, grounds, and equipment. Rosenwald's Rural Schoolbuilding Program operated on the basis of matching funds, and as Anderson points out, "Most of the cash, either through private contributions or public tax funds, came from rural Black citizens. Their additional contributions in the form of land, labor, and building materials were also substantial." In fact, it is estimated that 16.64 percent of the funding was provided directly by Blacks, 63.73 percent through tax funds to which Blacks were the exclusive contributors, 4.27 percent from White donations, and 15.36 percent from the Rosenwald Fund.[33]

As these examples show, even the truly benign forms of White philanthropy were not bestowed upon a helpless people. African Americans were active participants, and when the philanthropy of others included attempts at social engineering, the Black community resisted.

Some of the earliest Black mutual aid societies were modeled on White organizations such as the New York Manumission Society, an antislavery group founded by Whites whose mission was to agitate for passage of antislavery legislation and to protect freed slaves from being kidnapped and returned to the south. Over time, and as the number of Blacks in New York City increased, however, the Manumission Society's mission changed to that of social control. Subscribing to the nineteenth-century view of Black inferiority, the Society attempted to dissuade freedpersons from indolence or acts considered by the Society to be immoral. Its most important instrument in this regard was the establishment of the African Free School, an early example of the use of education for socialization within the context of charity.[34]

The African Free School opened in 1787. The school's objective was to socialize Blacks—through education—so that they would be morally suitable to enter society as freepersons. At first limited to boys, the school's enrollment reached nearly one hundred when it became coeducational. Its instruction was intended to separate children from the baser morals and behavior of their parents. To that end, the curriculum emphasized proper appearance, conduct to and from school, classroom behavior, respect for property and fear of God—to the exclusion, it seems, of academic training.[35] Although the African Free School was essentially an attempt to control Black children, it and other similar institutions in fact served to galvanize the Black community's resistance to such efforts. The formation and success of many of the early nineteenth-century Black mutual aid societies and schools can be traced in part to these attempts at social control disguised as benevolence.

In the postbellum era Black colleges were favorite recipients of White philanthropy, but these donations were often contingent upon the college's endorsement of the "Hampton-Tuskegee" model of industrial education rather than a classical-liberal curriculum. As James Anderson and others have pointed out, schools such as Fisk University were often forced to suppress a well-respected classical-liberal curriculum if they wanted to attract White donors. Funding was also withheld from Black schools whose administrators or student body were perceived as being too "radical" in their views on racial uplift. Although institutions like Fisk and Howard resented the White philanthropists' efforts to move them closer to racial accommodation and vocational education, they were in fact dependent upon this philanthropic funding. While they accepted the donations of the White philanthropists, they subverted their intentions by continuing to maintain (although not openly) a classical-liberal curriculum along with vocational courses. During the 1920s, students and Black leaders openly rejected the Hampton-Tuskegee model on the basis that it no longer met the needs of students in a changing educational environment.

In a discussion of the social scientific research conducted on "the Negro problem" between World War I and II, sociologist John H. Stanfield presents the case that conservative White philanthropists and philanthropic fund officials rewarded Black social scientists who favored racial assimilation. Those who exposed the elite origins of race theory were excluded from philanthropic funding and discouraged from publishing research results that were at odds with philanthropic positions.

According to Stanfield, the net effect during this "golden era of race-relations research" was to bias solutions to the "Negro problem" in the direction of racial grad-ualism.[36] Rather than press aggressively for full rights and privileges as citizens, the philosophy of gradualism posited that change occurred over generations. In other words, Blacks should be patient; they would eventually "evolve" into full citizenship. In effect, foundation officials chose to deny the existence of racial and social constructs as significant and used their funds to attempt to shape national race-relations policy.

As the nineteenth century drew to a close, Black philanthropy shifted from occurring only on a local level to include broad, national efforts. In the opening decades of the twentieth century three African American advocacy and philanthropic organizations were created that have proved to be enduring and highly successful efforts to extend the typical Black ethic of community support and care beyond the immediate neighborhood. The National Urban League, the National Association for the Advancement of Colored People, and the United Negro College Fund continued the philanthropic tradition of providing services and programs that historically addressed the needs of enslaved and freed African Americans. In response to racism, discrimination, and segregation, the voluntary associations and philanthropic organizations remained a buffer. During the Civil Rights era, they provided leadership and resources for the movement and fostered and supported Black self-determination.

The National Urban League was formed in 1910 as a social work and community planning agency for the purpose of expanding opportunities for Blacks. Trained social workers and other professionals assisted Blacks who had moved to urban areas with employment, housing, health care, and education. During the early part of the twentieth century, the Urban League opened craft union membership, skilled occupations, and vocational education to African Americans. Throughout its history, the Urban League based its program on the premises that poverty is not a character defect, that social science offers the solution to urban Blacks, and that the socioeconomic gap between African Americans and Whites can only be closed with the improved cooperation of the White elite. George E. Haynes, the Urban League's first executive secretary, was instrumental in launching a social work program at Fisk University to train African Americans as social workers. Currently, the Urban League is a community planning agency that emphasizes the expansion of equal economic opportunity for Blacks as a means of reducing class and racial tensions in urban areas.[37]

The National Association for the Advancement of Colored People (NAACP) was formed in 1910 by an interracial group including W.E. B. Du Bois and Mary White Ovington. Perhaps the best-known Black organization, its primary purpose was to achieve public safety and first-class citizenship for African Americans.

Relying initially on White philanthropy to ensure its survival, the membership burgeoned by 1920 as it emerged as the major civil rights organization in the United States. The goals of the NAACP have included the desegregation of society, the advancement of civil rights, and the inclusion of women in positions of importance. Throughout its history, the NAACP has provided legal counsel in court cases challenging desegregation. In the realm of education, its most important victory was the verdict by the United States Supreme Court to overturn *Plessy v. Ferguson* (1896) in *Brown v. Board of Education of Topeka* (1954), thereby ending school segregation.

The most purely philanthropic of the three associations, the United Negro College Fund (UNCF) was founded in 1944 by the presidents of twenty-seven Historically Black Colleges and Universities (HBCUs). Today, the Fund supports forty-one private Black institutions. While it initially raised funds for operating expenses including teacher salaries, scholarships and equipment, it now manages endowment funds and provides construction planning and oversight of physical facilities. Through capital campaigns and annual television and radio fund-raising events, the Fund not only raises money for colleges but also strives to increase public awareness of HBCUs and support for maintaining and strengthening them. This activity has assumed a higher priority in the post-*Brown* era, with the admission of African Americans to White institutions. The UNCF is, in fact, the major source of outside funding for private HBCUs. White philanthropists such as the Rockefeller-funded General Education Board, the Julius Rosenwald Fund, the Ford Foundation, and the Walter Annenberg Foundation have assisted it in its mission. Since the 1970s, the UNCF has embarked on a campaign of aggressive fund-raising techniques. In 1972, the organization started to run television and radio advertisements to solicit funds for HBCUs. In 1980, "The Lou Rawls Parade of Stars" was instituted as an annual event. The UNCF's slogan, "A mind is a terrible thing to waste," has been popularized through its fund-raising campaigns and its successful appeals have ensured the survival of most of its HBCU member institutions.[38]

As it continues to evolve, Black philanthropy exhibits distinct historical and cultural characteristics that crystallized in the nineteenth century. Fostered by the economic system of slavery, political disenfranchisement, and social segregation, Black philanthropy found its expression in discrete charity (both in-kind and monetary) to needy individuals such as the fugitive slaves and freedpersons, the collective efforts of mutual aid societies and churches, and the founding of Black institutions such as schools and colleges. Although the historical record of early nineteenth-century Black philanthropic efforts is often scant, research will benefit from the further revisioning of White philanthropy to elucidate African American contributions. In addition, the records of historically Black associations, churches, schools and colleges are potentially rich sources for discerning the motivations of individual donors and recipients. The enduring legacy of nineteenth-century Black philanthropy is the use of private funds to advocate public policy change. By equating education with liberation and self-determination, Black philanthropy not only placed education within the hands of African Americans but later put it beyond the reach of White control through the establishment of Black national advocacy and fund-raising associations.

NOTES

1. Toni Morrison, *Beloved* (New York: A. A. Knopf, 1987; New York: The Penguin Group, 1991), 305.
2. Ibid., 309.
3. William L. Pollard, *A Study of Black Self Help* (San Francisco: R and E Research Associates, 1978), 59.
4. Literature on the African American self-help tradition includes the following: W.E.B Du Bois, *Some Efforts of American Negroes for Their Own Social Betterment* (1898); Vincent P. Franklin, *The Education of Black Philadelphia: The Social and Educational History of a Minority Community, 1900–1950*; Dorothy Porter, "The Organized Educational Activities of Negro Literary Societies, 1828–1846," *Journal of Negro Education* (October 1939).
5. Merle Curti, "Philanthropy," in *Dictionary of the History of Ideas,* ed. Philip P. Wiener (New York: Charles Scribner's Sons, 1973), 3:486.
6. This is not unique to African-American minority populations. A useful book that discusses strategic questions about Black philanthropy, Asian American giving, contemporary Jewish philanthropy, and women donors and fundraisers is Charles H. Hamilton and Warren F. Ilchman, *Cultures of Giving II: Heritage, Gender, Wealth, Values* (San Francisco: Jossey-Bass, 1995).
7. See, for example, the history of the Rosenwald Fund, *Investment in People*; the history of the General Education Board, *Adventure in Giving*; and histories of the Peabody, Slater and Jeanes Funds.
8. Eric Anderson and Alfred A. Moss, Jr., *Dangerous Donations: Northern Philanthropy and Southern Black Education, 1902–1930* (Columbia: University of Missouri Press, 1999), 2.
9. James A. Joseph, *Remaking America: How the Benevolent Traditions of Many Cultures Are Transforming Our National Life* (San Francisco: Jossey-Bass Publishers, 1995), 85.
10. Pollard, *A Study of Black Self Help*, 57–59; Ira Berlin, *Slaves without Masters: The Free Negro in the Antebellum South* (New York: The New Press, 1974), 302.
11. Pollard, *A Study of Black Self Help*, 54.
12. Pollard, *A Study of Black Self Help*, 55–56.
13. Pollard, *A Study of Black Self Help*, 59.
14. John Hope Franklin and Alfred A Moss, Jr., *From Slavery to Freedom: A History of Negro Americans* 6th ed. (New York: McGraw-Hill, 1988), 206.
15. Berlin, *Slaves without Masters,* 304.
16. Julie Winch, *A Gentleman of Color: The Life of James Forten* (Oxford: Oxford University Press, 2002), 116; Linda D. Addo, "Sarah Mapps Douglass," in *Women Educators in the United States, 1820–1993: A Bio-Bibliographical Sourcebook,* ed. Maxine Schwartz Seller (Westport: Greenwood Press, 1994), 203–208.

17. Linda B. Selleck, *Gentle Invaders: Quaker Women Educators and Racial Issues During the Civil War and Reconstruction* (Richmond: Friends United Press, 1995), 39. For a history of Fanny Jackson Coppin's long tenure at, and influence upon, the Institute for Colored Youth, see Linda M. Perkins, *Fanny Jackson Coppin and the Institute for Colored Youth, 1865–1902* (New York: Garland Publishing, Inc., 1987).

18. W. E. B. Du Bois, *The Education of Black People: Ten Critiques, 1906–1960*, ed. Herbert Aptheker (New York: Monthly Review Press, 1973), 56.

19. Berlin, *Slaves without Masters*, 308–310.

20. John Rury, "Philanthropy, Self Help, and Social Control: The New York Manumission Society and Free Blacks, 1785–1810," *Phylon* 46, no. 3 (1985): 239.

21. For a discussion of punishments meted out to slaves and those who helped them escape, see John Hope Franklin and Loren Schweninger, *Runaway Slaves: Rebels on the Plantation* (Oxford: Oxford University Press, 1999).

22. Winch, *A Gentleman of Color*, 116.

23. Joseph, *Remaking of America*, 90–93; Dillard University website http://www.dillard.edu, Retrieved 2 January 2004.

24. Jean E. Fairfax, "Black Philanthropy: Its Heritage and Its Future." In *Cultures of Giving II*, Charles H. Hamilton and Warren F. Ilchman, eds., 9–21, 12.

25. For comprehensive works on the Underground Railroad, see William Still, *The Underground Railroad: A record of facts, authentic narratives, letters & c., narrating the hardships, hair-breadth escapes and death struggles of the slaves in their efforts for freedom, as related by themselves and others* (1886, revised ed. Philadelphia: People's Publishing Company, 1879); and Wilbur H. Siebert, *The Underground Railroad from Slavery to Freedom* (1898, reissued New York: Russell and Russell, 1967).

26. Catherine Clinton, *Harriet Tubman: The Road to Freedom* (New York: Little, Brown and Company, 2004), 158.

27. Clinton, *Harriet Tubman*, 191.

28. Clinton, *Harriet Tubman*, 203.

29. Clinton, *Harriet Tubman*, 209–210.

30. Henry A. Bullock, *A History of Negro Education in the South from 1619 to the Present* (Cambridge: Harvard University Press, 1970), 18–19, 27.

31. Bullock, *A History of Negro Education*, 28.

32. Ronald E. Butchart, *Northern Schools, Southern Blacks, and Reconstruction: Freedmen's Education 1862–1875* (Westport: Greenwood Press, 1980), 171–172.

33. James D. Anderson, *The Education of Blacks in the South, 1860–1935* (Chapel Hill: University of North Carolina Press, 1988), 153–154. For a global perspective on White philanthropy, see Robert F. Arnove, ed., *Philanthropy and Cultural Imperialism: The Foundations at Home and Abroad* (Bloomington: Indiana University Press, 1980).

34. Rury, "Philanthropy, Self Help, and Social Control," 231–241.

35. Rury, "Philanthropy, Self Help, and Social Control," 235.

36. John H. Stanfield, *Philanthropy and Jim Crow in American Social Science* (Westport: Greenwood Press, 1985), 191.

37. Jesse T. Moore, Jr. "National Urban League," in *Organizing Black America: An Encyclopedia of African American Associations*, ed. Nina Mjagkij (New York: Garland Publishing, Inc., 2001), 486–490.

38. Tiffany Ruby Patterson, "United Negro College Fund," in *Organizing Black America: An Encyclopedia of African American Associations*, ed. Mjagkij, 669–670.

CHAPTER TWO

Standing on Their Own

African American Engagements with Educational Philanthropy in Antebellum America

JEFFREY A. MULLINS

In a fiery letter to his chief benefactor in 1844, former slave David McDonogh proclaimed his resolve "never more to look up to the White man, whatever may be his profession or condition in society, as a true friend." Although most immediately occasioned by the refusal of medical schools to admit him following his graduation from Lafayette College, McDonogh founded his conclusion upon years of experience with white beneficence. After all, his famously benign former master had in fact made him purchase his own freedom over the course of fifteen years. Once free, his white benefactors in the American Colonization Society only allowed McDonogh to obtain an education on the condition that he would then promptly leave the country to settle in the colony of "returned" blacks in Liberia. And although he was charged by these same philanthropists to study medicine, he found the doors of all institutions for this purpose shut to him. So it was that McDonogh found such whites to be failures "as Philanthropists, as Colonizationists, and as Christians."[1]

If David McDonogh's experience was similar to that of many African Americans who received aid from white benefactors as a means to obtain an education, his response to his situation was only one among a range of possible courses of action in such circumstances. A fellow recipient of such aid, Washington McDonogh, typically took a more conciliatory route. Writing from Liberia to his former master to thank him for some parting advice he had given, he exclaimed that "there is nothing on earth that gives me more pleasure than it does to think that I have such an adviser and friend as you are."[2] Although Washington's circumstances had been similar to those of David, he adopted a different stance towards his benefactors. Along with condemnations of the hypocrisy of white philanthropy, then, we find among black students at Pennsylvania's Lafayette College reactions to educational support that included straightforward compliance with white expectations, diplomatic negotiation of the circumstances, and reversals of the application of guiding principles in order to pressure white philanthropists towards particular ends. At various points in his educational career David McDonogh employed all of these modes in order to better direct his own destiny, and so we can use his experience to illuminate different ways in which African Americans responded to antebellum philanthropic culture.

The experience of African Americans with institutions like Lafayette and the American Colonization Society allows us to see a cultural dynamic not usually explored: black appropriations of white-directed philanthropy. As one of only a few colleges in the period to accept black students, and as an institution with loose ties to the American Colonization Society, Lafayette College in the 1830s and 40s provides an excellent opportunity for exploring engagements with educational philanthropy across racial lines. Prior to the Civil War, only a few localities in America had a critical mass of blacks sufficient to build self-generated and controlled institutions, a dynamic usually found in the larger urban centers. In most places, however, this was not possible, so blacks had to participate in white-controlled institutions. Here we find a middle ground between two extremes that have long framed scholarly debates on slavery (and black experiences in early America more generally). On the one hand, the McDonoghs neither experienced a pervasive debilitation of their psyches nor engaged in total submission to authority. On the other hand, they did find the possibilities for self-control often quite limited, and they did routinely demonstrate deference to white authority. Instead of either extreme, then, we find creative appropriations of the network of white-originated reform and philanthropic movements so pervasive in antebellum America. Although historians have closely examined related areas, black engagements with white social reform and philanthropic institutions remain relatively unexplored. Scholars have studied the range of "benevolent" white viewpoints and practices as directed towards blacks, including the various forms of anti-slavery activism (moral suasion, political reform, use of direct force), and the tensions between abolitionists and colonizationists.[3] Similarly, in recent years scholars have turned their attention to the dynamics within and among black-originated social institutions in antebellum America, including political gatherings, cultural organizations, and reading groups.[4]

David McDonogh's encounter with Lafayette College and the American Colonization Society also allows us to revisit some assumptions about the meanings and forms of philanthropy. Scholars such as Kathleen McCarthy and Susan Ryan have recently reminded us that earlier generations of Americans had a quite different understanding of philanthropy than that often entailed by our present-day use of the term. Rather than being just about giving or just about giving financially—and that usually done by those in the upper end of the economic scale—philanthropy in the early nineteenth century was understood to include all forms of helping others and to involve people across the social spectrum. Among other things, philanthropy meant "giving *and* volunteering," and it was a key arena in which different groups and individuals "publicly contested for authority and power during the nation's youth."[5] Social reformers in antebellum America aimed at nothing less than a transformation of society through aggregate individual change. Not all reformers had the same vision of what society should look like, however, and the range of issues in such competing visions only partially overlaps with those that concern us today. In understanding benevolent or philanthropic activities in the past, therefore, we need to set aside most of our notions about the meanings and consequences of such behavior.

In reconsidering our recently narrowed rendering of the notion of philanthropy, is there an alternate definition we can invoke that will be less contextually limited? One scholar has recently framed the concept in terms of activities that "advance society by providing necessary social, cultural, and educational services which are not provided by the state or the market for political or economic reasons or which are provided by the state but not in a way that satisfies philanthropists."[6] However, along with the behavior being described, we also need to consider the motives, both conscious and unconscious. A recent major forum on philanthropy in American history stresses that, for all of its differing forms across time and space, philanthropy "has its roots in the desires of individuals to impose their visions, ideals, or conceptions of truth upon their society." Leaving aside the false dichotomy between pure-minded "benevolence" and nefarious "social control" that guided historical inquiry in the 1970s and 80s, scholars now acknowledge that anyone engaged in philanthropy and social reform partakes in a complex mixture of both benevolence and social control. That is, people who strenuously reach out to others do so because they believe their aid to be in the others' best interest. At the same time, all such aid is directed toward a particular outcome, which necessarily furthers a particular vision of the world; people without such a motivating vision rarely commit the personal resources necessary for philanthropy. The activities that individual philanthropic motives inspire, though, will be very much dependent on—and only comprehensible in terms of—that particular cultural context.[7] A full understanding of African American involvement in philanthropy in the early decades of the United States is impossible without fleshing out black appropriations of white-initiated philanthropy. As recent debates—in the academy and in more public venues—have demonstrated, many present-day issues regarding African American roles in U.S. society are directly structured by the racial dynamics of antebellum America, and only by understanding these structures can we hope to adequately address our own pressing problems.[8]

In considering what light the case of David McDonogh can shed on the dynamics of race, education, and philanthropy in nineteenth-century America, we need to begin with a central piece of disciplinary translation. What many students of contemporary policy and practice tend to refer to as either "philanthropy," "charity," or "social outreach," those discussing the early nineteenth-century (both then and now) refer to as "moral reform" or "social reform." The literature on this topic is extensive, but for the moment it will suffice to note that antebellum reformers hoped to change society as a whole by reforming the personalities and behavior of a critical mass of individuals. The various reforms of the period frequently overlapped with each other. Furthermore they were interwoven with the emergence of a middle class and its attendant shifts in gender and race relations, such as the development of "separate spheres" for each gender and a widespread reduction of liberties for free blacks.[9]

Although sometimes portrayed as lying at the margins of antebellum reform, the above description most certainly applies to the American Colonization Society (ACS). Between its foundation in 1816 and the Fugitive Slave Law in 1850, the ACS earned more scorn from black Americans and their abolitionist allies than almost any other institution excepting, of course, slavery itself. Modern historians have likewise tended to be critical of this effort to remove all free blacks from the U.S. and resettle them in western Africa. Both antebellum Americans and recent historians, however, have been forced into a reconsideration of colonization efforts. In the case of nineteenth-century African Americans, after the Fugitive Slave Law erased the freedom from enslavement previously promised by the northern states, many escaped slaves and free-born blacks chose to leave the nation. For their part, historians increasingly realize that the colonization movement—including all of its racist assumptions—was no radical extreme but rather was pivotal to the entire nineteenth-century discussion about race in America.[10]

The idea of establishing a colony to which European Americans might transport all of their neighbors of African descent—thereby leaving the continent free of their debilitating presence—had its roots in the eighteenth century. Thomas Jefferson contemplated the idea, although he also recognized the logistical hurdles that made any complete realization of this vision unlikely. Americans also could look to the example of Sierra Leone, the colony that Britain had established on the west coast of Africa for precisely this purpose. And some African Americas embraced the idea as a means of escaping white oppression, as was the case with the boatload of colonists that the wealthy Paul Cuffee helped to emigrate to Africa in 1816.[11]

Although initially embraced by several black leaders, most free blacks in the north quickly and overwhelmingly rejected the ACS plan to "return" them to Africa. In a decisive meeting of three thousand free blacks in Philadelphia in 1817, participants unanimously concluded that African colonization assaulted their rights and status as citizens and free persons. Had they not been born in America? Did they not, through their labor and service, help make the nation what it was? Did they not have at least as much claim as any white man to the liberty promised by the Declaration of Independence? In the years before 1850, then, almost no free black leaders spoke in favor of colonization to Africa.

For slaves, however, the situation was different. In many instances masters were only willing to manumit slaves on the condition that they leave the nation. This sentiment was not new. Indeed, some colonies had made it a legal requirement that freed slaves leave the colony upon their release. Arising from a concern that blacks and whites could not successfully live together in freedom and that the former would degrade the liberty of the latter, many white Americans concluded that co-existence with free blacks was impossible. Whatever they might think of the motives of those whites willing to pay for their Atlantic passage, for slaves emigration was sometimes the only path to freedom. Furthermore, even some well-established free blacks (such as Bowdoin college graduate and newspaper editor John Russwurm) thought that the hardships of Liberia would be preferable to the unremitting oppression of America.

Whites participated in the colonization movement for a variety of reasons. Most of these reasons were grounded in some form of the racial bias that contemporary critics charged motivated the ACS, but the relationship between colonization and racism was more complex than those critics generally allowed. Some colonizationists thought that they might literally empty the continent of blacks, leaving it for whites. These were probably in the minority. Others no doubt held out some vague hope for a complete racial removal but contributed to colonization more as one element in a larger drive to figuratively erase the presence and contributions of free blacks from America.[12] Still others believed it was the kindest and most ethical thing to do. Such was the case with people like radical abolitionist William Lloyd Garrison, who initially supported colonization before having a change of heart.

John McDonogh, the one-time owner and namesake of David and Washington McDonogh, brought his own personal history to his decision to manumit his slaves and send them to Liberia. Many of the officers of the ACS did not themselves own slaves, and so the process by which McDonogh arrived at the conclusion to both join the ACS and to free his own slaves helps us to understand the intersection among the pecuniary interests of slaveholders, the philanthropic interests of colonizationists, and the racial assumptions that guided both groups. Born and educated in Baltimore, McDonogh gained experience in merchant houses before moving to New Orleans in 1800 at the age of twenty-one. Over the next two decades he flourished both in terms of wealth and reputation and acquired a large number of slaves on his plantation directly across the Mississippi from New Orleans. Although he officially retired from the business world in 1817, McDonogh continued to build his fortune on his plantation through the labor of his slaves.

According to his own account, McDonogh's philanthropic sentiments towards his slaves crystallized in 1825, when he landed upon the idea of having all those slaves who were willing engage in a process of purchasing their own time in increments. In this manner they might "obtain freedom for themselves and [their] children" in approximately fifteen years, "without loss or the cost of a cent to myself." McDonogh made it clear to his slaves, however, that even this delayed freedom came at a cost. They would not only have to work during that portion of Saturday normally designated for rest, but also add on up to four additional hours of labor to each of their other normal working days. Furthermore, any slaves found to have violated the code of moral conduct that McDonogh set out would not only lose all investment in themselves but would be immediately sold off to another owner. And not least, he required that every slave thus freed proceed directly to Liberia on a ship that he would provide. As with other philanthropic and reform movements of the day, McDonogh's benevolence was designed to bring about his own social vision in those to whom he offered aid.[13]

Like most people participating in philanthropy, McDonogh believed that his vision ought to be widely adopted, and to this end once the first group of freed slaves set sail for Africa in 1842 he wrote and published a pamphlet describing his methods. He waited until his plan bore its initial fruit so that he could reliably recommend this course of action to others. However, McDonogh did not wait until then to play an active role in the national colonization movement, serving as a Vice President of the ACS from 1834 to 1841. In doing so he joined Henry Clay, Francis Scott Key, and a number of other national figures in advocating for the removal of all free blacks to Africa.

Even for the most optimistic of colonizationists, however, the experiences of the initial waves of ACS sponsored-colonists made it plain that African Americans were more American than African and that further preparation of colonists would be necessary if the Liberian experiment were to succeed. In addition to the fact that black Americans died from disease at rates equal to white Americans, the emigrants were no better prepared than whites to deal with the circumstances present in Liberia and were disposed (as were the few whites in Liberia) to survive through trade with the indigenous people rather than through the "self-sustaining" farm and craft labor that ACS officials envisioned. As a consequence, as their experiment progressed, colonization supporters often sponsored artisan training for some of the colonists, and in some cases even went to far as to arrange college-level education for those individuals whom they hoped would make effective ministers and teachers when the colonists returned to the "land of their fathers."

As the fifteen-year cycle for his slaves' self-purchase neared its end, John McDonogh likewise realized the benefit of having some individuals with advanced education among the slave cohort. The very life of the colony required trained physicians, and the Christian mission of the colony required trained clergy. In this vein he sent David and Washington McDonogh to Lafayette College in 1838, when both were about eighteen. How he selected these two individuals is not clear. Nor do we know why he chose Lafayette in particular, although some institution outside of the south was clearly preferable, since many states (including Louisiana) had outlawed the education of blacks. Like many white students they began in the "preparatory department" of Lafayette, what we would today understand as a "secondary" school, before matriculating to collegiate studies. Aside from the course of study, however, not many aspects of the experiences of whites and blacks at Lafayette were shared.

When David and Washington McDonogh arrived at Lafayette, they were not the first black students to attend that institution. Although racial mixing at colleges—as in most social institutions of the era—was extremely rare, at least one other African American attended Lafayette, coming in 1832. Additionally, a half-dozen more black students would come to Lafayette during the 1840s, the recent precedent having been deepened by the two students from New Orleans.[14] The receptivity of Lafayette only went so far, however, and the McDonoghs found themselves eating, studying, and lodging separately from the white students.

As much as blacks were systematically excluded from white colleges, there is one sense in which David and Washington McDonogh might have expected to find better arrangements at Lafayette. As a manual labor college, Lafayette participated in a philanthropic tradition that sought to expand access to higher education by allowing students to do agricultural and craft work to pay for their tuition and expenses. This novel system, created in part as a reaction to the social tensions attending the market revolution of the 1820s, was almost always linked with some other form of social outreach. In many cases manual labor schools were designed to train ministers for service on the expanding frontier, and the movement as a whole was suffused with the language of breaking down barriers between the laboring and the professional classes. Furthermore, antislavery advocates had used the conceptual and logistical aspects of manual labor education to craft institutions such as Oberlin College and the Oneida Institute that would further their goals and sometimes made racially integrated student bodies a part of this. Also, throughout the 1830s leaders of the nation's free black community had made plans in their annual meetings for a black-initiated and operated manual labor college as a means of educational and social advancement.[15]

The particular origins of Lafayette College, however, saw this philanthropic practice put to somewhat different ends. The college began its life as a more radical institution, founded by Rev. John Monteith in 1829 in Germantown (just north of Philadelphia) as the Manual Labor Academy of Pennsylvania. Monteith had come most recently from the Oneida Institute in upstate New York, where evangelical fervor mixed with abolitionism in a manual labor institution. Rev. George Junkin took over the Germantown institution in 1830, but when his Old School Presbyterian beliefs clashed with the New School outlook of the board of trustees in 1832, he took advantage of the opportunity to remove the school to Easton, which had a charter to found Lafayette College, but little else. As part of this merger, however, the new college continued its commitment to having students engage in artisanal and agricultural labor, but dropped its specifically Presbyterian focus. Like other manual labor schools, then, Lafayette was born out of the drive to train young men of modest means for the evangelical ministry; yet the college increasingly served a more mainstream audience.[16]

As the founding president of the new college, George Junkin himself embodied several ideas that directly affected the students from John McDonogh's plantation. In many ways Junkin was a socially leveling Presbyterian, both personally familiar with students from all classes and self-sacrificing in his efforts to keep alive the institution's core mission of cross-class access and understanding. On matters of race, however, Junkin held more conservative opinions. He was a firm supporter of the ACS, and also believed that the Bible provided justification for slavery (a practice in which the Junkin family themselves eventually engaged).[17] It is not surprising, then, that he agreed to help McDonogh and the ACS in their plan.

Leaving aside the structural segregation in lodging, instruction, and dining, we do not know a lot about the earliest years of David and Washington McDonogh at Lafayette. Neither entered the record for formal discipline, which is more than can be said for many of their peers. In an era when youth at academies and colleges were using colleges not only to reaffirm and reinvent the social hierarchy but to expand its upper reaches, student disorder and rebellion were fairly common. At Lafayette in 1840, for example, one student stabbed another in the dining hall in retaliation for a social slight. More common were individual and collective student assertions of honor in dealings with faculty and trustees, such as student celebrations (in defiance of trustees' directions) for the 1844 return of Junkin as Lafayette's president. As students whose very presence was already against the boundaries of acceptability, however, neither of the McDonoghs could afford any such assertions.[18]

By the time David McDonogh entered the collegiate course, however, Junkin had taken another position, and in 1841 he was replaced as president by John Yeomans. This brought a number of changes to Lafayette. Shortly before he left office, Junkin concluded that the manual labor system was not financially tenable and so abandoned the system. While this meant a decline in students, Yeomans helped to compensate for this by using his close ties with the Presbyterian establishment to secure students who had scholarships from the Presbyterian Board of Education.[19] There were additional shifts in the faculty and in the dynamic between the faculty and the board of trustees, which added tensions to the institution. Throughout his three-year stint as president, Yeomans appears to have experienced challenges to his leadership, including struggles with the trustees over leadership of the institution and appropriate forms of student discipline.

One such set of challenges came from David McDonogh. By this point McDonogh was three years removed from the New Orleans plantation and had become accustomed both to a life of freedom and to the attributes of honor and self-respect required to be "manly." Apparently McDonogh began to put into practice the calls for "self-government" that he so frequently heard impressed upon the students. Not long after Yeomans took his new position, he wrote to John McDonogh that "David has the power of becoming a good scholar," but that he was "quite high minded & needs occasional checks" to be placed on his "temper & disposition."[20] Yeomans wrote this in 1841, when his charge still had three years ahead of him in his collegiate course. More challenges lay ahead.

One of the conflicts between the college president and his student came in 1842. In preparation for his eventual role as an ordained minister, McDonogh directed a local Bible class on Sundays. He was proud of the work he did among Easton's free blacks, and he often invited white students and faculty down into town to observe. One elder member of the Bible study group, however, apparently felt challenged by this arrangement, since he was accustomed to leading the group. The elderly man took advantage of his position as a servant to Yeomans and complained to the president of the new practices of the Lafayette student. Yeomans sided with his servant, even though McDonogh was the assigned leader of the group, leaving the latter feeling undermined.

McDonogh wrote of the event to Walter Lowrie, a Pennsylvania merchant and politician who was an agent of the ACS and David's financial trustee and his legal guardian (an arrangement required due to the complexities of the interstate slave traffic). Reflecting upon all of the other forms of exclusion to which he was subject at Lafayette, McDonogh concluded: "I do not think that I am treated right by President Yeomans. He wants me to submit to all the rules and regulations of college, whereas I enjoy none of the privileges." He expressed his willingness to abide by every college rule, but he wanted consistency in their application and did not believe that Yeomans was conducting himself properly in this regard. In support of his case, he appealed to the authority of white observers, noting that "teachers from the white schools . . . said that our school is conducted better than any other of its like in the Borough of Easton."[21] In a subsequent letter, he also detailed how many of the students and faculty at Lafayette supported his position, again deploying white standards and status to further his own ends.[22]

Perhaps aware that he was pressing the limits of acceptable norms to be writing one elite white benefactor to complain about another, in the latter part of his letter McDonogh began to shift his tone. He noted that, "Were it not, sir, for the advantages I possess here, I would readily desire you to find some other institution for me." The advantages, however, were too great, and he acknowledges how important they were to him. In particular, he expressed his appreciation that he could simultaneously pursue the regular collegiate course, which prepared him for the ministry, and engage in medical training through his medical apprenticeship with Easton physician Hugh Abernathy. As he emphatically framed it, "I would sooner undergo the most severe and rigid discipline, that can be given, than to give up my medical studies."[23] So it was that even as he stressed the injustice he thought had been done to him and his desire to continue leading the Sunday school, he wrote Lowrie that "if you think I had better *give it up*, just say the word and it will be done immediately." McDonogh here employed the accepted forms of redress of a subordinate (in terms of both race and class) to a benefactor. Appealing to his guardian for advice and aid, and offering to accept any decision he thought just, McDonogh simultaneously used his role as recipient of philanthropy to his advantage while not challenging prevailing norms.

In the case of the McDonogh students we find the prevalent relations of paternalism taken to an extreme. Southern planters saw themselves as "prime movers, fathers writ large," but usually this relationship was expressed indirectly.[24] Although neither David nor Washington McDonogh appear to have had any blood relationship to John McDonogh, both unfailingly address him as "father" in their correspondence, and likewise refer to him as such when writing to third parties. Of course, we must bear in mind that there is always some degree of utilitarian motive in such a relationship and that it would be a grave mistake to take everything a person in this position wrote as representing his unfiltered view of the world. Indeed, deference was a key component of the polite (and professional) society that the McDonoghs hoped to enter.[25] On the other hand, some of Washington McDonogh's expositions go well beyond what is necessary, and the intensity and length suggest the power of the paternalism involved in most of antebellum philanthropy. Washington McDonogh went so far in one letter as to suggest that—although John McDonogh forcefully separated him from his birth parents—his former master made a better parent than his actual kin could ever be.[26] At points, then, we find the internalization of the gratitude and obligation that reformers desired from the recipients of their beneficence, indicating the power involved in the dynamics of reform.

John McDonogh apparently basked in the attention from his former slaves. His understanding of philanthropy entailed receiving this reward of gratitude. In his 1842 description of his plan for manumitting and exporting his slaves, he repeatedly expounded upon how grateful and joyful his slaves were to him, and how even upon the docks of departure the emigrants exhorted those remaining in bondage to look after their dear master. Even as he wrote these lines, the New Orleans plantation owner apparently saw no irony in observing that he would use the proceeds from the labor of those slaves whom he was so graciously liberating to buy yet more humans on the auction block of the slave market.[27]

David McDonogh, however, saw things differently. For him, genuine philanthropy would entail a relationship of equals. Equality, however, was decidedly not what most reformers had in mind. The philanthropic relationship was intrinsically one of inequality, and in most reform movements those distributing the fruits of benevolence worked to solidify, not blur, those lines of difference.[28] Such was certainly the case at Lafayette, where the McDonoghs had to constantly petition Walter Lowrie, their legal guardian, for money for the smallest things, and just as often to purchase an item on their behalf. Sometimes this was because an item was not available in Easton (such as medical equipment), and sometimes because this seems to be the standing arrangement for many everyday items (such as hats). The arrangement kept the McDonoghs from exercising independent judgment: anything but the smallest decision required consultation with a white benefactor.

In response to such constraints, over time David McDonogh displayed less of the deference that he exhibited in the Sunday school affair and increasingly asserted his own capacity for choice. Such was the case in April of 1844, when he learned from Lowrie that his guardian and his former master had concluded that he ought to sail to Liberia immediately following his graduation in the fall. Addressing his guardian as an equal, he wrote to Lowrie, "Hitherto, dear sir, there has been a perfect unanimity and agreement between us three; but now sir, we must differ—and that materially—in as much as I am decidedly, utterly and radically opposed to the above decision, and for the following reasons." McDonogh went on to reaffirm his willingness to go to Liberia, but only after his medical studies were complete, which would mean at least two years of study at a medical school following his graduation from Lafayette. After all, he observed, there were "no medical colleges in Africa, and, of course, no anatomical or dissecting apparatus." How could he become a skilled professional in the absence of these?[29]

In writing a similar letter to his former master, the student showed he had indeed learned something at college, and put his education in the cultural mores of elite whites to good use. After telling John McDonogh what he had heard from Lowrie of the New Orleans gentleman's decision, David McDonogh then expressed his disbelief that such news could possibly be true. After quoting directly from an earlier letter that his master had written to him, in which he exhorted the young man to pursue his studies beyond his graduation from Lafayette, the former slave exclaimed, "No, I can not, for a moment, think that you have changed your mind. I know you too well to believe that you are thus mutable." And citing his own promise to his master to pursue and fulfill these education goals, he then continued, "Why, I would suffer Martyrdom rather than violate a promise mate [sic] especially to you."[30] For David McDonogh, one could only claim the mantle of benevolence if one kept one's promises. He thus used the standard of honor and character that was central to elite white culture against the ACS and his former master in his effort to further his case.

Using these and other tactics to appropriate white-initiated philanthropy for his own ends, it was the slave who eventually triumphed over the master. Although David McDonogh had initially agreed to his white benefactor's requirement that he go to Liberia upon the completion of his studies, he made this agreement only to gain his aid and with intentions of staying in the United States. After graduating from Lafayette College in 1844, David McDonogh managed to secure an unofficial entrance into the College of Physicians and Surgeons of New York. Although the College refused to grant a diploma to a black man, officials did acknowledge that McDonogh had completed all elements of a medical education, and they never challenged his claim that he had a degree from their institution. One of the professors there secured for him a position at the New York Eye and Ear Infirmary, and afterwards McDonogh set up a private practice in New York City. He enjoyed success in his profession, and used his own position to contribute to a variety of African American-run charitable organizations. In recognition of his prominence and generosity, after his death the McDonogh Memorial Hospital—which accepted patients of all races—was named after him when it opened in 1893.[31] Although David McDonogh's story is only one of many types of interaction across racial lines in nineteenth-century educational philanthropy, it enables us to see some of the ways in which both monetary philanthropy and African American-initiated institutions had their origins in practices run on fundamentally different principles.

NOTES

1. David K. McDonogh to Walter Lowrie, 26 November 1844, Special Collections, Skillman Library, Lafayette College.
2. Washington McDonogh to John McDonogh, 7 October 1846, in *African Repository* 23 (1847), 175–176.
3. Classic works include Winthrop Jordan, *White over Black: American Attitudes Toward the Negro, 1550–1812* (Chapel Hill: University of North Carolina Press, 1968); George M. Frederickson,

The Black Image in the White Mind: The Debate on Afro-American Character and Destiny, 1817–1914 (New York: Harper & Row, 1971); Ronald Walters, *The Antislavery Appeal: American Abolitionism After 1830* (Baltimore: Johns Hopkins University Press, 1978); Aileen S. Kraditor, *Means and Ends in American Abolitionism: Garrison and His Critics on Strategy and Tactics, 1834–1850* (New York: Random House, 1967).

4.   Among the more prominent recent studies are Patrick Rael, *Black Identity and Black Protest in the Antebellum North* (Chapel Hill: University of North Carolina Press, 2002); Mia Bay, *The Black Image in the White Mind: African-American Ideas About White People, 1830–1925* (New York: Oxford University Press, 2000); Elizabeth Rauh Bethel, *The Roots of African-American Identity: Memory and History in Antebellum Free Communities* (New York: St. Martin's Press, 1997); Elizabeth McHenry, *Forgotten Readers: Recovering the Lost History of African American Literary Societies* (Durham: Duke University Press, 2002).

5.   Kathleen D. McCarthy, *American Creed: Philanthropy and the Rise of Civil Society* (Chicago: University of Chicago Press, 2003), 3; Susan M. Ryan, *The Grammar of Good Intentions: Race and the Antebellum Culture of Benevolence* (Ithaca: Cornell University Press, 2003).

6.   "Introduction," in Thomas Adam, ed., *Philanthropy, Patronage and Civil Society: Experiences from Germany, Great Britain, and North America* (Bloomington: Indiana University Press, 2004), 4.

7.   Lawrence J. Friedman and Mark D. McGarvie, eds., *Charity, Philanthropy, and Civility in American History* (Cambridge: Cambridge University Press, 2003), frontispiece, 1–21.

8.   K. Anthony Appiah and Amy Gutmann, *Color Conscious: The Political Morality of Race* (Princeton: Princeton University Press, 1996); Eric Lott, *Love & Theft: Blackface Minstrelsy and the American Working Class* (New York: Oxford University Press, 1993).

9.   Ronald G. Walters, *American Reformers, 1815–1860* (New York: Hill & Wang, 1997 revised edition; 1978); Robert H. Abzug, *Cosmos Crumbling: American Reform and the Religious Imagination* (New York: Oxford University Press, 1994).

10.   Wilson Jeremiah Moses, ed., *Liberian Dreams: Back-to-Africa Narratives from the 1850s* (University Park: Pennsylvania State University Press, 1998), xx–xxxiv; Bruce Dorsey, *Reforming Men and Women: Gender in the Antebellum City* (Ithaca: Cornell University Press, 2002), 136–194.

11.   On some of these early thoughts and efforts, see Floyd J. Miller, *The Search for a Black Nationality: Black Emigration and Colonization* (Urbana: University of Illinois Press, 1975), 21–53; Philip J. Staudenraus, *The African Colonization Movement, 1816–1865* (New York: Columbia University Press, 1961), 1–11; Early Lee Fox, *The American Colonization Society, 1817–1840* (Baltimore: Johns Hopkins University Press, 1919).

12.   On some of the larger patterns of racial erasure, see Joanne Pope Melish, *Disowning Slavery: Gradual Emancipation and "Race" in New England, 1780–1860* (Ithaca: Cornell University Press, 1998).

13.   John McDonogh, *Letter of John McDonogh, on African Colonization; Addressed to the Editors of the New Orleans Commercial Bulletin* (New Orleans, 1842).

14.   For further details about the various attendees at Lafayette, see Selden J. Coffin, *The Men of Lafayette, 1826–1893: Lafayette College, Its History, Its Men, Their Record* (Easton: George W. West, 1891).

15.   Theodore Dwight Weld, *First Annual Report of the Society for Promoting Manual Labor in Literary Institutions, Including the Report of their General Agent, Theodore D. Weld. January 28, 1833* (New York: S.W. Benedict & Co., 1833); Jeffrey A. Mullins, "'In the Sweat of Thy Brow': Education, Manual Labor, and the Market Revolution," in Scott Martin, ed., *Cultural History and the Market Revolution in America, 1815–1860* (Lanham: Madison House Press, 2004); Paul Goodman, "The Manual Labor Movement and the Origins of Abolitionism," *Journal of the Early Republic*, 13

(1993), 355–88; Milton C. Sernett, *Abolition's Axe: Beriah Green, Oneida Institute, and the Black Freedom Struggle* (Syracuse: Syracuse University Press, 1986), 33–41.

16. *Second Annual Report of the Board of Trustees of the Manual Labor Academy, of Pennsylvania. November 9, 1830* (Philadelphia: William F. Geddes, 1830); David Bishop Skillman, *The Biography of a College: Being the History of the First Century of the Life of Lafayette College* (Easton: Lafayette College, printed by The Scribner Press, 1932).

17. Mary Price Coulling, *Margaret Junkin Preston: A Biography* (Winston-Salem: John F. Blair Publisher, 1993), 63.

18. Jeffrey A. Mullins, "Honorable Violence: Youth Culture, Masculinity, and Contested Authority in Liberal Education, 1800–1830," *ATQ: Nineteenth Century Literature and American Culture* 17 (2003); Rodney Hessinger, "'The Most Powerful Instrument of College Discipline': Student Disorder and the Growth of Meritocracy in the Colleges of the Early Republic," *History of Education Quarterly* 39 (1999), 237–262; Steven J. Novak, *The Rights of Youth: American Colleges and Student Revolt, 1798–1815* (Cambridge: Harvard University Press, 1977).

19. John Yeomans to Rev. M. B. Hope, November [no date], 1841, Special Collections, Skillman Library, Lafayette College.

20. John Yeomans to John McDonogh, 18 November 1841, Special Collections, Skillman Library, Lafayette College.

21. David McDonogh to Walter Lowrie, 13 September 1842, Special Collections, Skillman Library, Lafayette College.

22. David McDonogh to Walter Lowrie, 23 September 1842, Special Collections, Skillman Library, Lafayette College.

23. David McDonogh to Walter Lowrie, 13 September 1842, Special Collections, Skillman Library, Lafayette College.

24. Ira Berlin, *Many Thousands Gone: The First Two Centuries of Slavery in America* (Cambridge: Harvard University Press, 1998), 118.

25. Richard L. Bushman, *The Refinement of America: Persons, Houses, Cities* (New York: Vintage Books, 1993); C. Dallett Hemphill, *Bowing to Necessities: A History of Manners in America, 1620–1860* (New York: Oxford University Press, 1999); Jay Fliegelman, *Prodigals and Pilgrims: The American Revolution Against Patriarchal Authority* (New York: Cambridge University Press, 1982).

26. Washington W. McDonogh to John McDonogh, 7 October 1846, in Bell I. Wiley, ed., *Slaves No More: Letters from Liberia, 1833–1869* (Lexington: University Press of Kentucky, 1980), 141–142.

27. John McDonogh, *Letter of John McDonogh, on African Colonization; Addressed to the Editors of the New Orleans Commercial Bulletin* (New Orleans, 1842).

28. Susan Ryan, *Grammar of Good Intentions* (Ithaca: Cornell University Press, 2003); Christine Stansell, *City of Women: Sex and Class in New York, 1789–1860* (New York: Alfred A. Knopf, 1982).

29. David K. McDonogh to Walter Lowrie, 26 November 1844, Special Collections, Skillman Library, Lafayette College.

30. David McDonogh to John McDonogh, 5 April 1844, Special Collections, Skillman Library, Lafayette College.

31. Russell W. Irvine, "Pride and Prejudice: The Early History of African-Americans at P&S," *The College of Physicians and Surgeons of Columbia University* (winter 2000): 13–16.

CHAPTER THREE

Booker T. Washington

Philanthropy and Aesthetics

MICHAEL BIEZE

Why did wealthy northeastern white people give Booker T. Washington so much money, and what can his story tell us about successful fund-raisers in the world of philanthropy who solicit from an outsider culture?[1] When the question is examined only via the economic motivations of northern capitalists, the answer is usually that Washington could provide them with a compliant, uneducated workforce willing to postpone civil rights for a bowl of materialistic pottage. In other words, with relatively painless monetary donations northern capitalists were able to preserve the social and economic hierarchy while also creating a pipeline of laborers readily available for their own use. Or so the argument usually goes. For example, James D. Anderson, in discussing the history of white philanthropy, has described the "core of industrial philanthropic ideology as being focused on squelching civil rights" and the "affirmation of black subordination."[2] Thinking about the philanthropic relationship in this way makes the grave error of assuming that the 'outsider' fundraiser is always merely a pawn in someone else's game.

Anderson's assessment exemplifies two blind spots in what has become the familiar way of interpreting Washington and philanthropy. First, by focusing only on the motivations of those who gave money, this interpretation completely overlooks the motivations of Washington himself. The issue has never been examined from the vantage point of the fund-raiser. This angle requires a journey into what Washington biographer Louis Harlan called "the secret life" of Washington and reveals a man convinced that fund-raising depended upon a constant, artful display to prove to donors and potential donors that his programs yielded results.[3] In other words, he deliberately made himself an attractive recipient. This, in turn, points to the second blind spot. The traditional way of interpreting Washington's philanthropic relationships assumes that the methods he used to raise funds were successful only at the expense of reinscribing white notions of black inferiority; in this analysis, Washington is seen as a mere 'Uncle Tom.' A more nuanced reading is necessary. There has been little research done on the ways and reasons fund-raisers, and in particular those struggling for favorable recognition by the mainstream, sometimes deliberately employed their outsider or exotic cultural traditions to attract and land donors. Washington's performance for elite white audiences can be located within the nineteenth-century tradition of a privileged world that projected nostalgia, simplicity, and allegories of modernism upon those they perceived as being on the lower rungs of the civilization ladder and can be seen as successful progressive efforts that helped uplift the race.[4]

Washington's call to the Deep South in 1881 to launch a normal school for blacks occurred during what sociologist Rayford Logan called the nadir of American race relations, a shadowy period witnessing the death of nearly all the hopeful advances in policies and laws enacted during the Reconstruction period. Ironically, the reason that Tuskegee was founded, which was for a white politician to win an Alabama state senate seat by giving local blacks a school in exchange for their vote, would be gone within a generation as disfranchisement and Jim Crow laws would take away that very right. But Washington—the former slave who never knew his white father, had worked as the lowest of wage laborers and domestic help, been twice a widower, seen slaves whipped as a child, witnessed freemen's lynched bodies hung along rail lines for his viewing, and was vilified in the southern press whenever he stepped out of line—always saw the glass as half full. At least he led everyone to believe that, resulting in his later depiction as a Panglossian figure hopelessly unaware of the vicious racism all around him. In reality, Washington functioned beneath a mask of compliance to affect change, believing that the times would allow only bottom-up, gradual change. Tuskegee Normal School opened on the fourth of July, 1881, with a small appropriation from the state, in a space borrowed from the local African Methodist Episcopal Zion church. Since he did not want any denominational assistance nor received much state or federal funding, Washington's growing vision of building a black industrial acropolis would require that he live a life on northern roads constantly in search of money. He was so successful that he became the first black college president of national recognition and the first black media celebrity.

Washington marketed himself and Tuskegee as simultaneously primitive and modern. That is, he knowingly provided images of a peaceful, bygone era of the south within the new Victorian Arts and Crafts aesthetic, appealing to both his donors' sense of Christian charity and their socially conscious taste. The Arts and Crafts Movement in America, the dates of which roughly parallel the lifetime of Washington, was a broadly eclectic movement originally based on the writings of John Ruskin and William Morris. It was a reaction against factories, mass-produced design, and the elimination of the worker in the creative process, and emphasized handcrafted, functional, simple, communal efforts of the working class. Ruskin, whose aesthetics may be simplified to the concept that art should advance the harmonious interplay of labor, art, and morality, was at the forefront of the movement. True beauty was moral; the worker was a craftsman who developed mind and body and created works communally for the betterment of society. Furthermore, if material culture could inculcate values and transform social ills, then it would be in the interest of social reformers to employ proper taste.[5]

The Movement's socialist leanings in England shifted into a capitalist form in America, exemplified in the ideals of Washington's friend Elbert Hubbard and his Roycroft community in East Aurora, New York. Washington and Hubbard were kindred spirits. Both rose to fame in 1895, oversaw publications, ran large communities, and were powerful self-promoters. Both reduced their philosophy to the same phrase—"head, heart, and hand"—to challenge liberal education's separation from practical knowledge.[6] Washington's mastery of the media in creating compelling images reflective of this philosophy and aesthetic was the source not only of his financial success but also of his social activism in the philanthropic world. Whereas it claimed to represent and be an art for the common working man and woman, its style was most often highbrow.

Like many Victorians, Washington saw art as an expression of the highest attainment within culture, a symbol of the apex of civilization as it was conceived of in the nineteenth century. This meant that a sliding scale of art existed for each class as it found its natural and rightful expression. Most blacks had not reached, in his estimation, a level of economic and cultural attainment commensurate with, for example, owning a piano, learning French, reciting poetry, or dressing in fancy clothes. As he wrote in 1902, "the southern white people had the idea that every Negro educated would become a minister, or teacher, or dude: that an educated Negro meant as a rule a high hat, a big walking-cane, kid gloves and patent leather shoes."[7] Instead, he espoused a restrained high taste in the rising Arts and Crafts style of simplicity, one that modestly matched blacks' artistic expressions with their economic and cultural realities.

Washington successfully matched a mythic image of an Old South to well-intentioned northerners' visions of an "uncivilized" and yet spiritually pure region of the United States. Part of Washington's philanthropic genius lay in his ability to covertly advance his social, political, and educational ideals while he appeased a white audience's taste for nostalgic images of the black worker presented at a safe distance.

Art theorist Hal Foster offers one way of understanding this idealized notion of uncivilized purity, writing "[t]he primitive is articulated by the west in derivative or supplemental terms: as a spectacle of savagery or a state of grace."[8] However, historian Leo Marx suggests that the "state of grace" may be further split into a Rousseau-like noble savage or the shepherd described by Virgil as a man of culture who chooses a distant, agrarian retreat.[9] The latter was the image Washington constructed. For northern white elites—a world comprised of businessmen, educators, and philanthropists—Washington performed the role of the highly civilized man of taste, albeit one who knew his place. He countered the savage racist images in white popular culture with soft-focus photographs of student labor and of himself in a state of bucolic grace at Tuskegee. A pastoral shepherd, he made certain to never be confused as a dandy or flaneur of the city. Washington made it abundantly clear that he was at home in the rural south. It was here, in nature and not in books, Washington stated, that the true and the good waited to be discovered: "To me there is nothing more delightful and restful than to spend a portion of each Sabbath afternoon in the woods with my family, near some little stream where we can gather wild flowers and listen to the singing of the mocking-birds and the ripple of the water. This, after a good sermon in the morning, seems to take us very near to nature's God."[10]

As America's first black media celebrity, Washington was a master of appealing to white northerners by sending paradoxical messages. His formula for success was simple. He simultaneously presented both a progressive and a nostalgic view of black life in the south, picturing the present in a modern photographic style that rendered life timeless through painterly, soft-focus filtering [Figure 1]. Washington's aesthetic performance for white philanthropists was deployed in at least four specific ways: (1) through images of racial progress (material and spiritual), (2) through images of passivity (compliance), (3) through flattery of his patrons, and (4) through support of the arts as a demonstration of progress. We will look at each in turn below.

Demonstration of racial progress was Washington's most common fund-raising tactic. Starting with his own story, Washington himself served as the primary object lesson in progress. He loved to repeat his tale of founding Tuskegee in a storm-drenched shanty teaching beneath an umbrella. His favorite method of showing progress was the "before and after" format, a formula Washington embraced in the late 1890s and utilized throughout the rest of his life [Figure 2].[11] The Tuskegee Machine constantly provided white readership with visual evidence of how poor, unkempt black men and women were transformed into upstanding Tuskegee men and women. As Emmett J. Scott, Washington's personal secretary, pointed out in a white Boston charity journal, one could continue to live in a "wretched one-room cabin" or, with knowledge provided by Tuskegee, live "in comfortable homes" [Figure 3]. [12] Northern white readers could see for themselves, in photographs supplied by Washington, how the former sharecroppers now lived in New England charm.

Washington's second strategy was to present an image of both himself and Tuskegee as one of passivity for white audiences. In photographs, he remains seated or reflective while those around him seem to confront the camera, sending a message that Washington's goal was not to radically challenge whites' sensibilities. At times this passivity could be subtle, such as his pose in the popular stereograph from Tuskegee's twenty-fifth anniversary in which Washington slouches in the middle of a group including Harvard's President Charles W. Eliot, industrialist Andrew Carnegie, and publisher Lyman Abbott [Figure 4].

Yet much more blatant examples of a willingness to present an image of southern passivity exist, falling under the visual rubric of the Sunny South. For example, the New England photographer Clifton Johnson's 1901 visual story for *The Outlook*, fully supported by Washington, evokes an expression of the Tuskegee president most at home in the faraway south, nearest to God, nature, and animals [Figure 1]. [13] Shot in the soft-focus, high-art style known as Pictorialism, it is the photographic aesthetic closest to the Arts and Crafts movement. An even more nostalgic visual essay was created by Julian Dimock, who offered northern white readers softly lit images of the old days, including antebellum survivors such as "a mammy" and "typical pickaninnies." [14] At the end of these photographs is a portrait of Booker T. Washington. A few years later, Washington used the Dimock photographs to illustrate a four-part series he wrote for the lavish New York journal *The World's Work*. [15] It is unclear if this busy man surrounded by books, a telephone, and cut flowers is guiding blacks away from the past or not. These sets of photographs, both done by white photographers, are particularly striking when juxtaposed with the highly active performances Washington distributed through the black press. This Washington was a defiant man, whose dramatic oratory skills were demonstrated on outdoor stages in the Deep South before enchanted seas of admiring black faces. Unknown to the white media was the long list of black photographers Washington employed to distribute these kinds of images. [16]

Washington's third strategy for fund-raising was to flatter his benefactors. The most obvious expression of gratitude was to name buildings after patrons. The more subtle form of flattery was to package his school's success story and marketing productions in the Arts and Crafts taste of his philanthropist friends. As a grateful recipient of funds, Washington never failed to recognize the philanthropists' generosity. The Tuskegee campus was a vast expanse of naming opportunities. [17] A campus walk reveals a who's who list of powerful men of the age. Over the doors of campus buildings are found names such as Carnegie, Huntington, Phelps,

Rockefeller, and Slater. When elaborate donor recognition was needed, Washington set his team in motion. In order to recognize the death of Tuskegee Trustee William Henry Baldwin Jr., Washington staged a massive outpouring of lamentation centered on a huge photograph of Baldwin. Washington assured Mrs. Baldwin that her husband's portrait was "hung in the Chapel in the place you designated, and it is a constant source of satisfaction to all of us to have it there."[18] Everywhere on and around the Tuskegee campus, philanthropists could witness success in terms that they understood. Washington's home, the large two-story mansion known as The Oaks, was the epitome of bourgeois Victorian taste. The campus became a rambling collection of classical buildings, a black acropolis serving as a showcase for moneyed visitors. Even the faculty housing in the area known as Greenwood was created with donors in mind. Emmett J. Scott noted that it was intended to recreate a New England village, an environment that would be reminiscent of home and thereby reassure philanthropists that their money had been well spent.[19]

Washington's benefactors were approached by the Tuskegee president with productions made in their elite style, showing them that he shared their tastes. His first book, *Daily Resolves*, was designed in an Arts and Crafts illuminated manuscript revival style, a lavish and detailed work clearly not made for mass distribution [Figure 5].[20] In fact, when the black organizers of the 1900 Paris World's Fair attempted to include all known publications by African Americans authors for their exhibition space, it was not listed.[21] This sumptuously decorated collection of Washington phrases, as richly embellished as any book production of the era, was made for a select elite. The best known example of Washington's display of refined taste is found in Gertrude Kasebier's frontispiece photogravure portrait of Washington for *Up from Slavery* [Figure 6].[22] Whereas his previous autobiography, *Story of My Life and Work*, was conceived with black audiences in mind, *Up from Slavery* was Washington's perennial gift for white donors.[23] When Washington sat for the New York-based Kasebier in December of 1900, he was having his picture taken by one of the leading portrait photographers in the world. The publishers, Doubleday, Page & Co., had just begun to serialize the book in *The Outlook* and it did not include the Kasebier portrait. As the book neared completion, however, the publishers dropped all of the original photographs and illustrations and replaced them with this one photograph showing Washington as a dignified, seated scholar. There is no doubt that Washington, who rigorously controlled all of his media productions, chose the image. This dignified, classical pose, seen slightly from below to increase his stature, became his best-known image as the book enjoyed constant distribution as a gift for wealthy friends. Yet, at the same time, there is a self-consciousness in the portrait which maintains Washington's submissive positioning of himself. The awkward hands, holding papers meant to depict him as a noble thinker, are arranged by the photographer in a contrived manner revealing a willingness to be posed. Later images of Washington show a man who gave rather than received such directions.

Fourth, and finally, Washington sought to bring in northern financial support through strategic deployment of the arts. The Tuskegee campus was an artistic show-case deliberately designed to display the aesthetic and ethical sophistication of an institution that surrounded its students with high culture. Washington's attempt to contract Frederick Law Olmstead, the country's leading landscape architect, to help design the grounds is further evidence of his commitment to creating a thorough-ly cultured environment for the students.[24] Olmstead ultimately did not landscape the campus, but the grounds were nonetheless spectacular, and Washington distrib-uted images of them that were nothing short of a utopian vision [Figure 7].

Although Tuskegee was known primarily as an industrial school—and justifi-ably so—Washington took great pains to fill daily campus life with uplifting cul-ture beyond its architecture and landscape. The institute hosted Paul Laurence Dunbar to read poetry, offered a leading architecture school, had a series of famous photographers on the grounds, placed Raphael prints in the classrooms, and hung pictures on the dormitory walls from the well-known Knoedler Gallery in New York. There was even a campus museum space with African artifacts. Northern sup-porters grew to know the campus through an endless stream of photographically illustrated stories exemplifying the mission and success of Tuskegee.

Washington supplemented these visual representations of his institution with live performances that further bound the interest of white supporters to his college. He learned early on that white audiences were drawn to what were called planta-tion songs, the period's term for spirituals, and he began incorporating them in his northern fund-raising tours. As a student, he had watched the Hampton Singers recreate the Old South for potential donors in what can be described as both an attempt to preserve and romanticize black culture. By the 1890s booking agents for Atlanta University, Fisk University, Hampton Institute, and Tuskegee Institute were all competing for dates in the north.[25] Tuskegee first explored this possibility in the spring of 1889 when Washington wrote to General Armstrong, suggesting that a group of singers could bring in significant donations from the north by hav-ing them sing songs "confined to that which is peculiar to this part of the South."[26] Eventually this effort became a standard part of the Washington tour. One of Washington's ghost writers, Max Bennett Thrasher, reported in 1900 that Washington was obliged to keep going north for money "by personal solicitation and by public addresses, frequently having in the latter the assistance of the songs of a quartette of young men from the school."[27]

Washington's support of these singing tours, like his marketing of images of the Old South, was filled with ambiguities. While Washington certainly played to white audiences' enjoyment of these concerts as a means of experiencing a nostalgic, albeit fictional past, he also passionately supported spirituals as an authentic form of black art to be treasured.[28] Art served as a propagandistic tool both for fundraising and for establishing black art. As Washington aged, he became increasingly outspoken in his call for black history as well as a black art. However, what he meant by that was never clearly defined. In 1906 Washington wrote, "so long as the Negro was taught that everything that was good was white and everything that was bad was black . . . it was natural and inevitable that he should desire to become in everything—in style, manners, thought, and in the color of his skin—white."[29] He commented that:

> the feelings that divided my mind and confused my purposes when I was a young man, have also divided members of my race. The continual adverse criticism has led some to disavow our racial identity, to seek rest and try our successes as members of another race than that to which we were born. It has led others of us to seek to get away as far as possible from association with our own race, and to keep as far away from Africa, from its history and from its traditions as it was possible for us to do.[30]

Washington's efforts fall within the history of individuals and groups willing to perform nostalgic scenes of a simpler time in order to raise money from those with kindly hearts, deep pockets, and a self-appointed sense of enlightenment.[31] Washington's rise to national prominence in Atlanta in 1895 at the Cotton States and International Exposition occurred only two years after the Chicago Columbian Exposition, which became a world stage for attempting to display the hierarchy of cultures from around the globe as an act of public anthropology. As historian Curtis Hinsley writes, "At Chicago in 1893, public curiosity about other peoples, mediated by the terms of the marketplace, produced an early form of touristic consumption."[32] Yet the cultures being consumed on the Fair's Midway were enactments by groups now savvy enough to know how to act the part in order to raise money through sales of so-called authentic goods. However, unlike the Chicago Midway, blacks in Atlanta in 1895 now controlled their own displays within the Negro Building. Instead of greeting visitors as Aunt Jemima, black painters, sculptors, photographers, and craftsmen displayed their skills. Among the largest displays was that of Tuskegee Normal and Industrial Institute. All aspects of the school's agricultural and industrial work were exhibited. In a clear attempt to distance themselves from the so-called primitive displays of the Chicago Midway, the organizers of the Negro Building juxtaposed their work against a section of the building titled "Uncivilized Africa."[33]

Within a short time, Washington would join the growing strategy being used by other southern college presidents who, in order to raise money, discovered how to sell northerners a new version of a nostalgic and exotic Dixieland. Washington's contemporary and friend, Berea College president William Goodell Frost, was a kindred spirit in the effort of crafting a southern identity as a marketing strategy. Berea College, located in Kentucky, was on the edge of bankruptcy when Frost took charge. Frost, who was white, employed the same tactic as Washington by playing into southern myths for northern philanthropists.[34] As author John O'Brien observed, Frost turned to wealthy New Englanders, weaving new "layers of invention" about the south in *The Atlantic Monthly* to meet "the immediate needs of outside missionaries."[35] Each article slowly helped in creating the identity of Appalachia as a land filled with the contradictory image of romanticized hillbillies: God-fearing, pure Anglo-Saxon folk cut off from the evils of modernity.[36] A few years earlier, also in the pages of *The Atlantic Monthly*, readers were told by Booker T. Washington about a new Black Belt comprised of educated, black Christian farmers raised up through New England virtues.[37] Washington's ambiguous portrait of progressive black workers set within the nostalgia of a simpler, agrarian south was similar to Frost's except for one key point; Washington also furtively spoke in another voice to black audiences.

Part of Washington's fund-raising success was due to his ability to sell different identities to black and white America. Both were necessary parts of the money equation. He needed to raise money from whites in order to fund his projects in the black world. He developed status in the black world by having social capital in the world of the philanthropists. These connections slowly enabled him to build the Tuskegee Machine, a complex assemblage of political connections which generated his power to affect the black press, influence local and national political appointments, secure jobs for friends, run the National Negro Business League, and raise the profile of the Hampton-Tuskegee model of education. The ability to demonstrate success in the black world, in turn, made him increasingly attractive to white power brokers. Each audience required different representations. To white philanthropists, he sold a passive image of Tuskegee's success packaged in a style based upon New England aesthetic taste. For black elites, he presented an active image of power in the black press.[38]

His efforts were necessarily Janus-headed because the very nature of his project required him to please two groups moved by vastly different ideas. He perpetuated images of what was called in the white press the "Old Time Negro," believing it to be a necessary tactic to garner white approval and support in Jim Crow America.[39] But, Washington's shrewd manipulations among whites masked his role in supporting black artists and the creation of a separate set of representations for black audiences. For all of his accommodationism, he was also the architect of a new image of black identity which countered the prevailing racist images in mainstream American culture.[40] With stealth, Washington operated under the aegis of a particular aesthetic, nostalgic Victorian compliance, so that he could slowly develop the more radical goal of the New Negro.

In addition to performing a Sunny South routine and directing his message to different constituencies, Washington knew how his patrons were motivated by their faith. He understood that the philanthropists of the Progressive Age, who were primarily northern industrialists, perceived themselves to be enlightened and aesthetically sophisticated followers of Social Darwinism, not mere labor bosses. What sold them on the Tuskegee Plan was Washington's ability to deliver proof of the so-called "civilizing" forces of industrial education.[41] Though paternalistic, the philanthropists believed that they were not supporting an uneducated labor force but helping to create schooled workers with Christian character and good manners. Northerners read in Lyman Abbott's *The Outlook* how Washington's students were following the words of St. Paul: "But if any provide not for his own, and especially for those of his own house, he hath denied the faith, and is worse than an infidel."[42] It was this emphasis on religion and character building, often summarized by Washington as his gospel of the toothbrush, which made him a household name among the northern elite. Appealing as a Christian to Christian charity was often the tactic that opened philanthropists' doors for Washington.[43] He was a brother in what became known as the Social Gospel movement, the aesthetic of which united labor, God, and moral taste. He represented in images and words the promise of what the philanthropists' support could achieve.

Washington's powerful white supporters saw him as the very essence of the successful, progressive, African American man. Nearly all of his philanthropic supporters, including the Tuskegee board of trustees, were Protestant leaders in the Social Gospel movement. They saw cities as inherently immoral, upheld traditional gender roles, valued moderate versus radical change, and firmly believed in a hierarchy of cultures ranging from barbaric to civilized.[44] For the Social Gospeler, the new man of faith was like Theodore Roosevelt, a man of means and mind who took robust physical action when the needs of justice called. This led to a social philosophy, as Janet Fishburn writes, which "made it possible to accept personal success and be aware of social problems at the same time."[45]

As Christian captains of industry, Social Gospelers believed it was the duty of the church and its members to act as agents of change in the state. In particular, they believed that they could use their power and money to solve the so-called "Negro Problem" through education rather than legislation, and they saw their "Brother[s] in Black" as equals in Christian faith who simply needed some help in order to achieve their own social uplift.[46] In this view, one could be a rich Christian as long he or she was charitable and demonstrated modest taste.[47] Washington deliberately exhibited a public demeanor of self-control, temperance, modesty, and the simple tastes that inspired the confidence of these eager philanthropists. As a shrewd black businessman, Washington knew the limitations of his place in Jim Crow society. He made sure to keep the peace with southern whites so that no concerns could be raised for his patrons.[48] Moreover, Washington assured northern white audiences that black institutions, including Tuskegee, were being substantially helped from within the black community.[49] What could be more appealing to these men and women of great wealth than to hear that he had even abandoned lofty dreams of becoming a lawyer in order to "help his race to help itself"?[50] The philanthropists were funding a fellow philanthropist.

Philanthropists sent Washington money, offered advice, and used their influence to help him because he seemed to be like one of them without demanding to really be one of them. Like the philanthropists, Washington lived in luxury. He lived in an Eastlake-style Victorian home and kept a second residence in the north. He not only sent his children north for schooling but also exhibited his affinity for white culture by, for example, naming his daughter Portia after a character in Shakespeare. He had traveled to the continent to dine with Queen Victoria in London and had walked through the Luxembourg Palace in Paris to look at the works of the African American painter Henry O. Tanner. At the same time, he never traveled in the northern philanthropists' Pullman cars, was seen dining with them in public, or stayed at their homes. Washington lived a life commensurate with theirs, yet clearly separate, and he always played to his audience. Nothing seemed peculiar about the ease with which his voice shifted from the round tones of a southern dialect to New England crispness.

Washington's images of what he repeatedly called "the dignity of labor" were located at a safe distance for northerners by their placement in the exotic setting of what was being called the Sunny South.[51] His cultural performance fit perfectly within his white supporters' progressive blending of philanthropy with an aesthetic of moral superiority. Washington presented himself and Tuskegee in the modern Arts and Crafts aesthetic taste of his benefactors by linking morality, labor, and beauty. Across the country, socially progressive thinkers found a path to uplift within the Arts and Crafts aesthetic. Building upon the philosophy of the English writer, critic, and artist John Ruskin, Progressives believed in creating communities and community centers fostering the handmade as an antidote to a vast range of social ills from industrialism to poverty.[52] In the face of the proliferation of anonymous, mass-produced machine artifacts of modern life, handmade objects represented traditions shared within a community. The catch phrase of both Washington and the Arts and Crafts movement was "head, heart, and hand." It was believed, from Boston Settlement Houses to Chicago's Hull House, that the downtrodden could find hope and moral light in the handcrafted object. Boston's *Home and Club Life*, a journal for women supporting charitable efforts, routinely offered advice on how the tasteful home provided comfort and moral object lessons by surrounding the tenants with visual models of uplift.[53] Journals such as the *Christian Herald* championed new efforts at bringing refinement to tenement dwellers by hosting "slum socials," showing how exposure to taste and Victorian manners would raise them up from their squalor.[54] For many in the north, Washington was the Ruskin of the Black Belt, working to uplift blacks through a simple yet powerful aesthetic and labor ethics. Northerners read stories and saw pictures verifying that, among the magnolias and antebellum columns, was the man from Tuskegee who led with unaffected simplicity.[55]

Washington's images of the black worker handcrafting objects in the agrarian south provided precisely the romantic image of progress that good-hearted, enlightened white philanthropists sought. Washington repeatedly reminded white leaders that "labour" must not be seen as drudgery, but as having "beauty, dignity, and civilising [sic] power."[56] According to Washington and his followers, nothing symbolized the climb up the social ladder more than owning and decorating an attractive home. Washington's multiple writings on the subject are traceable to the educational philosophy of his mentor, Hampton Institute founder, General Samuel Chapman Armstrong. These writings culminated in a 1908 article in *The Century*, in which Washington outlined the climb for the next generation as being from log cabins to homes of "taste and culture."[57]

For a century, scholarship on Washington has taken as a foundational presupposition W.E.B. Du Bois's critique that Washington's work was retrogressive for the race. In 1903 Du Bois asserted that Washington's leadership led blacks to lose the vote, accept Jim Crow segregation, and that it diverted funding from true higher education toward "mere" industrial schools.[58] Within a few years, that critique grew to include Mary Church Terrell's charge that Washington was even willing to stoop so low as to tell "dialect stories at the expense of the race" in his efforts to maintain inferiority in social life and education.[59] These kinds of portrayals grew to create the Booker T. Washington readers are most familiar with in this country. The basic problem with these portrayals is that they are built exclusively from the perspective of those who opposed Washington rather than also looking at the issue from his perspective.[60] These appraisals, accurate or not, tell us about a particular contemporary black critical understanding of Washington that ignores other contemporary opinions as well as the reasons northern white philanthropists responded to his calls for support for Tuskegee. Washington and Du Bois have too often been reduced to oversimplified caricatures of themselves when their views and actions are examined by scholars, a simplification which flattens the complexity of their relationship and ignores the nuances in their beliefs. A similar process has taken place whenever Washington's relationship to northern philanthropists is studied; it is past time to begin unfolding these complexities.

So why did the philanthropists give Washington so much money? Because, in effect, he showed them a flattering image of themselves and their philanthropic dreams. They saw a bucolic, Christian, exotic black world in the distant south rising up the Darwinian social and intellectual ladder, projected in an aesthetic that matched their own sense of high culture and service. Washington showed them idealistic views of progress being made as a result of their money and counsel.

Washington's double-life made him the most successful black fundraiser in America. Like many Victorians, including Du Bois, Washington saw art as both propaganda and an expression of cultural progress.[61] Needing the economic and political support of this audience, Washington built on the history of the "primitive" by performing for white civilization as he had learned as a student and teacher under General Samuel Chapman Armstrong at Hampton Institute. It is certainly possible to read these performances as acts of compliance. Houston Baker writes that these performances of labor amount to "a zealous aestheticization of slavery as 'modernity.'"[62] However, it is also possible to read his performance of a nostalgic aesthetic as a calculated posture providing him with a public façade while he covertly pursued his educational, political, and social concerns. While appearing to be only conservative, these visual efforts read differently when contextualized against a backdrop of ubiquitous racist media productions from the mainstream. As art critic Peter Scheldahl recently stated, "All racism, on some level, is aesthetic, as a projection of 'the ugly.'"[63] Washington's understanding of the aesthetics of racism are evident in his attempts to counter the demeaning images of poor, unkempt blacks in the popular media with positive examples of the black worker, asserting black equality as measured by the white Victorian taste of his benefactors [Figure 8]. These demonstrations of culture and refinement served to represent intellectual, moral, and economic equality on the part of blacks. In this way, his efforts should be recognized as an attempt—during a dark and violent period of this country's history—at racial uplift for the illiterate, southern masses offered within the protected, segregated space of a black utopia. He may have stooped to raise money, but he also forged the first generation of self-determined media images of black men and women wholly created by blacks, laying the foundation for the New Negro movement of the next generation.

NOTES

1. An earlier version of this chapter was presented at the National Association of African American Studies national conference in Houston, Texas, in February of 2003.

2. James D. Anderson, "Philanthropic Control over Private Black Higher Education," in *Philanthropy and Cultural Imperialism*, ed. Robert F. Arnove (Boston: G.K. Hall & Co., 1980), 156.

3. Louis Harlan, "The Secret Life of Booker T. Washington," *The Journal of Southern History* 37, no. 3 (1971): 393–416.

4. Marianna Torgovnick, *Going Primitive* (Chicago: University of Chicago Press, 1990), 244.

5. For a general discussion of the Arts and Crafts Movement, see Eileen Boris, *Art and Labor: Ruskin, Morris, and the Craftsman Ideal in America* (Philadelphia: Temple University Press, 1986).

6. Elbert Hubbard, *The Philosophy of Elbert Hubbard* (New York: Wm. H. Wise & Co., 1930), 132. Paralleling Washington's head, heart, and hand philosophy, Hubbard wrote that "The Artist is one who is educated in the three H's—head, heart, and hand."

7. Booker T. Washington, "Problems in Education," *The Cosmopolitan*, September 1902, 514.

8. Hal Foster, *Recoding: Art, Spectacle, Cultural Politics* (Seattle: Bay Press, 1985), 196.

9. For a discussion of the primitive versus the pastoral, see Leo Marx, *The Machine in the Garden* (New York: Oxford University Press, 1964; 2000), 22.

10. Ibid., 299.

11. Booker T. Washington, "The Story of Tobe Jones," *New England Home Magazine*, 22 January 1898, 140–143;———*Making Useful Citizens* (Tuskegee: Tuskegee Institute Press, c. 1912). The date of this promotional material is based upon the image being used in a 1912 advertisement, "The Bee" Printing Co. to BTW, 14 September 1912, Booker T. Washington Papers in the Division of Manuscripts of the Library of Congress, Library of Congress, Washington D.C., Reel 409. Hereafter letters and documents contained on microfilm reels in the Library of Congress will be identified as [LC]. LC Reel 337.

12. Emmett J. Scott, "Tuskegee's Great Gathering," *The Christian Herald and Signs of Our Times*, March 1901, 233.

13. Booker T. Washington, "Chickens, Pigs, and People," *The Outlook*, 1 June 1901, 291–299.

14. A. W. Dimock, "The South and Its Problems," *The Metropolitan Magazine*, October 1907, 1–-11.

15. Booker T. Washington, "Chapters from My Experience, I." *The World's Work*, October 1910, 13505–13522.

16. A partial list includes C. M. Battey, A. P. Bedou, William E. Benson, Peter Jones, Charles D. Robinson, Addison Scurlock, Harry Shepherd, and Addison Turner. For detailed account of their work for Washington, see Michael Scott Bieze, "Booker T. Washington and the Art of Self-Representation" (Ph.D. diss., Georgia State University, 2003).

17. Richard Kevin Dozier, "Tuskegee: Booker T. Washington's Contribution to the Education of Black Architects" (Ph.D. diss., University of Michigan, 1990).

18. Booker T. Washington to Mrs. William H. Baldwin, Jr., 4 December 1905, LC Reel 23.

19. Emmett J. Scott and L. Stowe, *Booker T. Washington: Builder of a Civilization* (New York: Doubleday, Page & Company, 1918 [1916], 162.

20. Booker T. Washington, *Daily Resolves* (New York: E.P. Dutton & Co., 1896).

21. Daniel Murray, *Preliminary List of Books and Pamphlets by Negro Authors for the Paris Exposition and Library of Congress* (Washington, D.C.: Library of Congress, 1900). Washington's other two books published by that date, *Black Belt Diamonds* and *Future of the American Negro*, were listed.

22. Booker T. Washington, *Up from Slavery* (New York: Doubleday, Page & Company, 1901).

23. Booker T. Washington, *The Story of My Life and Work* (Atlanta: J.L. Nichols & Company, 1901).

24. Louis Harlan, BTW to Jabez Lamar Monroe Curry, 21 September 1894, in Louis R. Harlan and Raymond W. Smock, eds., *The Booker T. Washington Papers*, 14 volumes (Urbana: University of Illinois, 1972–1989), 3: 469. Hereafter these volumes will be cited as *BTW Papers* with the volume number and page number.

25. Thomas Calloway to Booker T. Washington, 26 December 1895, LC Reel 122.

26. Booker T. Washington to Samuel Chapman Armstrong, 4 April 1889, *BTW Papers*, 2: 522.

27. Max Bennett Thrasher, *Tuskegee: Its Story and Its Work* (Boston: Small, Maynard & Company, 1901), 187.

28. Both Washington and Du Bois found spirituals to be a profound works of art. While white culture described anything of African heritage as uncivilized and barbaric, Washington embraced spir-

ituals as a gift from Africa. Washington asserted that, "According to the testimony of African students at Tuskegee there are in native African melodies strains that reveal the close relationship between the Negro music of America and Africa, but the imagery and sentiments to which the plantation songs give expression are the outcome of the conditions in America under which the transported children of Africa lived." See *Twenty-Four Negro Melodies Transcribed for the Piano by S. Coleridge Taylor*, with a preface by Booker T. Washington (Boston: Oliver Ditson Company, 1905), viii.

29. Booker T. Washington, "Tuskegee: A Retrospect and Prospect," *North American Review*, April 1906, 523.

30. Washington, *The Story of the Negro*, 12.

31. He should be seen as the culmination of a century which saw artists like the self-promoter George Catlin parade American Indians before Noble Savage-hungry European audiences in the 1840s or Black Elk's Sioux perform before Queen Victoria in 1886. See George Gurney and Therese Thau Heyman, eds., *George Catlin and His Indian Gallery* (Washington, D.C.: Smithsonian American Art Museum, 2002).

32. Curtis M. Hinsley, "The World as Marketplace," in *Exhibiting Cultures: The Poetics and Politics of Museum Display* (Washington, D.C.: Smithsonian Institute, 1991), 363.

33. "Is He a New Negro?," Chicago Inter Ocean, 18 September 1895, *BTW Papers*, 4: 38–39.

34. In addition to Berea, perhaps the best-known example of a southern institution of higher education generating a regionalist craft tradition to find donors is Newcomb College. Tulane University's sister school, Sophie Newcomb Memorial College, was founded in 1895 as an effort to train young women in aesthetically useful skills such as ceramics. "The whole thing was to be a southern product, made of southern clays, by southern artists, decorated with southern subject," wrote its founding director. See Leslie Green Bowman, *American Arts & Crafts: Virtue in Design* (Los Angeles: Los Angeles County Museum of Art, 1990), 160.

35. John O'Brien, *At Home in the Heart of Appalachia* (New York: Anchor Books, 2001), 250–251. Frost recognized the burgeoning interest in southern crafts. He helped establish the Berea Fireside Industries to have students produce works to help market the school. To entice northern philanthropists, "Dr. Frost often took old coverlets [of traditional Appalachian weavers] with him on trips to attract funding and publicity for the school." See Gillian Moss, "Art as Philanthropy," in *"The Art That Is Life: The Arts & Crafts Movement in America, 1875–1920*, ed. Wendy Kaplan (Boston: Boston Museum of Fine Arts, 1987), 309.

36. For example, see William Goodell Frost, "Our Contemporary Ancestors in the Southern Mountains," *The Atlantic Monthly*, March 1899, 311–320.

37. Booker T. Washington, "The Awakening of the Negro," *The Atlantic Monthly*, September 1896, 322–328.

38. Washington saw in black art the clearest demonstration for white America that blacks were their intellectual equals by creating works at the highest level according to the mainstream's standards. Blacks achieved cultural, and eventually social, equality by gaining economic stability, the acquisition of a well-designed, tasteful home serving as the primary sign. Therefore, he increased his efforts over his lifetime to advancing the artistic careers of writers, musicians, architects, painters, and photographers to speak to this black audience by developing black culture. In particular, the photographs of A. P. Bedou show Washington as an active, fiery speaker in a manner never depicted in white newspapers or journals.

39. Thomas Nelson Page, "The Old-Time Negro," *Scribner's Monthly*, November 1904, 522–532. Page and his peers believed that slaves and masters shared a harmonious, familial relationship which was now being destroyed by those who failed to recognize the "bond of friendship" they once enjoyed. Page lamented how the "old-time negro," "like the last leaves on the tree," was vanishing.

40. Henry Louis Gates, "Harlem on Our Minds," *Critical Inquiry* 24 (1997): 1–12.

41. The meaning of the term 'civilized' was clearly defined by Howard professor Kelly Miller in 1901. Like Washington and other education leaders, Miller had internalized the mainstream's conception of a hierarchy of humankind, resulting in the view that Africans were barbaric. Miller wrote that "Civilization may be defined as the sum total of those influences and agencies that make knowledge and virtue. . . . The essential factors of civilization are knowledge, industry, culture, and virtue. . . . The African was snatched from the wilds of savagery and thrust into the midst of a mighty civilization." African Americans would not turn in significant numbers to Africa for inspiration until the Harlem Renaissance. See Kelly Miller, "The Education of the Negro," *Report of the Commissioner of Education for the Year 1900–1901, volume 1* (Washington, D.C.: Government Printing Office, 1902), 803.

42. Booker T. Washington "On Our Racial Problems," *The Outlook*, 6 January 1900, 16.

43. Even Washington detractors noted the evangelical nature of his business crusade. For example, see E. Franklin Frazier, *Black Bourgeoisie* (New York: The Free Press, 1957; New York: Collier Books, 1962), 133–134. "The religious nature of this crusade was indicated in the annual address by Booker T. Washington which was delivered in the form of a 'Business Sermon' based upon the Biblical text, 'To him that hath shall be given.'"

44. Ronald C. White, *Liberty and Justice for All: Racial Reform & The Social Gospel (1877–1925)*, with a foreword by James M. McPherson (New York: Harper & Row, Publishers, 1990), 66. White lists the Social Gospelers on the Board of Trustees for several Black colleges, including Tuskegee.

45. Janet Forsythe Fishburn, *The Fatherhood of God and the Victorian Family: The Social Gospel in America* (Philadelphia: Fortress Press, 1981), 13. Fishburn argues that the Social Gospelers saw it as their duty, being at the apex of civilization in terms of wealth and culture, to assist in the moral and economic uplift of those lower on the ladder.

46. "The Jubilee of the New South," *The Century Magazine*, January 1896, 470. The author, writing about the Atlanta Cotton States Exposition of 1895, summarized the "negro problem" as consisting of the "moral, intellectual, and material conditions" of blacks.

47. William Henry Baldwin, Jr. to William P. Bancroft, 6 April 1899, *BTW Papers* 5: 76–77. Baldwin, a Social Gospel Tuskegee Trustee, was responding to a letter Bancroft sent to Washington about the Tuskegee president's new mansion, The Oaks. Bancroft wondered if such a large home was necessary or appropriate. Baldwin responded by writing, "It is imperative that if we expect Booker Washington to live and do good work, for him to have comfortable surroundings. . . . The great charm and strength of Booker Washington lies in his extreme modesty. His simpler tastes and habits and the quiet strength of his modesty appeal very strongly to me."

48. White southerners constantly checked him for signs of seeking social equality. The best-known examples are his social engagements with President Theodore Roosevelt and John Wanamaker, both of which brought the southern press out in force, attacking the public stance of not seeking social equality. On 16 October 1901, Washington dined in the White House with President Roosevelt. An onslaught of cartoons and articles raised fears among Whites of the forbidden racial social mixing. See Louis Harlan, *Booker T. Washington: The Making of a Black Leader, 1856–1901* (New York: Oxford University Press, 1975), 311–324. On 14 August 1905, Washington dined with department store owner John Wanamaker and his daughter in his Saratoga, New York, home. The next day's *Atlanta Constitution* headline read, "Booker T. Washington's Arm Aided Wanamaker's Girl as She Walked To Dinner." *BTW Papers* 8: 343. How did he respond to these sorts of events? Washington did speak out against his benefactors as he aged, albeit privately. For example, he wrote to Robert Ogden in 1906 complaining about the Southern Education Board's fail-

ure to help black schools, stating they had done little "so far as the Negro schools are concerned."
See White, *Liberty and Justice For All*, 88.

49. Booker T. Washington, "Negro Self-Help," *The Independent*, 23 November 1905, 1208.
Washington failed to mention that by 1910 about $1203.00 a year was being raised from blacks
while a pittance of $74.00 was raised from southern whites. The majority of funds still came from
northern whites. See Roy Finkenbine, "Law, Reconstruction, and African American Education,"
in *Charity, Philanthropy, and Civility in American History*, ed. Lawrence J. Friedman and Mark D.
McGarvie (New York: Cambridge University Press, 2003), 167. Washington reported in 1912 that
"For the first time in the history of the school we have made an especial effort to secure gifts from
colored people." He reported that $1,992.00 was collected from 1,022 black supporters. *Report
of the Principal to the Trustees of the Tuskegee Normal and Industrial Institute for the Year Ending May
30, 1912* (Tuskegee: Tuskegee Institute Press, 1912), 10.

50. "A Great School," *Hawaiian Gazette*, 3 December 1897, LC Reel 409.

51. The fantasy of the Sunny South in popular imagery should be seen as part of a broader colonial-
ist context. Writing about Orientalist fantasies of Europeans at the same time, Malek Alloula
writes, "The postcard does it one better; it becomes the poor man's phantasm: for a few pennies,
display racks of dreams....It is at once their [colonialists'] poetry and their glory captured for the
ages; it is also their pseudoknowledge of the colony....The postcard is ubiquitous. It can be found
not only at the scene of the crime it perpetuates but at a far remove as well." See Malek Alloula,
The Colonial Harem (Minneapolis: University of Minnesota Press, 1986), 4. It could be argued that
the philanthropists were already experienced in this kind of aestheticized struggle in the work of
Jacob Riis. In New York, journalist-photographer Jacob Riis served as a tour guide through
Bowery squalor, his slide shows for the wealthy showing aestheticized poverty. See K. Gandal, *The
Virtues of the Vicious: Jacob Riis, Stephen Crane, and the Spectacle of the Slum* (New York: Oxford
University Press, 1997).

52. Boris, *Art and Labor*.

53. For example, see *Home and Club Life*, 19 June 1897. This "Official Organ [of the] Women's City
Relief Association" offered essays on charity, art, music, science and fashion.

54. "The Tenement-House Social," *Christian Herald*, 13 March 1901, 232–233.

55. For example, see Clifton Johnson, "Tuskegee, A Typical Alabama Town," *The Outlook*, 1 November,
1902, 519–526. Along with white writers traveling south as artistic tourists, were a number of
major white photographers. The list includes such photographers as F. Holland Day, Julian
Dimock, Clifton Johnson, Leigh Richmond Miner, and John H. Tarbell.

56. Booker T. Washington, *The Future of the American Negro* (Boston: Small, Maynard & Company,
1899), 43.

57. Booker T. Washington, "Negro Homes," *The Century Magazine*, May 1908, 73.

58. W.E.B. Du Bois, *The Souls of Black Folk* (Chicago: A.C. McClurg & Co., 1903; New York: Signet
Classic, 1982).

59. Louis Harlan, *Booker T. Washington: The Wizard of Tuskegee* (New York: Oxford University Press,
1983), 95.

60. In addition to James D. Anderson, see W. Watkins, *The White Architects of Black Education* (New
York: Teachers College Press, 2001).

61. See Keith Byerman, *Seizing the Word: History, Art, and Self in the Work of W. E. B. Du Bois* (Athens:
University of Georgia Press, 1994). For a contrast between Washington's support of photography
produced in a Pictorialist style and the documentary style preferred by Du Bois, see Deborah Willis
and David Levering Lewis, *A Small Nation of People: W. E. B. Du Bois and African American Portraits
of Progress* (New York: Amistad, 2003).

62. Houston Baker, *Turning South Again: Rethinking Modernism/Re-reading Booker T* (Durham: Duke University Press, 2001), 60.

63. Peter Scheldahl, "Hitler as Artist," *The New Yorker*, 19 & 26 August 2002, 171.

Illustrations

A YOKE OF INSTITUTE OXEN

Fig 1a. Booker T. Washington touring Tuskegee's farm, p. 296. From Booker T. Washington, "Chicken, Pigs and People," *The Outlook*, 1 June 1901. Photograph by Clifton Johnson.

AMONG THE DOGWOOD BLOSSOMS

Fig 1b. Booker T. Washington stopping to look at dogwood blossoms, p. 299. (original photo owned by author). From Booker T. Washington, "Chicken, Pigs and People," *The Outlook*, 1 June 1901. Photograph by Clifton Johnson.

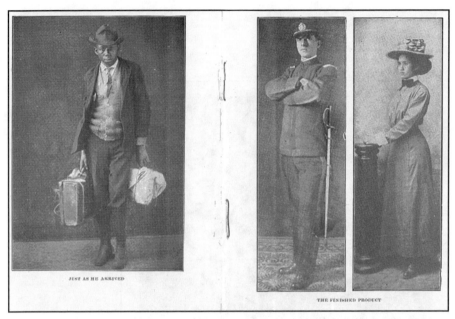

JUST AS HE ARRIVED

THE FINISHED PRODUCT

Fig 2. "Making Useful Citizens" (Tuskegee: Tuskegee Institute Press, 1912), 4–5. Fund-raising brochure describing the financial needs of the school (original brochure owned by author).

A TUSKEGEE COTTAGE
The Successor of the Negro Cabin

BOOKER T. WASHINGTON
The Founder of Tuskegee

A NINE-ROOM HOUSE
Its Owner Owns 600 Acres of Land

Fig 3. Emmett J. Scott, "Tuskegee's Great Gathering: The First Conference of the New Century Full of Promise for the Negro," *The Christian Herald and Signs of Our Times*, 13 March 1901, 233. Detail from the bottom of page. (original owned by author).

Fig 4. Stereograph. Booker T. Washington and Distinguished Guests, Tuskegee Institute, Alabama, 1906. Photographs taken at Tuskegee's 25th Anniversary Celebration. Back row from left to right: J.G. Phelps Stokes, Lyman Abbott, Hollis Burke Frissell, Andrew Carnegie, and Charles W. Eliot. Front row from left to right: George McAneny, Robert C. Odgen, and Booker T. Washington. (original owned by author).

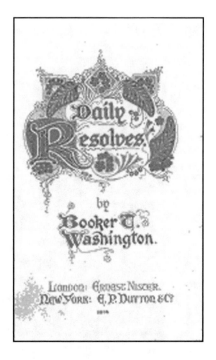

Figs 5a, 5b, and 5c. Booker T. Washington's first book, *Daily Resolves*, 1896. Cover, title page, and pages 1 and 2 (original owned by author).

Fig 6. Gertrude Kasebier, Booker T. Washington. Published in the same year in *The World's Work* (New York: Doubleday, Page, & Co., 1901) and as the frontispiece to *Up From Slavery* (New York: Doubleday, Page & Co., 1901). (original owned by author).

BIRD'S-EYE VIEW OF
GROUNDS AND BUILDINGS OF TUSKEGEE NORMAL AND INDUSTRIAL INSTITUTE
TUSKEGEE, ALABAMA

Courtesy of The Henderson Lithographing Co., Cincinnati, O.

Fig 7. Idealistic bird's-eye view of the Tuskegee campus, 1900. In Booker T. Washington, *Working with the Hands* (New York: Doubleday, Page & Co, 1904), between pages 244 and 245. Originally distributed as a lithographic print. (original owned by author).

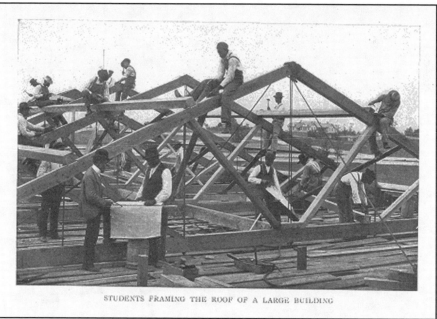

STUDENTS FRAMING THE ROOF OF A LARGE BUILDING

Figs 8a and 8 b. Comparison between typical racist image of Black labor and a contemporaneous Tuskegee photograph. Top (8a): *Postcard, Southern Labor.* Copyright by Brock, 1898. Bottom (8b): Frances Benjamin Johnston, Students Framing the Roof of Large Building, 1902, in Booker T. Washington, *Working with the Hands* (New York: Doubleday, Page, & Co, 1904), between pages 84 and 85.

CHAPTER FOUR

Creating AN Image FOR Black College Fundraising

An Illustrated Examination of the United Negro College Fund's Publicity, 1944–1960[1]

MARYBETH GASMAN AND EDWARD M. EPSTEIN

A photograph shows Black college students wearing nicely pressed, collegiate clothing [Figure 1]. They are holding their schoolbooks tightly across their chests. They are neat, clean, and studious. Across the page, the title reads "Access to education . . . in the American way."[2] Interspersed with crisply organized, modern looking type, this kind of image was the mainstay of 1940s and 50s United Negro College Fund (UNCF) publicity.[3] But what is the visual pedigree of these images and the layout and design in which they are situated? What did they say about the role of Black colleges in American society? Lastly, how did they serve the purposes of the UNCF, and shape the public's, and, most importantly, the donors' understanding of Black colleges and African American philanthropy?

A conglomeration of colleges and universities dedicated to fundraising in support of Black higher education in the United States, the UNCF came together in an effort to streamline the fundraising process for these institutions. In addition, the UNCF acted as a united voice for private Black colleges. These colleges were founded primarily in the South after the Civil War (with the exception of a few in the North) by White and Black missionary philanthropists with the express intent of educating the former slaves. Until the advent of desegregation, these colleges were the only option available for Blacks seeking higher education in the South and, in many cases, the North as well.[4]

The image of Black college students expressed in the above example of UNCF publicity is conservative and patriotic. The design is quite similar to mainstream forms of publicity that were used at that time. But it was by no means the only type of visual identity available to a Black organization. By the mid-1940s, there was a vast field of Black-run publications that had developed their own version of the modernist design idiom. Beginning in the 1920s, the thriving Harlem Renaissance had "produced a distinctive literary language, combining the folklore of Africa and southern black America."[5] The Renaissance was also the impetus for the modernist Black arts movement in the United States.[6] This artistic influence spilled over into graphic design and could be seen on the covers of *The Crisis*, *Opportunity*, *The Messenger*, and *Fire*. According to Michele Y. Washington, "Multifaceted visual artists mastered the skills of designing, illustrating, and hand-lettering type. With vigor and passion, they turned out dust jackets, illustrations for book interiors, covers of race journals, and posters for film and theater."[7] As well as exhibiting African influence in their design, the photography in these publications tended to take a more assertive and critical stance on issues of race. Given the fact that uniquely African American approaches to graphic design already existed, it is curious that an organization like the UNCF, founded by Blacks and for Black institutions, would choose such a mainstream representation for itself.

Informed by bell hooks' claim that "all art is situated in history, that the individual choice of subject matter reflects that situatedness," this chapter explores the fundraising solicitations made by the UNCF during the 1940s and 50s.[8] Why did the UNCF, in its efforts to secure funds for Black higher education, choose not to adopt the Black-inspired designs being used for publicity by other African American organizations but instead to stick to a conventional style with themes that reflected loyalty and patriotism? What messages were embedded in the style as well as the content of the publicity? How did the UNCF fundraising publicity address the political, social, and educational situation at the time? How did the UNCF break new ground in philanthropy by creating a unified image and agenda for a whole group of institutions within the spectrum of educational choices available in the post-war period?

As noted in the above example, photographs play an important role in UNCF publicity. Theorists of the image such as Roland Barthes have noted that photographs are not as important for the actual events they document, as the way they communicate their meanings to the audience. Details of a photograph, we are told, are interpreted using systems of symbols and meanings applied by the individual viewer.[9] Moreover, the techniques of photography allow for the selection and alteration of the material captured on film, making it easy for the photographer to construct and manipulate a reality that is independent of what he or she experienced.[10] Historian Joan Burstyn says of the choices photographers make about composition, lighting, and lens, "when we make such decisions, we, as photographers, at the most control, and at the least influence viewers' emotional and cognitive response to the world we have created."[11]

A number of scholars have applied the methods of visual communications to the analysis of images in education. In an essay entitled "Questioning the Visual in the History of Education," for example, Kate Rousmaniere analyzes classroom photographs and how they have been used to construct a conventionalized understanding of school practices. She has shown how the exact circumstances under which the photos are taken can be quite different from the messages they conveyed to the viewer, especially in light of their placement and use.[12]

Our chapter uses visual communications as a way to illuminate race relations and higher education fundraising practices from 1944–1960. It analyzes photographs, and also draws on the history of graphic design, to discuss the style of the publications in which they are placed. The pieces that we analyze are historical— drawn from the papers of the United Negro College Fund. On the most basic level, our chapter looks at the appearance of individual publicity pieces (their style, layout, and the correspondence of text and image) and compares them to other materials available at the time, including publications from both the Black and White worlds. It gleans several themes, including attitude toward social integration; the curriculum and needs of the Black college; and idealization, loyalty, and patriotism. Finally, the chapter compares these messages to the desired goals of the UNCF— in particular, the need to appeal to Black leadership, Black alumni, and White donors. It situates the UNCF's overall approach within the history of post-war and Cold War politics. As well as adding to our understanding of the role of fundraising publicity in higher education, this chapter uncovers an African American perspective on the history of graphic design.

UNCF BACKGROUND AND MAKEUP

At the end of the nineteenth century, Black colleges had exhausted funding from missionary sources. Simultaneously, a new form of support emerged, that of White northern industrial philanthropists. Among these leaders of industry were John D. Rockefeller, Andrew Carnegie, Julius Rosenwald, and John Slater. Although as individuals some of these industrial moguls may have had altruistic motives, the funding system that they created showed a strong tendency to control Black education and produce graduates who were skilled in the trades that served their own enterprises. Above all, the educational institutions they supported were extremely careful not to upset the segregationist power structure that ruled the South by the 1890s.[13] The philanthropists' philosophy was in direct conflict with that of many

Black intellectuals who favored a liberal arts curriculum. Black colleges such as Tuskegee and Hampton were showcases of industrial education. It was here that students learned how to shoe horses, make dresses, cook, and clean under the leadership of individuals like Samuel Chapman Armstrong (at Hampton) and Booker T. Washington (at Tuskegee).[14] On the other hand, institutions such as Fisk, Dillard, Howard, Spelman, and Morehouse were more focused on the liberal arts curriculum favored by W. E. B. Du Bois.[15]

Beginning around 1915, there was a shift in the attitude of the industrial philanthropists, who started to turn their attention to those Black colleges that emphasized liberal arts.[16] Realizing that industrial education could exist side by side with the more academic curriculum, the philanthropists opted to exercise control over all forms of Black education and create a conservative Black leadership class ensuring that future Black leaders would be educated in an environment that accommodated segregation. Attention from the industrial philanthropists was not necessarily welcomed by institutions like Fisk University, where rebellions ensued against autocratic presidents who were assumed to be puppets of the philanthropists.[17] In spite of these conflicts, industrial philanthropists provided major support for individual Black colleges up until the late 1930s. As this support began to wane, Black college leaders started to seek their own means of securing funding; this situation eventually led to the creation of the United Negro College Fund.[18]

Although a major player in the areas of fundraising, philanthropy, and higher education, the UNCF has received very little attention in these literatures. For example, Scott M. Cutlip's book, *Fundraising in the United States*, gives an exhaustive overview of the development of fundraising: important personalities, key organizations, and major donations.[19] However, he provides only three paragraphs on the UNCF. To his credit, he does acknowledge the Fund's role in popularizing the idea of a federated campaign—one in which many institutions band together for the good of the group.[20] Likewise, historians of education have focused their attention on the large sums of money that were contributed by philanthropists to Black colleges beginning after the Civil War through 1935 and the motivations behind these contributions.[21] However, there is little interest in the period after 1935—precisely the period in which the UNCF was created.

In 1935, Frederick D. Patterson became president of Tuskegee Institute in Tuskegee, Alabama. Patterson quickly acknowledged that he lacked the fundraising skills and personal ties of past Tuskegee presidents Booker T. Washington and Robert S. Moton. Typically, a new president would look to the trustees of an institution for assistance with fundraising, but Tuskegee's trustees had become accustomed to a more passive role due to the prominence of the institution's past presidents. Patterson found it difficult to run Tuskegee in an efficient manner while meeting the needs of poor Black college students—many of whom lacked the means to pay their tuition. After much frustration, he began to correspond with a cadre of Black college presidents about the challenges of fundraising and possible solutions to these problems. The majority of college presidents wrote back to him detailing their dire financial situations and providing many anecdotal stories about their difficulties in approaching foundations for funds. Patterson realized from his correspondence that Black college presidents were competing against each other by soliciting the same organizations and donors—usually the large industrial philanthropies. Most prominent among the foundation supporters of Black colleges was the Rockefeller-sponsored General Education Board (GEB). Founded in 1902 as an outgrowth of John D. Rockefeller, Jr.'s Negro Education Board, the GEB was a consortium of industrial philanthropies which had focused a portion of its giving on Black education.[22]

In 1944, Frederick D. Patterson established the United Negro College Fund as a combined fundraising appeal on behalf of 32 private Black colleges.[23] As a result of his previous interactions with the GEB, Frederick D. Patterson was easily able to convince John D. Rockefeller, Jr. to publicly endorse the UNCF and serve as its national chairman.[24] This affiliation connected the Fund to the corporate world. In addition to Rockefeller, Jr., men such as Alfred P. Sloan (General Motors Corporation), Harvey S. Firestone (Firestone Tire and Rubber Company), Richard K. Mellon (Mellon Bank), and Robert Woodruff (Coca-Cola Company) were on the national UNCF board. Thus, the constituency of the organization was broad. The Black college world itself encompassed revolutionaries such as W.E.B. Du Bois, moderates such as Charles S. Johnson, and was heavily supported by members of the Rockefeller, Ford, and Rosenwald families.[25] It was the goal of the UNCF to keep all of these constituencies on board and satisfied at a time when attempts by the National Association for the Advancement of Colored People (NAACP) to overturn legalized segregation placed the future of Black higher education in flux.[26] This goal was reflected in all of the organization's activities, including its publicity.

COMPARING UNCF FUNDRAISING PUBLICITY TO OTHER POST-WAR DESIGNS

In this section of the article we situate UNCF design within the spectrum of styles available during the mid-twentieth century. In doing so, we present a brief history of design from the early to mid-twentieth century—first showing the progression of mainstream design, and then that of other African American organizations. Typical of post-war American design, the UNCF fundraising booklets had a clean, modern appearance. For example, the typography blended hard-edged sans-serif fonts with type that had a hand-lettered look such as Brush Script. A representative example is the 1945 publication entitled "Thirty-two Steps Forward to a Better America" [Figure 2].[27] On the cover of this piece, the title is splashed across the names of the 32 member colleges, which appear in a smaller, upper-case lineal typeface. The Brush Script title font provides a tasteful counterpoint to the modern looking letters behind it. The copy on the inside is set with plenty of white space; photos are neatly placed, usually in an off-center position.

The Evolution of Modernism

This piece exhibits many of the features of modernist design as it was popularized in the United States during the 1940s and 1950s.[28] After World War I, many design styles had emerged in Europe that were associated with avant-garde art: Bauhaus, Constructivism, de Stijl, and art deco. These early modernist approaches later coalesced into a unified design approach referred to loosely as the international style.[29] This style was characterized by the strict use of a grid, a preference for sans-serif typefaces, off-center layout, and an overall economy of means.[30] In contrast to these rationalist tendencies, the international style also inherited from modern art a strong dose of surrealism.[31] The collage and photo montage, which placed images of vastly different scales and types on an equal plane, first appeared in cubism and dada,[32] and became a staple of the surrealist art of the 1920s. This type of image making was a regular feature of advertising design in the 1930s in Europe and later in the 1940s in the United States. An excellent example is the Swiss tourism posters designed by Herbert Matter in the mid-1930s. With their angled type, enormous faces, and tiny figures arrayed in every direction, they sweep the viewer into the space of the image and create a sense of speed and vertigo.[33]

Another prominent part of surrealism was the interest in spontaneously generated lines and shapes—figures that were said to emerge from the depths of the subconscious. These can be seen in the amoeba-like forms of Joan Miro's work, and the child-like drawing in work by Pablo Picasso and Paul Klee.[34] Again, this type of expression found its way into graphic design in the form of broad, flat biomorphic shapes and chicken-scratch illustrations. The tension between the rational, minimal, and geometric on the one hand, and the loose, freeform, and whimsical on the other, is characteristic of modernist design. In the UNCF publication "Thirty-two Steps" these tendencies are evident in the contrast of the Brush Script with clean, geometric letter forms.

Graphic artists such as Paul Rand, Saul Bass, and Lester Beall adapted these modernist design ideas to corporate advertising and publicity in the United States.[35] Rand was well known for his comprehensive visual identity package for the IBM Corporation—elements of which are still in use today. This visual identity extended from logo designs on packages to signage in stores and offices and pioneered the idea that the entire visual image of an organization should be carefully planned.[36] Modernist design became the standard in corporate identity and continued to be used through the 1970s. Thus, what had begun as a visual revolution came to be a comfortable part of the corporate mainstream in America.

A Black Take on Modernism

Aspects of modern design were adapted to very different ends by Black journals and organizations. These uniquely African-influenced designs were prevalent throughout the country in Black newspapers, on Black organizational publicity, and on Black literary publications such as Alain Locke's *The New Negro*.[37] They continued to be used through the early 1960s when they were supplanted by more art nouveau[38] designs, which were still heavily influenced by African and southern Black culture. An early example is the National Association for the Advancement of Colored People (NAACP) publication, *The Crisis*, which sociologist W.E.B. Du Bois edited during the 1920s. Throughout the 1920s and into the 1930s, *The Crisis* covers included an interesting blend of art deco and African elements. A March 1928 cover uses deco-like zigzag patterns in its type but also presents an array of African masks and figures.[39] The January 1932 issue of *The Crisis* uses similar deco type on its cover and features an Aaron Douglas fresco in its pages. Douglas was known for his depiction of African and African American subjects in a flat geometric style that was strongly reminiscent of cubism.[40] Later editions of *The Crisis* blended deco and Bauhaus-inspired elements—bold sans-serif type and flat stylized illustrations.[41] From the late 1930s on, the type became secondary to the cover photograph on *The Crisis*, which often featured a famous African American who had broken the color boundary.[42] These photographs were bold in their stance and composition.

An interesting collage of photos appears on a July 1940 cover of *The Crisis*— which has a hint of the surrealist dislocation of scale and place. It presents a wartime production theme using a bold array of photos and type—similar to modernist advertising done for The Container Corporation of America around the same time. However, rather than an uncritically patriotic message, the words "FOR WHITES ONLY" are splashed across photos of military aircraft.[43] While both *The Crisis* and the UNCF designers drew inspiration from modernism, *The Crisis* designs were much bolder and more challenging to the status quo.

Appealing to a Corporate Audience

Another typical feature of modernist design overall is the use of visual schema to present data. The pictograph or schematic Black and White figure first appeared in 1920s Bauhaus-inspired publications as a way of showing numeric data.[44] By the 1950s, this type of figure was standard corporate fare. Examples of this can be seen in the 1952 UNCF report entitled "What Are the Answers?" This piece presents itself as a casual exchange of information between two corporate leaders who happen to be members of the UNCF board: Alfred P. Sloan, Jr. (General Motors) and Devereux C. Josephs (New York Life Insurance). The publication opens with letters from each correspondent, reproduced as if photographed directly from the desk top: off-center, slanted, with the original letterhead, signature, and typewriter print. The pages that follow give a "scientific" answer to the questions raised by Sloan to Josephs. Each page has a visual presentation of quantitative data, with multiple pictograph figures, maps, and bar and line graphs. The publication culminates in a table, which lays out the financial needs of the UNCF member colleges.[45] Thus, "What Are the Answers?" is a typical display of quasi-scientific information about complex social problems.[46] The use of the graphs and pictographs follow a pattern of objectification of individual experience that typified many early to mid-twentieth century graphic presentations.[47] This type of display appeared in many corporate annual reports from the period as well as pamphlets such as those published by the United Nations Educational, Scientific, and Cultural Organization (UNESCO), which purported to deal with worldwide social problems.[48] By adopting a corporate style of design, and in particular, that of the annual report, the UNCF's "What Are the Answers?" appeals to its audience as if they were shareholders in a company rather than donors to a college.

VISUAL CUES: MESSAGES IN TEXT AND IMAGE

Like the layout and design, the messages conveyed by photography in UNCF fundraising publications were conservative. Among the themes stressed were the interaction of Blacks and Whites in UNCF events, the curricula and activities of students on the campuses, the physical conditions at Black colleges, and the loyalty and patriotism of students. In all of these categories, images and the pairing of images and text reinforced the needs of Black colleges but avoided any radical messages.

Mixed Gatherings, Mixed Messages

As mentioned, many images in the publications show the wealthy White benefactors of the UNCF colleges together with students, faculty, and administration. At a time when legalized segregation was still intact, the placement of Blacks and Whites together in a photograph was a delicate undertaking. Any image that suggested that the races were equal on a social level and that they were free to mix in all situations was likely to spark controversy. In film and on television, Black characters[49] were almost always stereotyped. Roles were usually subservient (e.g., maids, butlers, and gardeners); Black characters were portrayed as less intelligent, shiftless, and often the objects of ridicule.[50] Even the suggestion of familiarity between Blacks and Whites was enough to cause an outrage. An incident involving UNCF national chairman, John D. Rockefeller, Jr. and a Black child demonstrates this difficulty. During a 1944 UNCF radio broadcast, Rockefeller was photographed holding the girl on his lap. After the photo appeared in newspapers across the country, Rockefeller received many angry letters from Whites. The tone of the letters implied that somehow Rockefeller's actions would lead Blacks to believe that they were equal to Whites and would cause the country to dissolve into a lawless state.[51] The notion that Blacks, if left unrestrained, would degenerate into lawlessness was an almost religious tenet of the racist mythology of the time.[52]

Where mixed groupings are depicted in UNCF publicity photos, the images are either formally composed, collaged, or the White figure is shown in a dominant position. One such mixed group appears in "America Is Free to Choose" over the caption, "The Educated Are Tolerant" [Figure 3].[53] The grouping of White UNCF supporters with Black college leaders is shown standing in a line—there is no body contact, and each member has his hands at his side. Although the message might refer to toleration as a quality of liberal democratic society—a quality desired by both potential Black and White donors—it may also be read as a reference to the supposed lawlessness of Blacks. To at least part of the audience, the interpretation of the caption might have been "The educated behave themselves," a message that was nicely reinforced by Blacks standing in line with their White benefactors. Blacks are also shown behaving themselves under the tutelage of a White professor in a photograph in the "Thirty-two Steps" piece. Across from the subheading "Pointing the Way," a standing White figure points to a paper on a table, surrounded by a seated group of Black students.

Another photograph that shows the "correct" relationship between Blacks and Whites is on the cover of the June 1953 publication, *The Mobilizer*, a monthly newsletter distributed to UNCF donors and campaign directors.[54] The subordinate role of the Black participant is so carefully constructed as to obscure the true meaning of the image. In the photograph, Frederick D. Patterson, the President of the UNCF, shakes the hand of a much taller John D. Rockefeller, III, while Rockefeller holds an award certificate; Dwight D. Eisenhower stands behind the handshake but on the same side as Rockefeller, smiling. The slightly angled and more active stance of Rockefeller as he leans over toward the stiffer Patterson suggests that the philanthropist is giving an award—when according to the headline, he is actually the recipient of a citation from the UNCF [Figure 4]. According to Rockefeller, Jr.'s colleague Walter Hoving, it was not uncommon for the Black UNCF presidents to be asked to "step one step lower" in photographs.[55]

Other photographs seem to have been included to reinforce a sense of self-importance among the White benefactors. *The Mobilizer*, for example, has pages of photographs of corporate executives and their wives dining together; Black college leaders, if included at all, are relegated to a secondary role. In one particularly telling photograph, guests seated at a head table include John D. Rockefeller, III, General Motors Chairman Alfred P. Sloan, and numerous other executives who are conversing with one another. Seated in the center of the head table is Morehouse College president Benjamin E. Mays, whose gaze is focused on the table; none of the other guests are talking with him, and their backs are turned away.[56] *The Mobilizer* clearly belongs to a genre of donor publicity that supplies extrinsic rewards to the donor—showing them at the center of social networks.[57] That Blacks, with few exceptions, were not included in these networks is inadvertently conveyed by the pictures.

In addition to the many group photographs of wealthy donors in social situations, the publications contained numerous individual portraits of UNCF leadership, both Black and White. The presentation of these photographs again references the corporate report. Typical reports from the late 1940s and early 1950s included rows of portrait photographs of the company's board members as well as photographs of workers, shareholders, and customers in less formal settings.[58] Clearly, the UNCF wished to communicate with an audience comfortable with corporate styles of presentation.

A Focus on Industry

Images of students on Black college campuses showed them to be productive and hardworking. In the publication "America Is Free to Choose," the words "The Negro prefers to live by the American traditions of independence, thrift and self-help" appear under a photograph of a young Black man, presumably a student, driving a tractor [Figure 5].[59] Another page in the same publication is a collage of photos of Black students engaged in activities ranging from machine work to agriculture to medicine. The idea of productivity appears so often in the publication as to draw attention to itself. If not by the traditions of "independence, thrift, and self-help," what other tradition would the "Negro" prefer to live by? Accompanied by these photographs, the text seems to assume that part of the audience needs evidence to refute the racist myths of dependence and sloth.

Another curious aspect of the photographs of students at work is the continued prevalence of industrial and agricultural occupations. Again, it is important to note that by the time these publications appeared, the debate over liberal arts versus industrial curricula had all but ended.[60] Although at some Black colleges, industrial and liberal arts curricula existed side by side, according to Henry Drewry and Humphrey Doermann, "Industrial education lost much of its attraction well before World War II."[61] As mentioned, by 1915, northern philanthropists began to shift their donations from industrial to liberal arts colleges, and of the 27 colleges in the 1944 membership roster, less than a handful were noted for their industrial curricula.[62] True, UNCF founder F. D. Patterson was also the president of Tuskegee—a noted center of industrial education—but as a veterinary scientist, his idea of "industrial" might have included medical technology and aeronautics (programs he had supported), not tractors and sewing.[63] But of the nine photographs that depict work in the 1944 "America Is Free to Choose," four are of occupations generally considered manual: machine work, milking cows, driving tractors, and operating sewing machines.[64] In all of the photographs, there seems to be a deliberate selection of activities that emphasize making or doing as opposed to simply thinking. In short, given the opportunity to present its own picture of the activities at UNCF colleges, why would this Black organization choose to showcase the past of these institutions rather than their future?[65]

A possible interpretation of the persistence of photographs of industrial occupations is that the UNCF wanted to avoid challenging the accepted social status of Blacks in the South, in order to garner funds from more conservative donors. The photos reinforce the sense of productivity and industry as the result of a UNCF member college education. Another look at this material, however, shows it to be quite similar to photography in U.S. state department pamphlets from the same period. One publication in particular, "The UNESCO Story," provides an excellent comparison. This publication, which tied support for UNESCO to Cold War themes, has numerous photographs of industrious-looking workers and students from developing countries, usually in the presence of teachers and benefactors from the industrialized nations, taking advantage of the new tools and technologies provided to them.[66] That the publication is directed to wealthy benefactors as well as ordinary Americans is evident from the many photographs and lists of these individuals. The content and arrangement of these images send the message that donations of capital and technology from industrialized regions can contribute to the lives of those in underdeveloped areas. The similarity of the UNESCO materials to those of the UNCF suggests another interpretation of the UNCF's emphasis on industrial occupations: a desire to show the positive impact of technology and business capital in an "underdeveloped" region of the United States.

This message is further reinforced by another detail that occurs frequently in the publications: maps of the southern region in which the UNCF member colleges are located. Similar maps appear in publications from the same time from the World Health Organization and UNESCO to illustrate the distribution of food and supplies to various peoples of the world.[67] Like these UN graphics, maps in UNCF publications show its donors how their contributions are spread out over the "areas of need."[68]

Picturing Needs

Need is conveyed through a variety of means in the UNCF publicity. For example, the publicity piece entitled "A Significant Adventure," shows the experience of living at a Black college to be quite an adventure indeed. Under the heading "Poor Housing Discourages Faculty," there appears a photo of a ramshackle two-story, wood frame house—apparently suggesting that Black college faculty are living in substandard conditions.[69] In the same publication, a photograph of two faculty members inspecting books stacked up on the floor of a basement appears above the caption, "Limited Space Means Poor Library Service."[70] The identification of the space as a basement is clearly conveyed by the exposed brick wall that surrounds the books [Figure 6]. Again, the focus on these inadequate conditions can be interpreted as an example of Black colleges adopting a "beggar status." However, another view is that these conditions are likened to the sub-standard conditions depicted in United Nations' photographs of developing countries. Although in both interpretations the Black college is placed in a subordinate role, the second one carries with it the notion that improvement in education for Blacks is congruent with the goals of democracy and capitalism.

Patriotism and Loyalty

Another theme in UNCF fundraising publicity images is that of loyalty to the United States. The connection between UNCF colleges and themes of freedom and democracy is most apparent in the inclusion of photographs of Black students in uniform. Pictures of Blacks serving in various capacities of the military are spread throughout the pages of "Thirty-two Steps Forward to a Better America"—a publication that appeared near the end of World War II.[71] Likewise, the 1944 publication "America Is Free to Choose" features a row of Black airmen pictured in front of a bomber with the caption, "The Negro is making a substantial contribution to the war effort."[72] The text itself begins with the words "It is self-evident . . . ," an obvious reference to the Declaration of Independence. After the end of the war, UNCF photographs continued to suggest that activities at Black colleges were contributing to America's interests—showing that civilian efforts worked hand in hand with those of the military. An image that makes this connection is found in the 1950 publication "A Significant Adventure." This image depicts a Black man in uniform on the left with a group of young Black nursing students on the right.

The caption underneath, enclosed in a stylized coat of arms, reads "Loyal citizens serving their country."[73] This message seems to suggest that service to the United States may be either in the military or in any form of hard work. Once again, the images point to another interpretation of the focus on industry: that Black colleges contribute to or strengthen the United States.

Patriotism is also conveyed through the style of the photographs, which paints a picture of youthful life at the Black colleges. For example, in "America Is Free to Choose," an image of a male and female Black student appears over the caption "The private Negro colleges have been the major source of leadership in the past and are the hope for providing leaders for the future" [Figure 1].[74] The subjects are photographed from a low vantage point so as to emphasize their height. Their features, which are idealized, are softened slightly so as to emphasize geometric form over individual identity. Another nearly identical photograph appears in "A Significant Adventure," also with a male and female couple, also photographed from a low vantage point, and lit in a similar way.[75] The stance of these photographs is strikingly similar to 1920s and 1930s propaganda photos from the Soviet Union, such as those made by Alexander Rodchenko and El Lissitzky.[76] In an essay entitled "Photography and Electoral Appeal," Roland Barthes describes a similar idealization in campaign photographs from the 1950s. According to Barthes,

> A three-quarter face photograph [i.e., viewed from an angle] . . . suggests the tyranny of an ideal: the gaze is lost nobly in the future, it does not confront, it soars, and fertilizes some other domain, which is chastely left undefined. Almost all three-quarter faced photos are ascensional, the face is lifted towards a supernatural light which draws it up and elevates it to the realm of higher humanity. . . .[77]

In the UNCF's case, the idealization of Black youth reinforces a patriotic and optimistic view of America.

In light of the emphasis on patriotism, the connection between supporting the UNCF and the Cold War themes of freedom and democracy becomes even clearer. Numerous titles, headings, and captions in UNCF pamphlets advertise the link between the organization's goals and those of "the free world": "The Tools of Freedom"; "America Is Free to Choose"; "Education Means Progress"; and "Living Democracy." Similarly, the U.S. State Department's "UNESCO Story" links worldwide economic development and national security. It specifically mentions U.S.-Soviet competition as a reason to support United Nations efforts. It is also significant that many of the UNCF publications appeared at the same time that accusations of disloyalty were being made against many figures in higher education, government, and the media.[78] In certain cases, the House Un-American Activities Committee (HUAC), whose members included southern conservatives such as Senator Martin Dies, Jr. of Texas, brought charges against educators because they had shown support for the Black cause.[79] Thus it was necessary for the UNCF leadership to advertise to all the idea that its member colleges were on the right side of the struggle against Communism.

A STRATEGIC USE OF IMAGES AND TEXT

In the words of the UNCF founders, the most important goal set forth by the organization was to "help provide funds required for current operating budgets . . . 10 percent of [the] budgets" of the affiliate colleges.[80] However, an even more important goal was educating the American public as to the contributions that Black colleges and their graduates had made throughout the nation.[81] This effort was significant not only for its benefit to the fiscal well-being of the Black colleges, but for the effort to improve the status of Black higher education in the United States. In many ways, it was a revolutionary idea—although groups of colleges and universities had already emerged (e.g., Ivy League, the Seven Sisters).

Looking at the UNCF publicity materials, it would be easy to conclude that some of their contents undermined this effort. Certain aspects of the design and appearance of UNCF brochures were quite conservative. Comparing UNCF publications to other designs of the time and reviewing the history of graphic design in the early to mid-twentieth century, we see that their layout and typography were a bland distillation of modernist styles rather than the bolder use that had been developed in other Black publications such as *The Crisis*. The pages were filled with clichéd graphs and charts in the corporate style. Moreover, the text sometimes failed to repudiate racial stereotyping—leaving in references that might have affirmed the racist assumptions of some readers.

According to Roland Barthes, "a photograph is a mirror, what we are asked to read is the familiar, the known."[82] Certainly, the photography in UNCF publicity used a language that was well known to its audience. The Black subjects that appeared in the photographs were presented in roles that were deemed acceptable according to the racial politics of the day. They were portrayed as successful and optimistic but rarely assertive. The Black college pictured was one that fit in nicely with segregation-era notions of Black education: a place where one learned an industrial skill and above all the values of industry and self-sufficiency. Furthermore, the decrepit appearance of the campus reaffirmed conventional notions of charity: conveying the importance of the donation but also reinforcing the donor's sense of superiority. Finally, frequent juxtapositions of Black college students with the American flag and symbols of American military might suggested a kind of unquestioning loyalty. Thus, one interpretation of the UNCF publicity would be that it made a Faustian bargain: trading the long-term improvement of the image of Black colleges for financial success.

However, certain aspects of the publicity lend themselves to another interpretation. When looked at in the larger context of a nation emerging from war and entering an indefinite ideological struggle against Communism, the UNCF fundraising materials can be seen as having a larger purpose. The organization seized an opportunity to position itself within the Cold War struggle and in fact used this struggle as leverage against its adversaries. Leverage in this case included rallying powerful interests (corporations, government officials, and influential individuals) to the cause of Black higher education. It was well known that those who controlled wealth in the United States—notably John D. Rockefeller, Jr.—were engaged in their own public relations campaign designed to deflect the notion that capitalism cared little about the well-being of ordinary people.[83] It was for this reason that Rockefeller, Jr. had devoted the better part of his life to philanthropic endeavors.[84]

And the United States government itself had a role to play in this public relations game. As the superpower committed to defending capitalism as the superior economic and political system, it needed to show the world that life under this system was prosperous and just, even for those who lived in less-favored regions of the country.[85] A review of UNCF fundraising materials shows numerous maps of the South, pictures of good, corporate-looking people along with evidence—both photographic and schematic—of the benefits they were providing. This aspect of the publicity materials suggests a more savvy kind of bargaining on the part of the UNCF leadership. The financial gain of Black colleges was tied to their positioning as key players in a democratic and capitalist society. In fact, this positioning proved useful in the ongoing struggle for Black rights. Those who would advocate the continuation of Jim Crow claimed that Black colleges were havens of Communism and outside agitation.[86] In order to oppose segregation during the tense post-war period, it was necessary to situate Black leadership and Black college students among the loyal citizenship and disconnect them from ideas of dissent and treachery. The UNCF fundraising publicity helped sustain its member institutions through a difficult period, which saw the waning of industrial philanthropy in the south and the end of legalized segregation. In the process, the UNCF broke new ground, creating a unified image and agenda for a wide-ranging group of institutions, each of which had a unique history and mission.[87]

NOTES

1. An earlier version of this chapter was published as Marybeth Gasman and Edward Epstein, "Creating an Image for Black Higher Education: A Visual Examination of the United Negro College Fund's Publicity," *Educational Foundations* 18, 2 (Spring 2004).

2. America Is Free to Choose," 1944, General Education Board Papers, Record Group 5235–5240, series 1, sub-series 3, box 491, folder 5338, Rockefeller Archive Center, Sleepy Hollow, New York (RAC).

3. In this chapter, we use both present and past tense. Present tense is used when talking about specific documents that we are looking at now. Past is used when we talk about historical situations and context.

4. Although segregation was not mandated by law in the northern United States, White colleges and universities rarely accepted Black students.

5. Michele Y. Washington, "Souls on Fire," in Steven Heller and Georgette Balance, eds., *Graphic Design History* (New York: Allworth Press, 2001), 269.

6. David C. Driskell, David Levering Lewis, Deborah Willis-Thomas, and Mary Schmidt Campbell, *Art of Black America* (New York: Abradale Press, 1994); Richard Powell, David Bailey, and Paul Gilroy, *Rhapsodies in Black: Art of the Harlem Renaissance* (California: University of California Press, 1997).

7. Washington, "Souls on Fire," 269.

8. bell hooks, *Art on My Mind. Visual Politics* (New York: The New Press, 1999).

9. Roland Barthes, *Camera Lucida* (New York: Noonday Press, Farrar, Straus and Giroux, 1981); Roland Barthes, *Mythologies* (New York: Hill and Wang, 1971); Kate Rousmaniere, "Questioning the Visual in the History of Education," *History of Education* 30, 2 (2001): 109–116; Ian Grosvenor and Martin Lawn, "Ways of Seeing in Education and Schooling: Emerging Historiographies," *History of Education* 30, 2 (2001): 105–108; Ian Grosvenor, Martin Lawn, and Kate Rousmaniere, (eds.), *Silences & Images: The Social History of the Classroom* (New York: Peter Lang, 1999); Joan Burstyn, "History as Image: Changing the Lens," *History of Education Quarterly* 27, 2 (Summer 1987): 167–180.

10. Burstyn, "History as Image: Changing the Lens."

11. Burstyn, "History as Image: Changing the Lens," 168.

12. Rousmaniere, "Questioning the Visual in the History of Education."

13. James D. Anderson, *The Education of Blacks in the South* (Chapel Hill: University of North Carolina Press, 1988).

14. Anderson, *The Education of Blacks.*

15. Anderson, *The Education of Blacks;* Stephen J. Peeps, "Northern Philanthropy and the Emergence of Black Higher Education—Do-gooders, Compromisers, or Co-conspirators?" *Journal of Negro Education* 50, 3, (1981): 251–269; Eric Anderson and Alfred A. Moss, *Dangerous Donations: Northern Philanthropy and Southern Black Education, 1902–1930* (Missouri: The University of Missouri Press, 1999).

16. Anderson, *The Education of Blacks.*

17. Anderson, *The Education of Blacks.*

18. Anderson, *The Education of Blacks;* Peeps, "Northern Philanthropy and the Emergence of Black Higher Education."

19. Scott Cutlip, *Fundraising in the United States* (New Jersey: Rutgers University Press, 1965).

20. Although our focus for this paper is historical, there have been current writings on the topic of fundraising design. For more information, please see: Harold D. Lasswell, Ralph D. Casey, and Bruce Lannes Smith, (eds.), *Propaganda and Promotional Activities; An Annotated Bibliography* (Chicago: University of Chicago Press, 1969); George A. Flanagan, *Modern Institutional Advertising* (New York: McGraw-Hill Book Company, 1967); and A. Westley Rowland, *Handbook of Institutional Advancement* (San Francisco, CA: Jossey-Bass, 1986).

21. Anderson, *The Education of Blacks*; Peeps, "Northern Philanthropy and the Emergence of Black Higher Education;" Anderson and Moss, *Dangerous Donations*.

22. Although the GEB was funded as an outgrowth of the Negro Education Board, it gave only 19% of its donations to Black Education. For more information, see Anderson and Moss, *Dangerous Donations*. According to historian James D. Anderson, the GEB wanted to orchestrate the "systematic development of a few select institutions of black higher education." (p. 238). These institutions would " . . . produce college-bred leaders to acculturate black Americans into the values and mores of southern society. Second, it was very important that Black leaders be trained in the South by institutions 'in touch with the conditions to be faced by the young people in later life rather than in the North by institutions . . . out of touch with southern life.' Third, and most important, the development of a few strong institutions was viewed as a strategic means to reduce the number of existing black colleges" (p. 255). See Anderson, *The Education of Blacks*.

23. See Marybeth Gasman, "Frederick Douglass Patterson (1901–1988), College President and Founder of the United Negro College Fund," *The Encyclopedia of Philanthropy* (New York: Oryx Press, 2001).

24. Frederick D. Patterson to Jackson Davis, 28 May 1943, General Education Board Papers, Record Group 5235–5240, series 1, sub-series 3, box 490, folder 5231, RAC.

25. Patrick J. Gilpin and Marybeth Gasman, *Charles S. Johnson: Leadership beyond the Veil in the Age of Jim Crow* (New York: State University of New York Press, 2003).

26. Richard Kluger, *Simple Justice: The History of Brown v. Board of Education and Black America's Struggle for Equality* (New York: Knopf, 1976).

27. "Thirty-two Steps Forward to a Better America," 1945, General Education Board Papers, Record Group 5235–5240, Series 1, Subseries 3, box 491, folder 5238, RAC.

28. Philip Meggs, *A History of Graphic Design* (New York: John Wiley & Sons, 1998).

29. Meggs, *A History of Graphic Design*.

30. Meggs, *A History of Graphic Design*.

31. Jerry Jankowski, *Shelf Space. Modern Package Design, 1945–1965* (San Francisco: Chronicle Books, 1998).

32. Cubism and dada are two key movements in modern art. Pioneered by Pablo Picasso and Georges Braque, cubism dissected forms and represented them as flat, geometric shapes. Dada emerged as a revolution in literature and visual arts in the aftermath of WWI. A protest against the war and the established order, dada championed the anti-art gesture (e.g., Marcel Duchamp's *Fountain*, which consisted of an upside-down urinal placed in an art gallery) and the chaotic assemblage of what were then considered non-art materials.

33. Meggs, *A History of Graphic Design*, 298–299.

34. Werner Haftmann, *The Mind and Work of Paul Klee* (New York: Praeger, 1954); Glenbow Museum, *Four Modern Masters: De Chirico, Ernst, Magritte, and Miro* (Calgary: Glenbow Museum, 1981); Los Angeles County Museum of Art, *Picasso: Sixty Years of Graphic Works* (Los Angeles: L.A. County Museum of Art, 1966).

35. Jankowski, *Shelf Space*.

36. Jean-Marie Floch, *Semiotics, Marketing, and Communication: Beneath the Signs, the Strategies* (New York: Palgrave, 2001).

37. Alain Locke, *The New Negro* (New York: Atheneum Press, 1925).

38. Art nouveau refers to a style of art developed in the last decade of the nineteenth century. It is characterized by the free use of ornament based on organic forms and by its flowing lines and curves.

39. *The Crisis,* March 1928, NAACP, Robert W. Woodruff Library Archives, Atlanta University Center, Atlanta, Georgia.

40. *The Crisis,* January 1932, NAACP, Robert W. Woodruff Library Archives, Atlanta University Center, Atlanta, Georgia.

41. Meggs, *A History of Graphic Design,* 284.

42. *The Crisis,* September 1939, November 1947, NAACP, Robert W. Woodruff Library Archives, Atlanta University Center, Atlanta, Georgia.

43. *The Crisis,* July 1940, NAACP, Robert W. Woodruff Library Archives, Atlanta University Center, Atlanta, Georgia.

44. Meggs, *A History of Graphic Design,* 292.

45. "National Mobilization of Resources," April 1952, General Education Board Papers, III 2G, Box 492, folder 5241, RAC.

46. We use the term "quasi-scientific" to differentiate this presentation of data from that of scholarly social scientific research. Tables and graphs resulting from academic research might be accompanied by detailed descriptions of the methods, use a precise scale, and indicate the source of the data.

47. Meggs, *A History of Graphic Design.*

48. Lillian Doris, *Modern Corporate Reports* (New York: Prentice-Hall, 1948): 146–150; The U.S. National Commission for UNESCO, *The UNESCO Story* (Washington, D.C.: Department of State, 1950).

49. In most cases, Black characters were portrayed by Whites in blackface.

50. Kenneth W. Goings, *Mammy and Uncle Moses. Black Collectibles and American Stereotyping* (Bloomington: Indiana University Press, 1994).

51. Buford G. Lincoln, Life Insurance Counselor, Los Angeles, California to John D. Rockefeller, Jr., 3 June 1944, Messrs Rockefeller–Education, III 2G, box 96, folder 6620, RAC.

52. Leon Litwack, *Black Southerners in the Age of Jim Crow* (New York: Knopf, 1998).

53. UNCF's "America Is Free to Choose," 1944, General Education Board Papers, Record Group 5235–5240, series 1, sub-series 3, box 491, folder 5338, RAC.

54. "*The Mobilizer,*" June 1953, Rockefeller–Education, III 2G, Box 96, folder 664, RAC.

55. Walter Hoving was interviewed regarding his involvement in the UNCF in 1981 by historian Marcia Goodson. The interview is located at the Columbia University Oral History Collection, New York, New York (p. 31).

56. "*The Mobilizer*", June 1952, Rockefeller–Education, III 2G, Box 96, folder 664, RAC.

57. Cutlip, *The History of Fundraising.*

58. Del Monte Shield Annual Report, May 1952; Humble Oil & Refining Company Annual Report, 1948, Schomburg Center for Electronic Text & Image, University of Pennsylvania Library, Philadelphia, Pennsylvania (*www.library.upenn.edu/etext/collections/lippincott*). The Schomburg Center has hundreds of annual reports in PDF format located on its website.

59. UNCF's "America Is Free to Choose," 1944, General Education Board Papers, Record Group 5235–5240, series 1, sub-series 3, box 491, folder 5338, RAC.

60. Charles V. Willie and Ronald R. Edmonds, *Black Colleges in America. Challenge, Development, and Survival* (New York: Teachers College Press, 1978), 91; Anderson, *The Education of Blacks,* 274; Daniel C. Thompson, *Private Black Colleges at the Crossroads* (Westport: Greenwood, 1973).

61. Henry Drewry and Humphrey Doermann, "Stand and Prosper." *Private Black Colleges and Their Students* (Princeton: Princeton University Press, 2001), 92.

62. "Appraisal of a Venture. The United Negro College Fund's First Fifteen Years, 1944–1959," John D. Rockefeller, Jr. Papers, RAC.

63. Frederick D. Patterson, *Chronicles of Faith. The Autobiography of Frederick D. Patterson* (Tuscaloosa: The University of Alabama Press, 1991). While at Tuskegee, Patterson initiated many new programs related to science and technology, including commercial dietetics (1935), commercial aviation (1935), veterinary medicine (1935) and engineering (1948).

64. Anderson, *The Education of Blacks.* See the chapter entitled, "The Apostles of Liberal Education."

65. In the past foundations such as Phelps-Stokes, the Rosenwald Fund, and the General Education Board used images of industrial education to portray Black colleges. However, these were White-led organizations operating early in the century.

66. The U.S. National Commission for UNESCO, *The UNESCO Story* (Washington, D.C.: Department of State, 1950): 57–61.

67. The UNESCO Story (Washington, D.C.: U.S. National Commission for UNESCO, 1950), 54.

68. UNCF's "What Are the Answers?" 1952, General Education Board Papers, Record Group III 2G, box 492, folder 5241, RAC. See also, "Appraisal of an Adventure," Vertical Files, UNCF Papers, AU Center.

69. UNCF's "A Significant Adventure," ~1950, General Education Board Papers, Record Group 5235–5240, Series 1, sub-series 3, box 491, folder 5240, RAC.

70. UNCF's "A Significant Adventure," ~1950, General Education Board Papers, Record Group 5235–5240, Series 1, sub-series 3, box 491, folder 5240, RAC.

71. UNCF's "Thirty-two Steps Forward to a Better America," 1945, General Education Board Papers, Record Group 5235–5240, Series 1, subseries 3, box 491, folder 5238, RAC.

72. UNCF's "America Is Free to Choose," 1944, General Education Board Papers, Record Group 5235–5240, Series 1, sub-series 3, box 491, folder 5338, RAC.

73. UNCF's "A Significant Adventure," ~1950, General Education Board Papers, Record Group 5235–5240, Series 1, sub-series 3, box 491, folder 5240, RAC.

74. UNCF's "America Is Free to Choose," 1944, General Education Board Papers, Record Group 5235–5240, series 1, sub-series 3, box 491, folder 5338, RAC.

75. UNCF's "A Significant Adventure," ~1950, General Education Board Papers, Record Group 5235–5240, Series 1, sub-series 3, box 491, folder 5240, RAC.

76. Rodchenko was a Russian painter, sculptor, designer, and photographer; Lissitzky was a Russian painter, typographer, and designer. Alexander Lavrentjev, *Rodchenko Photography* (Munich: Schirmer/Mosel, 1982), 113; Philip Meggs, *A History of Graphic Design*, 268.

77. Barthes, *Mythologies.*

78. Mary L. Dudziak, *Cold War Civil Rights. Race and the Image of American Democracy* (Princeton: Princeton University Press, 2000).

79. Litwack, *Trouble in Mind.* John Egerton, *Speak Now Against the Day. The Generation Before the Civil Rights Movement in the South* (New York: Knopf, 1994); Marybeth Gasman, "Scylla and Charybdis: Navigating the Waters of Academic Freedom at Fisk University during Charles S. Johnson's Administration (1946–1956)," *American Educational Research Journal* 36, 4 (winter, 1999).

80. Frederick D. Patterson, "Development Programs at Negro Institutions," Speech given before the Council of Presidents of the National Association of State and Universities and Land-Grant Colleges, Chicago, Illinois, 11 November 1969. Located in vertical file, UNCF Papers, AUC Center.

81. Jackson Davis, General Education Board notes, 17 June 1943, General Education Board Papers, Record Group 5221–5234, series 1, sub-series 3, box 490, folder 5231, RAC.

82. Barthes, *Mythologies.*

83. Anderson, *The Education of Blacks*; Ron Chernow, *Titan. The Life of John D. Rockefeller, Sr. (*New York: Vintage Books, 1998); Edward Berman, *The Influence of the Carnegie, Ford, and Rockefeller*

Foundations on American Foreign Policy: The Ideology of Philanthropy (New York: State University of New York Press, 1983).

84. Peter Collier and David Horowitz, *The Rockefellers* (New York: Holt, Rinehart, and Winston, 1976); Marybeth Gasman, "A Word for Every Occasion: John D. Rockefeller, Jr. and the United Negro College Fund, 1944–1960," *History of Higher Education Annual* (Spring 2003).

85. Dudziak, *Cold War Civil Rights.*

86. Egerton, *Speak Now Against the Day;* Ellen Schrecker, *No Ivory Tower. McCarthyism and Universities* (New York: Oxford University Press, 1986).

87. For more information, see John Egerton, *Speak Now Against the Day*, 172–174.

Illustrations

Fig 1. "America Is Free to Choose," 1944, General Education Board Papers, Record Group 5235-5240, Series 1,   sub-series 3, box 491, folder 5338, Rockefeller Archive Center, Sleepy Hollow, New York (used with permission).

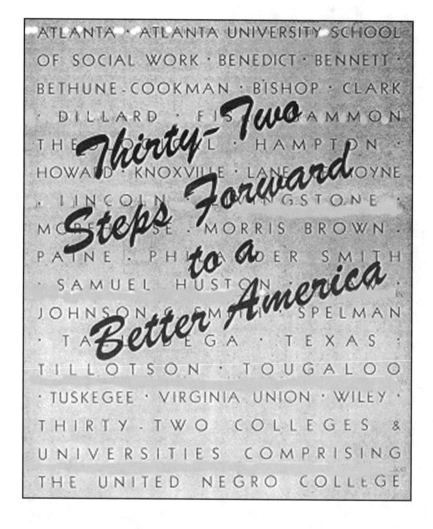

Fig 2. "Thirty-two Steps Forward to a Better America," 1945, General Education Board Papers, Record Group 5235-5240, Series 1, subseries 3, box 491, folder 5238, Rockefeller Archive Center, Sleepy Hollow, New York (used with permission).

Fig 3. America Is Free to Choose," 1944, General Education Board Papers, Record Group 5235-5240, Series 1, subseries 3, box 491, folder 5338, Rockefeller Archive Center, Sleepy Hollow, New York (used with permission).

Fig 4. *The Mobilizer*, June 1952, Rockefeller—Education, III 2G, box 96, folder 664, Rockefeller Archive Center, Sleepy Hollow, New York (used with permission).

Fig 5. "America Is Free to Choose," 1944, General Education Board Papers, Record Group 5235-5240, Series 1, subseries 3, box 491, folder 5338, Rockefeller Archive Center, Sleepy Hollow, New York (used with permission).

Fig 6. "A Significant Adventure," 1950, General Education Board Papers, Record Group 5235-5240, Series 1, subseries 3, box 491, folder 5240, Rockefeller Archive Center, Sleepy Hollow, New York (used with permission).

CHAPTER FIVE

Thurgood Marshall

A Study of Philanthropy through Racial Uplift

NOAH D. DREZNER

"Education and work are the levers to uplift people."

—W. E. B. Du Bois[1]

"Racial uplift . . . can be considered a form of African American philanthropy."

—CENTER ON PHILANTHROPY AND CIVIL SOCIETY[2]

When defining philanthropy within the Black community standard definitions—such as large monetary donations—are too limiting. The Center on Philanthropy and Civil Society at The City University of New York, through a report commissioned by the Ford Foundation and the Coalition for New Philanthropy in New York, recently suggested that there is a trend to include actions of both self-help and benevolence in a new definition of philanthropy. Self-help philanthropy includes "cooperative giving of time and/or money in response to the needs of the individual family, and immediate community," while benevolent philanthropy includes monetary donations.[3] Self-help and mutual benevolence within the Black community grew out of centuries of oppression and legalized segregation, factors that, despite the good will of many Whites, required African Americans largely to rely on themselves for racial uplift. For any community to advance, both financial donations and service are needed. Neither form of philanthropy could be successful without the other. Researchers agree that racial uplift has long been the greatest motivation for giving either time or talent.[4] It is often talent that successfully advances a cause farther than money.

The actions of those involved in the Civil Rights Movement of the twentieth century, concerned with gaining rights of full citizenship for all Americans, should therefore be understood as philanthropic. The Civil Rights Movement was propelled by contributions of both money and time. It was through the extraordinary gifts of time, expertise and service of civil rights leaders such as Thurgood Marshall that American law came to recognize the right of all individuals to be treated equally.[5] These changes also facilitated the movement of members of the Black community into positions of economic and political influence, arenas that had previously been all but closed to them.[6] As a direct result of Thurgood Marshall's and other civil rights leaders' efforts to uplift the race by overturning their subordinate legal status, Blacks "have become more affluent, gained political power, particularly in the urban centers, and in certain respects, developed a stronger sense of community."[7]

Although Thurgood Marshall is perhaps best remembered for his historic position as the first Black Supreme Court Justice and although other men, such as Martin Luther King, Jr., have garnered more fame for their leadership in the Civil Rights Movement, Marshall's most direct and lasting contributions to the advancement of the race came in the years before the Movement and laid the groundwork for it. In offering a definition of what characterized the best presidents, Franklin D. Roosevelt asserted that it was those who were "leaders of thought at times when certain ideas in the life of the nation had to be clarified."[8] Marshall, although he never held public office, was just such a leader at a time when not only the ideas but the very laws of the nation were deeply flawed and in desperate need of repair. Through his tireless work in the courtroom on behalf of African Americans, Marshall should be viewed not only as a great leader but also, under an emerging definition, as a philanthropist.

A study of African American philanthropy would therefore be incomplete without an understanding of the contributions of Thurgood Marshall to the Civil Rights Movement. Both as a lawyer for the National Association for the Advancement of Colored People (NAACP) and then later as a Supreme Court justice, Marshall was intimately and passionately involved with issues pertaining to equal rights for all men and women, regardless of race, ethnicity, or creed. His NAACP tenure, 1932 to 1961, was a pivotal time for the organization, when overturning racial segregation was one of its prime directives. Marshall's work for the NAACP until 1935 was without remuneration. It was at this point that the new lawyer began his work on his first segregation case, *Murray v. Pearson*. Marshall would not be officially brought on as NAACP council, in a temporary position, until 1936.[9] By the time Marshall joined the bench of the Supreme Court, he had argued thirty-two cases before that body and won twenty-nine of them, mostly in the name of racial desegregation and other civil rights causes.[10]

Thurgood Marshall's activism extended from his time at the NAACP through the opinions and dissentions he issued on the country's highest court.[11] However, for the purpose of this chapter I am going to look only at Marshall's tenure as a lawyer for the NAACP and the Legal Defense Fund (LDF). Studying Marshall and his work for uplift of a community will help provide a more complete understanding of African American philanthropy in the United States during the twentieth century.

A CIVIL RIGHTS LEADER IN THE MAKING

Thurgood Marshall was born Thoroughgood Marshall (a name he later shortened legally) in 1908 to Norma and William Marshall in the age of Jim Crow.[12] Even though this was the postbellum period and slavery had been abolished almost half a century before, racism was rampant. Blacks were barred from the polls through hurdles of literacy, property ownership, and poll-tax requirements that were imposed throughout the South at the turn of the twentieth century. Novelists glorified the image of Ku Klux Klan while journalists over-reported Black crime, charges of rape, and arrogance. The campaign for Black disenfranchisement had begun.[13]

Jim Crow laws and segregation were not the only issues that Blacks were forced to deal with. Their ability to handle and worthiness to receive education was under constant fire. In 1900 a University of Virginia professor, Paul B. Barringer, told the Southern Education Association that "the Negro race is essentially a race of peasant farmers and laborers . . . as a source of cheap labor for a warm climate he is beyond competition; everywhere else he is a foreordained failure, and he knows this; he despises his own color."[14] Barringer then argued for the end of the "fraud" of educational suffrage—a position that Marshall would successfully fight throughout his career.[15]

When Marshall graduated from high school he could not go to his home state's flagship institution of higher education, the University of Maryland at College Park, because African Americans were not yet admitted. He did not want to go to all-Black Morgan State, the only public university open to African Americans in Maryland, because it was not of the same academic caliber of the University of Maryland.[16] As a result, Marshall chose to attend Lincoln University, a small private school for Blacks in Oxford, Pennsylvania. While at college the young Marshall met and married his first wife, Vivien "Buster" Burey, who later influenced him to pursue a career in law. When applying to law school Marshall once again attempted to gain admission to the University of Maryland. Shortly after submitting his application, an aide to the president responded in writing to Marshall, reminding him that no southern professional schools, including the University of Maryland Law School, ever admitted Black applicants.[17] This categorical rejection would haunt him for the rest of his professional life and begin the civil rights leader's quest for educational equality for Blacks. Marshall received his law degree in 1933 from Howard University School of Law instead, a historically Black university in the District of Columbia. After practicing for a year Marshall was hired as a staff attorney by the Baltimore branch of the NAACP. Shortly thereafter he undertook his first school segregation case, and in 1935 he sued the University of Maryland for its discriminatory admissions policies.[18] Marshall knew that opening the flagship schools to Blacks would offer his race more opportunities to succeed and improve the current situation in which they lived.

Along with his law school mentor, Charles Houston, Marshall searched for a prospective law student who would be the perfect candidate for the lawsuit; he found one in Donald Gaines Murray. Murray was a native of Baltimore with more than adequate academic credentials for admission. The young plaintiff had received his bachelor's degree from Amherst College after four years. Maryland's statutes at the time only required two years of postsecondary education for consideration for the law school.[19] Murray therefore had double the coursework required for admission. Marshall convinced Murray to send a registered letter to the University of Maryland requesting admission to the law school. Just as Marshall received in 1930, Murray got a letter indicating that he would not be considered for admission because of his race; the letter went on to advise him to consider Howard University Law School, Marshall's alma mater.[20]

Prior to the trial, the University of Maryland's registrar acknowledged that the institution had not admitted a single Black student since its affiliation with the state in 1920.[21] The Regents of the University built their case around the fact that the state had a policy of educating Whites and Blacks separately, as far as public schools were concerned.[22] It was therefore a matter of legal procedure, they argued, and not base discrimination that led the University to categorically reject all Black applicants. Based on the famous 1896 *Plessy v. Ferguson* case that declared segregated public education constitutional as long as it was equal, this line of argument required that quality public education be available for Blacks. Marshall and the other lawyers in this precedent-setting trial would use the logic of *Plessy* to argue their case, waiting for a later battle to challenge the very system of "separate but equal" education.

During the proceedings Raymond A. Pearson, then president of the University, admitted that "the Princess Anne Academy, the separate-for-Negroes 'Easton branch' of the university," was really an unaccredited junior college whose faculty contained only one person with an earned college degree.[23] This clearly showed that the notion of separate but equal was nothing more than a myth in Maryland. Marshall and the NAACP further showed that the University of Maryland School of Law was, at the time, the only American Bar Association-accredited institution in the state, effectively leaving Blacks no means for a legal education in Maryland. The team argued that access to advanced education was not a privilege but a right and that it was the legal responsibility of the state to assure that access to its citizens. Additionally, the NAACP argued that Murray's application should be considered regardless of his race because "segregated education . . . violated the equal protection under the law."[24] This laid the argument for future court cases in Marshall's educational suffrage movement. As a result, Judge O'Dunne ruled that the university's Regents must review Murray's application prior to the beginning of the next academic year and admit him if he was a worthy applicant.[25]

Led by the newly appointed acting president, H. Curley Byrd, the Regents appealed the court's decision. After O'Dunne's decision other Blacks had applied for graduate degrees in law and pharmacy as well as undergraduate education, and Byrd feared that White flight would occur at the institution over fear that the Black men would rape the approximately five hundred female students.[26] In their oral argument the university counsel described the central issue of the case as the right of the Regents to "follow Maryland's traditional policy of separation of races in educational institutions, and to deny admittance solely on the basis of color or race classification."[27] Marshall and the NAACP were successful in the appeals. The Court of Appeals upheld the original decision, stating that the law school was discriminating against Black residents and that as the only accredited law school available, it had to admit all qualified applicants. Notably, the Court of Appeals never answered the implied question about the notion of separate but equal, and through its silence left open the door for the creation of a separate law school for Blacks in the state of Maryland. Thankfully, this never happened. In a separate case, *Missouri ex rel Gaines v. Canada* (1938), the Supreme Court did rule that opening a separate law school for Blacks, as long as the education obtained was equal to that of a White law school, was permissible.[28]

The gains made by the *Murray* decision were small. In fact over a decade after *Murray*, Blacks had to sue the University of Maryland again for admission to graduate chemistry, nursing, and sociology programs.[29] However, *Murray* was a significant step towards the larger educational accomplishments of Marshall and the NAACP. Over the next two decades leading up to the *Brown* case that overturned *Plessey*, Marshall's litigation steadily challenged the underpinnings of American law itself. His goal was not merely to remind the nation to keep its own rules—equal protection—but to demonstrate that the rules themselves were wrong.

MARSHALL AND THE NAACP LEGAL DEFENSE FUND

When Marshall joined the NAACP, the U.S. Treasury Department did not recognize the organization as an "educational" alliance because of the organization's history of political lobbying, and it was therefore denied tax-exempt status by the Internal Revenue Service. In response, Marshall established the NAACP Legal Defense Fund, Inc., commonly known as the "Inc. Fund" or the Legal Defense Fund, which was designed to argue select cases in which a committee found racial injustices to have occurred. Because of its "nonpartisan" role, the LDF met the government's requirements to receive tax-exempt status. The purpose of the new fund, according to Marshall, was to "establish in the courts a precedent for the benefit of Negroes in General. [It was a] legal aid society for the advocacy of Negro rights in the courts as contrasted to the legislative halls and areas of general protection handled by the NAACP."[30] The LDF's charter, granted by New York State in 1940, included as its function "to receive and administer funds, contributed solely for legal aid to worthy Negroes suffering from injustice because of race or color and for educational purposes in the promotion of equality in the distribution of public funds for education."[31] In essence Marshall's LDF had a mission of racial uplift.

Juan Williams, in a 1990 article in *The Washington Post Magazine*, quotes Juanita Jackson Mitchell, an NAACP activist in Baltimore at the time the LDF was established, as recalling the Black response to Marshall's court triumphs as "euphoric with victory. . . . We didn't know about the Constitution. He [Marshall] brought us the Constitution as a document like Moses brought his people the Ten Commandments."[32] Under Marshall's leadership the LDF moved from a subsidiary organization of the NAACP to a separate, yet closely tied, entity. Marshall held the title of director-counsel of the LDF while remaining in his position of special counsel to the NAACP until 1956. The LDF worked to secure equal justice under the law. The Fund specifically focused on education, political participation and economic justice.

Prior to being appointed to the Federal bench, and even prior to arguing *Brown*, Marshall took on the Supreme Court and its handling of issues of racial justice. In an article in the *Annals of the American Academy of Political and Social Sciences*, he admonished the high court for its historical lack of consistency and slow movement toward equality among all citizens:

> That many of the vestiges of slavery remain and that racial discrimination still is practiced in all sections of the United States is to a considerable extent the responsibility of the United States Supreme Court which spelled out this new constitutional provision. The Court's narrow, cautious, and often rigid interpretation of the [fourteenth] amendment's reach and thrust in the past gave constitutional sanctions to practices of racial discrimina-

tion and prejudice. Such practices have been permitted to become a part of the pattern of contemporary American society, in effective nullification of the constitutional mandate.[33]

In addition to lambasting the nation's highest court in print, Marshall took thirty-two different cases before that bench, arguing on behalf of those that society despised. In case after case Marshall fought segregation. While most of his cases dealt with educational equality, Marshall also fought for Blacks' right to vote in Texas primaries, the right to rent or buy any place of residence, and for equality of pay.

Marshall's victory on behalf of the LDF in *Smith v. Allwright* (1944), in which the Supreme Court ruled that Blacks could vote in the Texas primaries, was a significant step towards his goals of racial uplift and equality. The NAACP had tried three times before to open the Texas primary system to Blacks.[34] Although courts had ruled in the NAACP's favor in the past, the Texas Democratic Party continued to bar Blacks from voting in the primary. Prior to *Smith* the Court ruled that while the Fifteenth Amendment guarantees Blacks the right to vote, this privilege did not extend to primaries because they were considered actions of private groups.[35] Justice Stanley F. Reed, a southerner from Mason County, Kentucky, wrote the eight to one majority *Smith* opinion. In his decision, the southerner wrote that "the right to vote in such a primary . . . without discrimination by the state . . . is secured by the Constitution [of the United States]."[36] The court found the private primaries as integral to the electoral process and therefore a state action. The impact of this decision was significant. NAACP and LDF officials saw this case as one that would determine whether Blacks were viewed as "secondary or primary citizens."[37] The NAACP believed that without a vote in the primary process a citizen was disenfranchised and not given equal protection. Participation in the political process was necessary to secure for Blacks the voice needed to influence the political and legal system. One way to judge the results of *Smith* is to observe Black voter registration levels before and after the opinion was delivered. Prior to *Smith*, only three percent of Blacks in the south were registered to vote. In 1947, only three years after the decision, that percentage had risen to twelve, and by 1950 twenty percent of southern Blacks were registered.[38]

Fifty years ago Marshall argued his most famous case in front of the U.S. Supreme Court, *Brown v. the Board of Education, Topeka, Kansas.* The *Brown* case encompassed five school segregation cases in Virginia, South Carolina, Delaware, Kansas, and Washington, D.C.[39] After seventeen years of success in opening post-secondary and graduate education through a series of court cases, Marshall, the LDF, and the NAACP were ready to take on educational segregation on a primary school level. At the time it was clear that separate was unequal. This inequality was apparent in the numbers. Take Clarendo County, South Carolina, for example; per-capita spending for White students was $179 as compared to spending for Black students for which it was $43, and the student-to-teacher ratio in the White schools was 28:1, while in the Black school system it was 47:1.[40]

While this was the case in many parts of the South, it was not the conditions of Topeka, Kansas. In fact the facilities were considered equal. Marshall's argument in *Brown* went further than the need for equal facilities, lest the Court uphold *Plessy* and again rule that school segregation was permissible as long as facilities were equal. Marshall wanted educational integration. He focused on testimony presented by educational, psychiatric, and social experts about the terrible effects of state-sponsored segregation upon Black children. Marshall argued "that segregated schools, perhaps more than any other single factor, are of major concern to the individual of public school age and contribute greatly to the unwholesomeness and unhappy development of the personality of Negroes which the color caste system in the United States has produced."[41]

The case was not easily won; Marshall began arguing *Brown* in December of 1952, and by June of 1953 the high court was still requesting further information.[42] It was almost a year and a half after the Court began hearing the case that Chief Justice Warren finally read the Court's unanimous decision:

> We conclude that in the field of public education the doctrine of "separate but equal" has no place. Separate educational facilities are inherently unequal. Therefore, we hold that the plaintiffs and others similarly situated for whom the actions have been brought are, by reason of the segregation complained of, deprived of the equal protection of the laws guaranteed by the Fourteenth Amendment.[43]

The *Brown* decision had a reach beyond education.[44] The Supreme Court extended *Brown's* constitutional scope by expanding the principle to desegregate other public facilities. Through a series of cases and unsigned per curiam opinions,[45] the Court ordered equal access to public parking-lots, restaurants, cemeteries, hospitals, parks, golf courses, buses, beaches, and amphitheaters.[46]

Marshall himself realized the importance, power, and reach of the *Brown* decision. He believed that the Court's opinion "probably did more than anything else to awaken the Negro from his apathy to demanding his right to equality."[47] In essence the 1954 decision can be seen as the foundation for the Civil Rights Movement, yet Marshall did not think it alone was responsible for birthing it. In commenting on the importance of his victories in *Smith* and *Brown*, Marshall once said, "I don't know whether the voting case or the school desegregation case was more important. Without the ballot, you've got no goddamned citizenship, no status, no power, in this country. But without the chance to get an education, you have no capacity to use the ballot effectively. Hell, I don't know which case I'm proudest of."[48] The future would show that through the victory of *Smith*, giving the right to participate in primaries and therefore the political process, Marshall provided a privilege and a power to a people that forever changed the appearance of local, state, and federal governments as well as the political parties. The right to vote gave Blacks the power to influence the nation and its policies. However, without *Brown*, those with this newfound power would not be able to use it to its full potential. The powerful combination of *Smith* and *Brown* provided a significant source of uplift for Blacks. In a speech given four months before the *Brown* ruling, Marshall said that "there is no excuse under the sun for any young person, today, feeling that there is any ceiling whatsoever on whatever he might do that is based on race or color. There is no reason for it anymore."[49] Marshall was challenging his audience to be active, for he knew that the rights to equal education and to vote were useless if no one took advantage of them.

MARSHALL'S LIFE AS A PHILANTHROPIST

Throughout his life and after his death people realized the importance of Marshall's work for American Blacks. In 1968, *Newsweek* magazine declared that Marshall "had done as much to transform the life of his people as any Negro alive today, including Nobel laureate Martin Luther King [Jr.]."[50] Yet Marshall's work was never focused narrowly on achieving civil rights for some but broadly on assuring them for all. For example, in 1960 Marshall helped draft a constitution for the soon-to-be independent Kenyan republic that provided protections for the White minority.[51] His achievements in the United States were helpful to those beyond his own race as well. A. Leon Higginbotham, chief judge emeritus of the Third Circuit Court of Appeals, remarked that "if [Marshall] had not won the *Brown* case the door of equal opportunity would have been more tightly closed also to women, other minorities, and the poor."[52]

Thurgood Marshall's efforts to uplift his race advanced the United States as a whole. Charles Houston, Marshall's law professor and vice-dean while at Howard University, advised his students that Black lawyers should see themselves as "social engineers" whose job was to "interpret his groups [sic] advancement."[53] Marshall was taught that as a lawyer he was to "use the practice of law to reform society."[54] This is precisely what Marshall did. U.S. Supreme Court Justice William J. Brennan, Jr. celebrated his colleague's achievements by describing Marshall as "a man who had made extraordinary contributions to society . . . who was on the prevailing side when it was very difficult to be on the prevailing side."[55]

Marshall's work as a lawyer for the NAACP was philanthropic in the truest sense. Through legal rather than the more traditional channels of financial donation, Marshall cared for and uplifted the disadvantaged. His tireless efforts for civil rights on behalf of the disenfranchised won for Blacks more opportunities, more freedoms, more equality than the work of any of the other politicians, policy-makers, or lawyers of the twentieth century.

W. E. B. Du Bois, a noted Black Nationalist and academic, closed his famous work "The Talented Tenth" by saying:

> Education and work are the levers to uplift a people. Work alone will not do it unless inspired by the right ideals and guided by intelligence. Education must not simply teach work—it must teach Life. The Talented Tenth of the Negro race must be made leaders of thought and missionaries of culture among their people. . . . The Negro race, like all other races, is going to be saved by its exceptional men.[56]

Thurgood Marshall was one of these "exceptional men." Marshall's work was "inspired by the right ideals and guided by [his] intelligence."[57] Through Marshall's hard work he brought Blacks the opportunity for better education. It was through his accomplishments at the NAACP and LDF that he uplifted his race by fighting and advocating for equality. By ensuring that Blacks had the right to education and the opportunity to be involved in the democratic political process Marshall helped more than just the "Talented Tenth of the Negro race" to be "leaders of thought and missionaries of culture" for generations to come.[58] As his birth name suggests, through a "Thoroughgood," Marshall was a philanthropist. Perhaps former President Clinton said it best in a statement released upon Marshall's passing: "He was a giant in the quest for human rights and equal opportunity in the whole history of our country. Every American should be grateful for the contributions [Marshall] made as an advocate."[59]

NOTES

1. W. E. B. Du Bois, "The Talented Tenth," in *The Negro Problem: A Series of Articles by Representative Negroes of Today* (New York: James Pott & Co., 1903).
2. Center on Philanthropy and Civil Society, *African American Philanthropy Literature Review* (New York: Center on Philanthropy and Civil Society, 2003), 9.
3. Ibid., 3.
4. Center on Philanthropy and Civil Society, *African American Philanthropy Literature Review*.
5. Lawrence Otis Graham, *Our Kind of People: Inside America's Black Upper Class* (New York: Harper Collins, 1999).
6. Mary Frances Winters, "Reflecting on Endowment Building in the African American Community," in Cultures *of Caring: Philanthropy in Diverse Communities* (Washington, D.C.: Council on Foundations, 1999).
7. Center on Philanthropy and Civil Society, *African American Philanthropy Literature Review*, 10.
8. R.W. Apple, Jr., "Legacy of Reagan's Presidency Now Begins the Test of Time," *New York Times* (11 June 2004): 1A
9. Howard Ball, *A Defiant Life: Thurgood Marshall and the Persistence of Racism in America* (New York: Three Rivers Press, 2001).

10. Carl T. Rowan, *Dream Makers, Dream Breakers: The World of Justice Thurgood Marshall* (Boston: Little, Brown, & Company, 1993).

11. Marshall continued to further people's rights through rulings such as extending "double jeopardy" to state prosecutions in *United States ex rel George Hetenyi v. Wilkins* (1965), giving women the right to chose and the right to privacy in *Roe v. Wade* (1973) and extending defendant's rights through *Gideon v. Wainright* (1964) and *Miranda v. Arizona* (1965).

12. Mabel M. Smythe, ed., *The Black American Reference Book* (New Jersey: Prentice-Hall, 1976).

13. C. Vann Woodword, *The Strange Career of Jim Crow*, 3rd rev. ed. (New York: Oxford University Press, 1974).

14. Ibid., 95.

15. Ibid.

16. Rowan, *Dream Makers, Dream Breakers*.

17. Irwin Ross, "A *Post* Portrait: Thurgood Marshall," *New York Daily Post Magazine*, 13 June 1960, 23.

18. Ball, *A Defiant Life.*

19. H. L. Mencken, "The Murray Case," 1935, *The Evening Sun,* obtained electronically from the Maryland State Archives s455-D012225A.TIF.

20. Ibid.

21. Rowan, *Dream Makers, Dream Breakers*.

22. Mencken, "Murray Case."

23. Rowan, *Dream Makers, Dream Breakers*, 52.

24. Jean L. Preer, *Lawyers v. Educators: Black Colleges and Desegregation in Public Higher Education* (Westport: Greenwood Press, 1982), 42.

25. Mencken, "Murray Case."

26. Rowan, *Dream Makers, Dream Breakers*.

27. Quoted in Preers, *Lawyers v. Educators*, 43.

28. Ball, *A Defiant Life.*

29. Preers, *Lawyers v. Educators*, 43.

30. Ball, *A Defiant Life*, 59.

31. Ibid.

32. Juan Williams, "Marshall's Law," *The Washington Post Magazine,* 7 January 1990 obtained electronically from the Maryland State Archives s455-D012190A.TIF.

33. Thurgood Marshall, "The Supreme Court as Protector of Civil Rights: Equal Protection of the Laws" in *Annals of the American Academy of Political and Social Sciences*, vol. 275 (May 1951), reprinted in Mark V. Tushnet, ed., *Thurgood Marshall: His Speeches, Writings, Arguments, Opinions, and Reminiscences* (Chicago: Lawrence Hill Books, 2001).

34. These cases included: *Nixon v. Herndon* (1927); *Nixon v. Condon* (1932); and *Grovey v. Townsend* (1935).

35. Ball, *A Defiant Life.*

36. *Smith v. Allwright*, 321 U.S. 649 (1944).

37. Quoted in Rowan, *Dream Makers, Dream Breakers*, 126.

38. Ball, *A Defiant Life*, 78.

39. Fred Powledge, *Free at Last? The Civil Rights Movement and the People Who Made It* (Boston: Little, Brown, & Company, 1979).

40. Marilyn Miller and Marian Faux, ed., *The New York Public Library American History Desk Reference.* (New York: Macmillan, 1997)

41. Thurgood Marshall, "An Evaluation of Recent Efforts to Achieve Racial Integration in Education Through Resort of the Courts" in J. Clay Smith Jr., ed., *Supreme Justice: Speeches and Writing* (Philadelphia: University of Pennsylvania Press, 2003) 52.

42. Ibid.

43. *Brown v. Board of Education*, 347 U.S. 483 (1954).

44. Derrick Bell, *Silent Covenants: Brown v. Board of Education and the Unfulfilled Hopes for Racial Reform* (New York: Oxford University Press, 2004); Charles J. Ogletree, *All Deliberate Speed: Reflections on the First Half-Century of Brown v. Board of Education* (W. W. Norton & Company, 2004); Richard Kluger, *Simple Justice: The History of Brown v. Board of Education and Black America's Struggle for Equality* (New York: Vintage Books, 2004).

45. A per curiam opinion is issued in the name of the Court rather than specific justices. These decisions tend to be short and viewed as relatively non-controversial.

46. Bell, *A Defiant Life*, 147; these cases include: *Burton v. Wilmington, Delaware, Parking Authority; Johnson v. Virginia; Rice v. Sioux City Memorial Park Association; Simkins v. Cone Memorial Hospital; Watson v. City of Memphis; Holmes v. City of Atlanta; Gayle v. Browder; Dawson v. City of Baltimore; and Muir v. Louisville, Kentucky, Park Theatrical Association.*

47. Quoted in Ball, *A Defiant Life*, 147.

48. Quoted in Rowan, *Dream Makers, Dream Breakers*, 129, and Columbia University Oral history Project (Thurgood Marshall), New York.

49. Thurgood Marshall, "The Future Lies with Our Youth," address before the National Newspaper Publishers' Association's Mid-Winter Meeting, at Tuskegee Institute, Tuskegee, Alabama, 23 January 1954, in Smith, ed., *Supreme Justice: Speeches and Writing*, 75.

50. Quoted in Juan Williams, "Marshall's Law," *The Washington Post Magazine*, January 7, 1990, 14, obtained electronically from the Maryland State Archives s455-D012190A.TIF

51. Williams, "Marshall's Law."

52. Quoted in Albert Sehistedt Jr., "Retired Justice, 84, Led Many Civil Rights Battles: Baltimore Native Was First Black on Highest Court," obtained electronically from the Maryland State Archives s455-D012148A.TIF.

53. Ball, *A Defiant Life*, 30; Genna Rae McNeil, *Groundwork: Charles Hamilton Houston and the Struggle for Civil Rights* (Philadelphia: University of Pennsylvania Press, 1983), 71.

54. Maurice C. Taylor, "A Biography of Thurgood Marshall, Who 'Came to Personify the NAACP," *The Baltimore Sun*, 29 November 1992, obtained electronically from the Maryland State Archives s455-D012170A.TIF.

55. Quoted in Allegra Bennett, "Marshall Honored at Dedication of Statue as 'Symbol of Progress," obtained electronically from the Maryland State Archives s455-D012146A.TIF.

56. Du Bois, "Talented Tenth."

57. Ibid.

58. Ibid.

59. Quoted in *New York Times News Service*, "Marshall's Friends and Colleagues Mourn Passing of Larger-Than-Life Jurist," *The Baltimore Sun*, 25 January 25 1993, 7A obtained electronically from the Maryland State Archives s455-D012156A.TIF.

CHAPTER SIX

The Links, Incorporated

Advocacy, Education, and Service in the African American Community

KIJUA SANDERS-McMURTRY AND NIA WOODS HAYDEL

For centuries, black women, during slavery and in freedom, played a significant role in the creation of social, cultural and educational, religious, and economic institutions designed to improve the material conditions and to raise the self-esteem of African-Americans.

—DARLENE CLARK HINE[1]

Philanthropy is about hope . . . the act of giving service to others is an act of hope for them, for ourselves, and for unknown others whom we will never know.

—ROBERT PAYTON[2]

PREFACE

A young high-school dropout raised by a single mother entered a local community college with the goal of getting a better job. The young student excelled academically, while working various jobs and envisioning a brighter future, and was more hopeful than most people of similar backgrounds and experiences would dare to be. This young woman soon completed her studies at the community college and prepared to transfer to a four-year university but was unsure how to proceed due to a lack of familial and financial support. The student felt completely overwhelmed by the exceedingly high costs of attending a four-year college.

The student applied for several scholarships hoping that someone would believe that she was worthy of pecuniary assistance. Several months later she received notification that she had been select-

ed as a scholarship recipient by an organization of black women dedicated to providing hope to the disadvantaged members of their race. The student was honored at a special ceremony that encouraged and motivated other young people. The experience inspired her because she benefited from the investment of women who would serve as models for all that she could accomplish in the future. The student later completed college at a four-year university, and went on to continue a career in higher education while pursuing a doctorate degree. The college graduate vowed to honor the legacy of the organization whose gift lifted her up in a time of need; she determined that she would dedicate her life to racial and social uplift. The scholarship was her first introduction to The Links, Incorporated, and it left an indelible impression.[3]

The Links, Incorporated, was established in 1946 by two African American women whose vision was to form an organization that would invite friends to "link together in service to their communities."[4] Fifty-eight years later this organization—comprised solely of African American women—is one of the leading philanthropic organizations in the Black community, particularly in the areas of community service, fundraising, and monetary donations.[5] More than eleven thousand members in over two hundred seventy-five chapters in the United States, Germany, the Bahamas, and South Africa are committed to linking their social relationships and individual commitments to community improvement. The Links members have established initiatives within their local communities related to "black youth, the arts and national and international trends and services."[6]

There is a dearth of scholarship on women philanthropists, and the literature becomes even more sparse when narrowed to African American women philanthropists. This is unfortunate for, as some recent historians have shown, African American women have been vital to the philanthropic activity of the broader black community.[7] These histories are steps in the right direction, but there is still much work to be done to balance our understanding of African Americans—and especially black women—as philanthropists. This chapter will contribute to that growing body of scholarship.

African American philanthropy has traditionally included the giving of time, talent, and services in addition to monetary donations. As philanthropy scholar Emmett Carson contends, "nearly every traditional Black organization is not only membership based but relies heavily on those members to volunteer, contribute money, and solicit others to participate."[8] Carson argues that "Black nonprofit organizations may represent an ideal model for other nonprofit organizations to emulate" if their goal is to increase volunteerism and fundraising in their various communities.[9]

In these ways The Links is paradigmatic of African American philanthropy, yet the organization also has a unique history and purpose. Philanthropy comes in many forms and from various sources. When considering philanthropic organizations, the white male model of giving large monetary gifts to a cause is what generally comes to mind. Conversely, when considering the act of giving in the black community, service and fellowship are the images one often sees. Our intention in this chapter is to present The Links as a well-balanced model of the two traditional varieties of philanthropy. A Study of The Links illuminates the complex social workings of philanthropy in the black community as well as honors this noteworthy organization and the remarkable women who give it life. For over fifty years the women of The Links have worked tirelessly to improve the lives of people of African descent through the arts, education, mental and physical health programming, and overall self-esteem development. They have implemented strategic programs that have affected the lives of countless African Americans nationwide and people of African descent throughout the Diaspora.[10] As historian Darlene Clark Hine notes:

> The philanthropic work of black women contains a palpable undertone of muted defiance of the racial and gender inequalities pervading virtually every aspect of American society . . . each black boy and girl saved from the streets, educated to be a productive and self-respecting citizen, restored to good health, and trained for a skilled job, represented a resounding blow to the edifice of Jim Crow, patriarchy and white privilege. Those so reclaimed were able to return to the black community and become additional agents in the struggle for social change and liberation.[11]

The Links' efforts are similar to the many efforts of African American women to address the social problems affecting their communities yet also differ in important ways.

In addition to having a membership comprised exclusively of black women, The Links is also distinct from other philanthropic organizations in its stringent service and financial requirements of its members. Worldwide, The Links members have given over fifteen million dollars to their local communities. Links members also donate numerous service hours throughout their various chapters. Through our analysis of The Links' philanthropic efforts we intend to record and analyze the contributions of this organization of powerful professional black women who furthered the practice of service and philanthropy by using a confluence of money, time, and social and political connections to uplift a people. The Links' strong commitment to personal service is even more striking when one notes that the women who comprise its membership are busy professionals with full calendars of family, work, and various social obligations (including memberships in other organizations) who nonetheless give selflessly of their time and talents.

Our research provides the first comprehensive scholarly analysis of the philanthropic efforts of The Links within the black community. The authors have relied on historical documents of The Links, including two important histories written by Links historian Marjorie Holloman Parker. While Parker's text offers a history of the programmatic evolution of The Links, it is specifically designed to give Links' members more information about their organization's history from the perspective of an insider.[12] Our scholarly analysis engages the philanthropic work of The

Links through the perspective of academic outsiders. We believe this provides us with a different goal and purpose than previous histories published through The Links organization. Our hope is to share our investigation of The Links with a larger audience of individuals who may not know that the organization exists and to help others develop an awareness of the contributions of this African American women's organization.

LINKED TOGETHER: BENEVOLENCE AMONG FAMILY, FRIENDS, AND COMMUNITY

The Links was not the first organization of black women committed to community service. Prior to its creation there were at least four black sororities that had been organized to address community needs.[13] These sororities saw social and political change as one of the best ways to address community problems and therefore were frequently involved with political initiatives in addition to the community service work they did in their communities.[14] While the founding members of The Links had the means to be political agents, they chose to begin their work in a more modest way. They were more concerned with using the resources they had to bring about practical change without being political in their execution of community initiatives. The Links was committed to a vision that would utilize friendship as a mechanism to expand its organizational agenda, namely, improving the condition of black communities.

The women who founded The Links were dedicated to racial uplift, a goal they hoped to accomplish by establishing local networks of friends who would use their familial, financial, and social resources to "link" up and lift up disadvantaged members of their race.[15] These women hoped to promote cultural, educational, and civic activities as a means of social betterment, and they worked hard to ensure that future members of The Links would maintain these core principles even as the organization grew. The original chapter, established in Philadelphia, was comprised of nine women who were all successful in their chosen professions. They were accomplished educators, musicians, and artists and had risen to the heights of Philadelphia society through their professional experience and familial connections. These women had the vision to see that their cultural capital could be used not merely for their own benefit but also to improve their community.

METHODOLOGY

We employed several methods for collecting information on The Links, Incorporated. Our data was gathered from archives, books, Internet searches of websites of various chapters of The Links, newspapers and periodicals, and one-on-one interviews. Our objective has been to research the ways in which this group of black women pursued the mission and purpose of the organization in the areas of advocacy, education, and service.

Archival resources provided the foundation for the historical piece of this work and a guiding framework for comprehending the evolution of the organization from its inception to the present. We conducted extensive research on the activities of individual chapters of The Links as reported in national and international magazines and newspapers. This was a rich resource for documenting The Links' progress in addressing social issues. Through this analysis we were able to observe how The Links has remained current on various issues that have plagued black communities and adjusted their programs to meet the changing needs of the individuals they are committed to serve. Finally, interviews were a key source of information for this study. We chose to conduct one-on-one interviews with Links' members as a means of giving voice to the personal experiences of the members of The Links, as well as to gain a more in-depth understanding of the philosophies of the members as they relate to the ideologies of service and philanthropy. The interview questions were designed to reveal the beliefs and opinions of The Links members about African American philanthropy, the social movement to uplift the black race and the role of The Links as a philanthropic organization focused on social change. These conversations provided the knowledge base needed to develop a better understanding of the information we gathered regarding specific chapter programs since the founding of the organization.

HISTORIC BEGINNINGS: LINKING FRIENDS THROUGH SERVICE

The 1940s was a turbulent time for blacks in the United States. Black soldiers fought for the United States during World War II with all of the fervor and passion of freed men and women who believed in the ideals of their country. They traveled the world fighting for the liberation of the disenfranchised only to return to the United States still disenfranchised themselves. Despite their poor treatment at home and in the military, their families were proud of their service to this country. This experience was typical of the era; blacks felt the highs of freedom and involvement in their communities and nation along with the deep lows of prejudice and rejection.[16]

The year 1946—the year in which The Links was started—was a particularly paradoxical one for black Americans, full of striking examples of both the tragedy and the hopefulness that filled their lives. The National Association for the Advancement of Colored People reported that it was "one of the grimmest years [for blacks]" in the history of the organization. Its report documented accounts of "blowtorch killing and eye-gouging of Negro veterans freshly returned from a war to end torture and racial extermination." This report expressed the frustrations of many blacks who felt that the brutal lynching of their soldiers was a betrayal of everything they had fought for during the war. At the same time, 1946 contained strong elements of hope for blacks. Charles S. Johnson was elected the first black president of Fisk University and Thurgood Marshall was awarded the Spingarn Medal for his distinguished service as a lawyer before the United States Supreme Court.[17] Women who would be future Links members witnessed the despair ravaging America's black youth and decided that something needed to be done to bring hope to these communities.[18]

During this period many blacks, particularly women, recognized the need for community action and mobilization. In November of 1946, Philadelphia matrons Margaret Roselle Hawkins and Sarah Strickland Scott invited seven friends to join them in the formation of a new inter-city club designed to make use of their particular gifts in meeting the desperate needs they saw in the black community. They met in the home of Lillian Hudson Wall, who became one of the founding members, which began a tradition practiced by many contemporary Links members to have intimate meetings in the homes of members. According to Darlene Clark Hine and Kathleen Thompson, black women during this time "knew how to organize, were accustomed to working together, and felt a strong kinship with members of their community beyond their immediate families."[19] The Links' founders envisioned an organization that would respond to the needs and aspirations of the black community. The mission would be carried out in three realms: civic, educational, and cultural. Based on these aims the club would implement programs intended to foster cultural appreciation through the arts, develop richer intergroup relations, and help the women who became members understand and accept the social and civic responsibilities Hawkins and Scott believed accompanied privileged status.[20]

Margaret Hawkins and Sarah Scott were high achievers and leaders in their personal and professional lives prior to starting this new organization. Both women were college educated and involved in other organizations that were committed to service in the black community, including Jack and Jill of America.[21] Each woman's experience prior to the formation of the The Links helps explain how and why these two women founded it.

Margaret Roselle Hawkins grew up and attended schools in Philadelphia. She was noticed for her artistic talent while in high school and entered a special program in the field of art. There, her natural gifts for organizing and motivating others came to the forefront when, confronted with exclusion from the annual all-white senior prom, she led her fellow black classmates in a campaign to integrate it. Ultimately, the school officials chose to cancel the event rather than concede to the black students' demands.[22] After graduating from high school Hawkins entered the Philadelphia Normal School. Upon graduation, she was awarded a four-year scholarship to the Woman's School of Design, later known as the Moore Institute of Art. When she completed her studies in 1931, she began to teach art in Camden, New Jersey's public schools. Almost immediately she became active in many organizations, including the Eastern Arts Association, the National Arts Association, the New Jersey Teachers Association, Jack and Jill, and the Mothers' Study Club. Later, Hawkins brought her artistic talent directly to bear on the organization she co-founded by designing the memorable Links bracelet, worn by many members.[23] Hawkins' social connections as an artist, educator, and member of many organizations was instrumental to her later success in developing programs when she served as the second National president of the organization from 1953 to 1957 during which time The Links developed the Links-NAACP life membership program.

Sarah Strickland Scott majored in English at the University of Pennsylvania and later began a career as a teacher in the Philadelphia high schools. Scott also completed a Master's degree in guidance counseling at Columbia University and went on to work as a guidance counselor at the Philadelphia high schools. She was actively involved with organizations that served young people. Parker notes that "many of her activities were youth or family oriented."[24]

She also served a term as national president of Jack and Jill.[25] When the existing chapters of The Links voted to expand the organization beyond clubs on the eastern seaboard to include chapters throughout the United States, co-founder Sarah Scott became the first national president in 1953.

Through their own hard work as well as the good fortune of family and friends, Hawkins and Scott were each able to achieve professional, financial, and social success. Rather than using these resources solely as means to make their own lives more comfortable, each had a long history of giving of their time and money and using their social connections to work for the black community. Both women saw that the work they did benefited enormously from the unusual confluence of resources they were able to bring to bear on their efforts and thus began the idea of creating an organization designed to perpetuate precisely that kind of work. Hawkins and Scott wanted to encourage women with similar resources not to take their privilege for granted but to use their position and power to uplift and motivate the underprivileged of their race.

DEVELOPMENT AND GROWTH OF THE ORGANIZATION

The evolution and growth of The Links was rapid. The success of the first chapter led quickly to the establishment of additional chapters, all done through the linkage of friends. The Links members in Philadelphia contacted friends in other cities along the eastern seaboard, inviting them to establish new chapters. Later, the members of those chapters would urge friends in other cities to do the same. Many of these women had longstanding friendships and networks with each other through other organizations such as college sororities, Jack and Jill, the Urban League, and the NAACP. The philosophy of working together toward a common goal was already inherent in black women of this time, and this helped spur the rapid growth of the organization.[26]

New chapters emerged quickly in neighboring states, with Atlantic City (NJ) following the first chapter one year later in 1947. In 1948 chapters started in Baltimore (MD), Petersburg (VA), Pittsburgh (PA), St. Louis (MO), Washington D.C., Wilmington (DE), and the Wilson-Rocky Mount-Tarboro triangle in North Carolina. Five more chapters followed in 1949, established in New Jersey, Ohio, New York, and North Carolina.[27] Each chapter developed with a similar mission; as one charter member of the Washington, D.C. chapter remembered, "In those days, we were just trying to open the way for black women to help their own communities."[28]

In June of 1949, representatives from the first fourteen chapters, including the original chapter, met in Philadelphia to discuss the future of the organization. The name "Links" had initially been chosen in 1947 by the founding members and had spread to each new chapter; each was known by its location, as in the Philadelphia Links or the Baltimore Links. As it became clear that the organization was growing rapidly and the growth was likely to continue, the members of the fourteen original chapters decided in 1949 that it was time to officially establish a national organization. The following year the number of chapters doubled and spread to other cities throughout the United States. Each chapter maintained the characteristics of the original chapter: selective and limited membership; holding meetings in the homes of one member; family involvement in group activities; professional networks; and the joining of resources to fund important civic and social interests of the members. Having described the founding and early history of The Links we will now turn to a closer analysis of this organization's mission and the means it has used to carry it out.

ADVOCACY, EDUCATION, AND SERVICE THROUGH PHILANTHROPY

Inherent in the mission of The Links from the beginning was the goal to engage the community in three distinct areas—civic life, education, and culture. In the first few years of the organization's history each chapter worked fairly independently, but once the national organization was established and a national board of officers elected The Links began to plan a national program, and a special committee was convened to conceptualize its development. The committee's first recommendation, in 1952, was that each chapter pledge to purchase a life membership in the NAACP. The purpose of this program was to support an organization dedicated to championing and fighting for the civil rights of all Americans. As Links historian Marjorie Parker noted "the response to the NAACP life membership project is a milestone in social action programming by women's organizations" because it encouraged each of its members to individually offer their resources to a civil rights organization. The collective efforts of The Links were a challenge to all Black organizations to begin to support civil rights organizations. The NAACP program, the first of The Links' many successful programs, became an "integral part of chapter programs, raising a challenge and setting an example for many other groups."[29]

During the 1960s, The Links began to create what would become known as program facets—small, focused initiatives—to provide structured methods to assist each chapter in the fulfillment of the overall mission of the organization. In 1962, the facet "Services to Youth" was implemented, followed over the course of the decade by "the Arts," "National Trends and Services," and "International Trends and Services."[30] Today chapters seek to implement programs that will meet the needs of their community in multiple ways through the organizational facets. Each chapter creates particular programs to meet the national agenda, with changes depending on the particular needs of the communities in which the chapter operates. Despite the variations in individual programs, the manner by which each program operates is quite consistent. We provide here a thorough description and analysis of one of The Links' facets as a means of understanding how they operate. The "Services to Youth" facet offers a practical model for organizations that want to focus on implementing programs that will benefit economically and socially disadvantaged young people. Through this facet The Links have designed, implemented, and evaluated programs geared to improving the quality of life for children of African descent. This model can be easily adopted and modified by other black philanthropic organizations to meet their particular needs.

SERVICES TO YOUTH

This facet was designed to "respond to the challenge to help young people more fully realize their potential talents and abilities" by focusing on education, arts and culture, health and wellness, scholarship, and teen pregnancy. [31] Black youth bore the brunt of racism during the 1940s and 1950s because many of them were not given access to quality education or equal opportunities under the law. Historians note that "Black women knew that their freedom and that of their children was linked directly to education," and the organization's commitment to education was indicative of this.[32]

Programs implemented by The Links chapters under the Services to Youth facet have focused on the critical need for economic support for school resources, mentorship, and tutelage of black youth. Each chapter's initiatives typically concentrate on ways to improve the conditions of their people while addressing specific issues that are related to their communities. For the purpose of this analysis, we provide details of various chapter activities and their social implications.

Los Angeles, California, has been plagued with well-documented incidents of gang violence.[33] This has had a profound effect on countless young men over the years, and often the mass media has focused on negative stereotypes of African American males. In a city whose urban culture militates against young people's ambition for educational success, the Angel City Chapter of The Links has worked since 1981 to counter the negative images of African American males. The Angel City Chapter implemented the "Achievers" program to identify, educate, and prepare young men of academic promise who might not otherwise get the help they need to succeed in our society. In addition to helping individual students, these efforts also influence other organizations to do similar work.

Achievers are required to participate in a community service project, attend motivational workshops, and maintain contact with a male mentor.[34] Through this program over six hundred young men have received training that enhances their ability to complete college applications and participate in interviews and motivate them to success. In addition, $1,190,000 in scholarships has been awarded to young men through this program. Both the Sacramento and San Diego[35] chapters have implemented the Achievers program for young African American men in their areas.

Other chapters have done similar work in their communities to increase access to college for disadvantaged youth. The Brooklyn Chapter established the "Salute to Youth Project" in 1960, which provides financial awards to college-bound high school seniors. Over four hundred students have received awards and scholarships through this project.[36] In addition to helping students go to college, many Links chapters also work with younger children. The Denver Chapter established the "Tribute to Black Youth" twenty years ago, which honors children in seventh through twelfth grades for academic, artistic, and athletic excellence and dedication to the community.[37] The honorees receive trophies, savings bonds, and gifts from The Links. The purpose of this project is to encourage children to pursue long-term goals. The Portsmouth Chapter has sponsored workshops for latchkey students. They supply computers and training for students and parents and tutor fourth and fifth graders at a local elementary school. They have also taken fifth grade students on a trip to Washington, D.C., to see the nation's capital.[38]

The Links organizes programs on chapter levels but often has national initiatives that are supported and implemented by chapters throughout the nation. Two important previous national programs were "Links to Success: Children Achieving Academic Excellence"[39] and "Project LEAD: High Expectations."[40] "Links to Success" was a signature program initiated in 1999 that combined "new teaching techniques, parental and community support, and a unique learning environment in an effort to encourage academic achievement."[41] This child-centered education-based program was a three-year pilot program focused on children in pre-kindergarten through fifth grade and their parents or caregivers. The program operated concurrently with the school cycle and provided educational training and other resources to parents and children.[42] Components of the program included a two-week orientation and training session for parents. The Pasadena-Altadena chapter implemented their own version of the program, which works in cooperation with the Pasadena Unified School District to provide Scholastic Aptitude Test preparation workshops and has donated over $300,000 in scholarships to prospective college students. Through this initiative, this chapter has implemented a Saturday school program that serves eighty second, third and fourth graders each year by providing reading and literacy instruction.[43]

Project LEAD: High Expectations (PLHE) was an outreach program designed to direct children away from drug abuse, avoid teenage pregnancy, prevent sexually transmitted diseases, and instill self-esteem in high-risk black youth. The program was a "targeted, nontraditional, primary prevention demonstration project" that focused on African American youth who were defined by the Office of Substance Abuse and Prevention as "1) children of substance abusers; 2) children at risk of becoming adolescent parents; 3) children at risk of dropping out of school; 4) children who are economically disadvantaged; or 5) children in self-care arrangements (latch-key children)."[44] PLHE was designed as a destructive behavior prevention curriculum comprised of five modules: Values, Self-Image, and Self-Esteem; Decision-Making; Prevention of Alcohol, Tobacco and other Drug Use; Prevention of Premature Sexual Involvement, Unintended Pregnancy, and Sexually Transmitted Diseases; Academic Excellence and Vocational or Career Planning. The way that this initiative was implemented provides an excellent example of how the national programs are implemented through the chapters.

The PLHE staff initiated a call for Links chapters and other social service organizations to participate in the early stages of the project. Local chapters were required to identify two persons from their organizations that would be trained on the five modules prior to implementation of the project. Fourteen Links chapters in eight cities began the project in 1987; by 1990 the project had been implemented by seventy-seven chapters of The Links. Four thousand young people benefited through completion of the project, and nearly two thousand others completed some portion of the project. This program was evaluated and tested, and the findings indicated that trainers reported positive changes among the youth by the end of the project.[45]

The details of each facet and the means by which each chapter implements them change slightly, but the intense efforts of all demonstrate that The Links is a serious philanthropic organization with members dedicated to far more than merely writing checks.

LINKING MEMBERSHIP TO SERVICE

As early as its founding in 1946 The Links' unusual vision of harnessing socio-economic privilege for racial uplift required that the organization have a particular type of membership. From the first chapter founded, membership criteria were stringent and exclusive. Only a unanimous invitation from the current members of a chapter could grant membership to a newcomer. Before a vote was held, prospective members had to demonstrate their compatibility with the goals of the organization through such criteria as their socio-economic standing, educational attainment, and professional careers. But the women who were chosen to participate also had to demonstrate their worthiness and dedication through their actions and deeds, not merely through their social connections or financial portfolios. Prospective members needed to have already demonstrated their commitment to public service.[46]

The selectivity of membership served multiple purposes, the primary one being to ensure that the women accepted would be committed to upholding the principle of community service. However, as Links' historian Marjorie Parker notes, these women had "the adhesive agent of friendship" and wanted their "joint activities to be positive and their time together to be well spent."[47] This practice reinforced the philosophy of linking friends through service by restricting potential membership to those who were recommended by current Links. Once membership was granted to a nominee through a full vote of the chapter membership, her consistent commitment to the chapter was an obligation. The original charter stipulated that if a member missed three consecutive meetings and failed to participate in community service projects, she would be dropped from the roll. Furthermore, the membership was limited to fourteen members per chapter; the small size and stringent requirements of the membership served to ensure that The Links would be an active, committed organization.[48]

Today the women who are extended an invitation to join The Links are chosen by the chapter's full membership after an intense nomination process. The purpose of this rigorous process is to ensure that newly inducted members are not being selected solely on the basis of their social standing or financial portfolios, for it has always been important to Links that its members' very lives be demonstrations of the organization's principles. Former Links national president Patricia Russell McCloud notes that The Links is not merely a group of exclusive socialites but an "activist group that takes on important domestic and international projects that assist blacks, children, and others."[49] At the same time, Lawrence Otis Brown found that the high standards of membership indicate that one's "social background, lifestyle, physical appearance, and family's academic and professional accomplishments must [pass] muster with a fiercely competitive group of women."[50] The exclusive nature of The Links is integral to its structure and mission yet has also been a source of frustration for those who believe in its goals but do not measure up to its strict standards.

Links members have varied perceptions about their social status and wealth and their role in the organization. In commenting on this tension, Russell-McCloud said, "I think that because membership in this organization is by invitation only, it creates an aura or mystique, and it lessens the knowledge and understanding of the mission." She went on to point out that "the stereotypical portrayal that gets attached relates possibly, and unfairly, to an upper-middle class that is insensitive to the greater needs in the community." Russell-McCloud argues that nothing could be further from the truth, that in fact the very nature of The Links is to be aware of and empathetic to the greater needs of the community. She believes that "to whom much is given, much is required" and argues simply " . . . our record [of public service] speaks for itself."[51]

When asked whether she considered the membership of the organization to be wealthy or elitist, one member acknowledged that the organization was comprised of middle- and upper-class women. Nonetheless, she did not consider the organization elitist or wealthy because she and her fellow Links worked to raise funds and were not passively writing checks for their endeavors. They were required to give a tremendous amount of service, and she questioned how they could be considered elitist when they were actively working for the underprivileged in the community.[52]

Historian Marybeth Gasman notes "the charge of classism has been lodged against many elite organizations, including Greek fraternities and sororities, regardless of their racial make-up." Gasman contends that these criticisms may exist because "African American groups are held to a higher, harsher standard."[53] She argues that African American groups are expected to do community service and specifically focus on racial and social uplift for the disadvantaged members of their race. Other publications on The Links have focused on them as an elitist group, while barely mentioning their philanthropic work. Thus, perceptions of The Links within the African American community and among the general public may be skewed because scholars in the field have not focused on their philanthropic work.

It is also important to note that there are many complexities imbedded in an analysis on how and why people engage in philanthropic activities. Historian Cynthia Lynne Shelton notes that among Black women the "desire to uplift the race was tangential to the desire for self-actualization, inclusive of capital accumulation, intellectual achievement and professional status." Shelton argues that "black women did not view these desires as mutually exclusive" but rather engaged in race work[54] because they believed that it was essential to their development, maintenance, and survival in this country.[55] In a recent report issued by the Center on Philanthropy and Civil Society, researchers noted that "African Americans have conceptualized the individual, family and community as a fluid continuum and African American philanthropy has reflected this view."[56]

CONCLUSION

When considering African American organizations that have been instrumental in affecting the social uplift of the black community, The Links should no longer be overlooked. This organization began only fifty-eight years ago, during a time when the black professional class was largely disregarded in American society, and has risen to become a major change agent in the black community. During the past six decades The Links has grown from one chapter with nine members to 275 chapters with more than 11,000 members in four countries, all while remaining focused on its original purpose of social and economic uplift for descendents of the African Diaspora.[57]

The charter members of the first Philadelphia chapter had a vision to use their talents, education, and social connections—and that of their friends—to improve the lives of African Americans in as many realms as possible. Through speaking with members from chapters worldwide, we have learned how the bond of sisterhood and service has been the foundation for the organization to accomplish these goals.

In our interviews, we learned how chapter members have gone into communities to assess the needs of the people and then taken practical steps to make a difference. The Links' initiatives have been as simple as providing school supplies for neighboring children whose families could not afford paper and pens, to establishing an inner-city boys choir in an effort to keep at-risk youth away from trouble, to creating mentoring programs linking troubled youth to successful businessmen and women. Regardless of the project, the evidence is clear that the members of The Links have dedicated themselves and their resources to their communities.

Although The Links has been a large contributor to the black community, it has also been heavily criticized as an exclusive club for members of the black middle and upper classes. Marjorie Parker argues that The Links was founded during an era when blacks were highly aware of their kinship with each other regardless of differences on other levels, and when those of the professional class organized to work for social change, they were never interested only in their own well-being. According to Parker,

> [F]ew, if any, were able to put aside their feelings of identification with and responsibility for other blacks with whom life had dealt less kindly. So, it has been that when groups of men or women deemed 'privileged' react to natural desires, rarely if ever do they organize just for the fun of it. They retain some conscious or unconscious awareness that neither education, economic status, [n]or even personal attainment ever erases the color line in America.[58]

Philanthropy comes in many forms and from various sources. Our intention in this chapter has been to present The Links as a well-balanced model of the two traditional varieties of philanthropy. These women provide extensive financial support to their communities through personal donations and fundraising campaigns as well as give many hours of hands-on service. Our examination of The Links historic philanthropic activities suggests that this model of philanthropy, which explicitly links abilities with needs may be one of the most viable and useful for the African American community and beyond.

NOTES

1. Darlene Clark Hine, *Hine Sight: Black Women and the Re-Construction of American History* (New York: Carlton Publishing, 1994), 109.
2. Robert Payton, "A Defining Moment in American Philanthropy," speech delivered at the National College of Industrial Relations in Dublin, Ireland, 26 September 1995. Accessed on 28 June 2003 from *www.paytonpapers.org.*
3. Wisdom Quotes from Margaret Mead. Accessed on 22 May 2004 from Wisdom Quotes from *http://www.wisdomquotes.com/000216.html.*
4. Marjorie Parker, *A History of the Links, Incorporated* (Washington, D.C.: Links, Incorporated, 1982), 12.
5. Fundraising efforts have included requesting financial gifts from major corporations and individual donors, while members have continued to significantly contribute from their own resources through monetary donations. By "African American community" we follow James Blackwell in referring to a social system or central set of "commonly shared values and goals" that are embraced by a significant portion of the blacks in the United States (James Blackwell, *The Black Community: Diversity and Unity* (New York: Dodd, Mead, 1985), 14.
6. Mission Statement of The Links, Incorporated, *www.linksinc.org*, accessed 12 March 2003.
7. Marybeth Gasman, "Sisters in Service: African American Sororities and Philanthropic Support of Education" in Andrea Walton, ed., *Stewards, Scholars, and Patrons: Studies in the History of Women, Philanthropy, and Education* (Indiana: Indiana University Press, 2004); Hine, *Hine Sight*, 109–128.

8. Emmett D. Carson, "Black Volunteers as Givers and Fundraisers," 3 (paper presented at the Center for the Study of Philanthropy, City University of New York's Conference entitled "Volunteers and Fundraisers," 14 November 1990).

9. Ibid., 1.

10. The term Diaspora is used to refer to any people or ethnic population forced or induced to leave their traditional ethnic homelands and disperse throughout other parts of the world and the ensuing developments in their dispersal and culture. Diaspora philanthropy refers to philanthropic giving from those that constitute the Diaspora to their motherland/country of origin—Definition from The Resource Alliance website at *http://www.resource-alliance.org/*, accessed 21 June 2004.

11. Hine, *Hine Sight*, 128.

12. We note that Marjorie Holloman Parker was a member of the Links, Incorporated, at the time that she wrote both histories, which classifies her as an insider.

13. Gasman, "Sisters in Service,"121.

14. Ibid., 3.

15. Darlene Clark Hine, Elsa Barkley Brown, and Rosalyn Terborg-Penn, eds., *Black Women in America: An Historical Encyclopedia: Volume I, A-L* (Indianapolis: Indiana University Press, 1993).

16. National Association for the Advancement of Colored People. Annual Reports. New York, 1911–1981 cited in Lerone Bennett Jr., *Before the Mayflower: A History of Black America* (New York: Penguin Books, 1988), 543.

17. Ibid., 543.

18. Hine, Brown, Terborg-Penn, eds., *Black Women in America*, 722–724.

19. Darlene Clark Hine and Kathleen Thompson, *A Shining Thread of Hope: The History of Black Women in America* (New York: Broadway Books, 1998), 267.

20. Parker, *History of the Links*, 3.

21. Jack and Jill of America is a national association of mothers of young children that was founded in 1938 in Philadelphia, Pennsylvania. See *http://www.jack-and-jill.org/Home_history.htm*, accessed 5 January 2004.

22. Parker, *History of the Links*, 3.

23. Ibid., 3.

24. Ibid., 4.

25. Ibid., 4.

26. Hine and Thompson, *A Shining Thread of Hope*, 267–273.

27. Parker, *History of the Links*, 7–8.

28. Ibid., 7.

29. Ibid., 71.

30. Ibid., 72.

31. Ibid., 75.

32. Hine and Thompson, *A Shining Thread of Hope*, 271.

33. Sanyika Shakur, *Monster: The Autobiography of an LA Gang Member* (New York: Penguin Books, 1993).

34. Achievers program information located in the Angels City Chapter of The Links, Inc. Collection, 1962–1987, Series II, box 3 of 3, folder 2, The University Library's Urban Archives Center at California State University, Northridge, and Northridge California.

35. *http://www.sacramentolinks.org/achievers.htm*, accessed 16 February 2004; Burl Stiff, "Young Gentlemen Pave Their Ways for the Future," in *Diego Union-Tribune*, 8 May 2003.

36. Sadie Feddoes, "Brooklyn Links Celebrate 45th Anniversary" *New York Amsterdam News*, 11 September 1997.

37. Dahlia Jean Weinstein, "Links Pay Tribute to Black Youths," *Denver Rocky Mountain News* 4 February 2003, sec. D.

38. http://nia.ecsu.edu/nrts/lhayden/portsmouth_links/mainlink.html, accessed 13 April 2004.

39. Damon Hodges, "Links Foundation Plans Pilot Program," Las Vegas report of *View News*, 7 April 1999.

40. Flavia R. Walton, Valerie D. Ackiss, and Sandra N. Smith, "Education versus Schooling—Project LEAD: High Expectations!" *Journal of Negro Education* 60, no. 3 (1991): 441–453.

41. Hodges, "Links Foundation Plans Pilot Program," 1.

42. Ibid., 1.

43. Geoffrey Bilau, "Strong LINKS: Area Service Club Celebrates 40 Years of Quiet but Effective Work," *Pasadena Star News*, 13 March 2003.

44. Walton, Ackiss, and Smith, "Project LEAD: High Expectations!" 443.

45. Ibid.

46. Parker, *History of the Links.*

47. Parker, *History of the Links.*

48. Walton, Ackiss, and Smith, "Project LEAD: High Expectations!"

49. Ibid.

50. Graham, *Our Kind of People*, 101.

51. Graham, *Our Kind of People*, 101.

52. Florida Woods, interviewed by Nia Haydel, New Orleans, LA, 14, July 2003.

53. Gasman, "Sisters in Service," 7

54. Cynthia Lynne Shelton, "We Are What We Do: The National Program of Alpha Kappa Alpha Sorority, Incorporated. A Post-modern Corporatist Interpretation of African-Amerian Women's Philanthropy" (Ph.D. diss., University of Kentucky, 2003).

55. Ibid.

56. Center on Philanthropy and Civil Society, "African American Philanthropy Literature Review." Report issued by Center on Philanthropy and Civil Society, The Graduate Center, The City University of New York, 3.

57. www.linksinc.org, accessed 19 April 2004.

58. Parker, *History of the Links.*

CHAPTER SEVEN

A. G. Gaston

A Story of Philosophy, Perseverance, and Philanthropy

FRED H. DOWNS

When A.G. Gaston died in 1996, the news of his death received substantial attention in his home city of Birmingham, Alabama, as well as coverage by the national media.[1] Gaston had built a monument to African American entrepreneurship and
philanthropy in a city that once symbolized racial oppression. He had become the
president and owner of seven different companies worth in excess of thirty million
dollars. His philosophy—seeing and satisfying the needs of people—was the
humane foundation of a successful business empire that included an insurance company, funeral homes, motels, a realty and investment corporation, a farm, a savings
and loan association, a cemetery, and a housing development. Gaston also made
generous philanthropic donations to the community. He was instrumental in organizing and funding the A.G. Gaston Boy's Club and contributed heavily to educational scholarship programs at a variety of institutions. The fact that Gaston was
103 at the time of his death was noteworthy, but it was the legacy this man left to
the world that captivated the business, educational, and philanthropic communities of the nation for decades. How did this man, the grandson of slaves, become
a self-made millionaire, entrepreneur, and philanthropist?

To answer this question, the work and contributions of Gaston must be examined using a multi-dimensional framework that addresses the social, cultural, business, and philanthropic facets of his life. Consequently, this chapter will explore the
development of Gaston's vast economic empire, Booker T. Washington's influence

on him, and the redistribution of his wealth through charitable and philanthropic activities. This historical analysis is framed against the backdrop of the segregated South, the Civil Rights Movement, and post-integration business and community relations in Birmingham, Alabama. Throughout the work, the notion of Black philanthropy and its personification through Gaston will be discussed, highlighting his contributions to a variety of social, educational, and religious causes.

BACKGROUND AND HISTORY

Although he never completed high school, A.G. Gaston's entrepreneurial skills, catalyzed by virtues of courtesy, dependability, hard work, honesty, and thrift, enabled him to create a $34 million dollar empire.[2] Gaston's remarkable life began in Demopolis, Alabama on July 4, 1892—only twenty-nine years after President Abraham Lincoln's Emancipation Proclamation freed the slaves—and spanned the next hundred years with an odyssey-like adventure that was unparalleled for his race and time.[3] Demopolis, located at the junction of the Black Warrior and Tombigbee Rivers, had prospered in the Deep South as a cotton town. Its black earth had supported cotton plantations for generations, but slavery, which had made the town flourish, had ended. At the time of Gaston's youth, Demopolis still bore the physical and emotional scars of the Civil War and struggled to regain economic stability.[4]

When Gaston was still a baby, his father died; his mother left Demopolis to find work and left young Gaston in the care of her parents for some time. His grandparents, both former slaves, instilled in him the traits of honesty, hard work, respectfulness, and service to the church. During his early childhood and while still living with his grandparents, Gaston was introduced to the social norms of the period. He was taught to respect others, especially the White folks. In his autobiography *Green Power, the Successful Way of A.G. Gaston*, he stated, "Any 'nigger' who did not jump off the sidewalk when they [White folks] came by was considered 'biggety' by the whole community, and just not well brought up." Additionally, he grew up believing that, by definition, all White men were honest, so when he witnessed a lynching as a boy there was "no doubt in my mind that justice had prevailed and the punishment was surely deserved."[5] Later Gaston, having been victimized by White men in business relationships, realized this was an incorrect belief.

Gaston left Demopolis in 1900 to join his mother, now working as a cook for a prominent Birmingham family. As Gaston and his mother prepared to board the train to their new home, he was given admonishment that would shape much of his life. Over and over his grandmother told him, "Don't fall into bad company, Art; you be careful up there. There's killings up there." Thus began the trip to

Birmingham, a place Gaston would call home for the next ninety-five years. A place made famous as the "Magic City" for its coal and iron industries; a place where forty percent of the population was Black; a place where twice as many Blacks died each year as Whites; a place where the Ku Klux Klan was ever present; a place where being in "bad company" could get you killed—the prospects of such a place both excited and terrified the young Gaston. On that train ride Gaston made a vow to himself: "You, Arthur George Gaston, are one colored boy who will not fall into bad company or get into trouble or get himself killed."[6] This oath became a paradigm of personal deportment and decision-making that would characterize Gaston throughout his life and career.

Upon arrival in Birmingham, Ms. Gaston and her son moved into their quarters on the grounds of her employer's home located in a fashionable residential section of the city. Ms. Gaston's employer, Mr. A.B. Loveman, was founder and owner of one of Birmingham's finest department stores. The Lovemans were not only rich, they were kind to the Gastons, and their son Berney became a friend and playmate to young Gaston. Rosie Gaston was a favorite with the Loveman family, and her skills in the kitchen made her a favorite with the social elite of Birmingham whom the Lovemans frequently entertained. While life for the Gastons was quite good, Rosie believed that her son needed to take advantage of the educational opportunities available in Birmingham.

Rosie Gaston began to make plans for her son's education. She believed he needed to go to school and meet well-to-do colored people or he would end up "swabbing by the flames in the blast furnace and fall into bad company."[7] She enrolled Gaston in the Tuggle Institute, a residential school for Blacks located in the northwest section of Birmingham. The school's headmaster, Carrie Tuggle, was a Black woman of vision and strength; her advocacy for orphans and delinquent youth was the impetus for the organization that bore her name. The Tuggle Institute evolved over time from a home for orphaned Black boys and girls to a quality school noted by the citizens and education community for excellence in education, social work, and religion.[8] While at the Tuggle Institute Gaston applied himself to his studies and also worked at odd jobs where he developed a strong work ethic and a life-long habit of frugality. It was also there that he first observed the work and experienced the benefit of fraternal societies.

The Tuggle Institute was supported by the Order of Calanthe, the women's auxiliary of the Knights of Pythias. The Knights of Pythias was founded in Washington, D.C., in 1864 by Justus H. Rathbone, a White man, in response to the anger, hatred, and vengeance that was rampant during the Civil War years. Rathbone felt a need to rekindle brotherly love throughout the land and subsequently founded this fraternity on the trinity of charity, friendship, and benevolence. The Fraternal Order of the Knights of Pythias was and continues to be dedicated to the cause of universal peace and is committed to the promotion of understanding among men.[9] Lodges of the fraternity were soon established throughout the country. This benevolent fraternity, its Birmingham women's auxiliary unit (headed by Carrie Tuggle), and prominent members of the community (including Mrs. A. B. Loveman) helped to establish and sustain the Tuggle Institute. This broad base of community support allowed the Institute's program of youth training to expand and, when combined with Carrie Tuggle's advocacy role as welfare officer for delinquent boys, was credited by Birmingham citizens with "saving wayward black youths from a life of mischief and possibly prison."[10]

While at Tuggle, Gaston heard Booker T. Washington speak on several occasions, and he made a deep and lasting impression on the young student. Gaston recalled in his autobiography,

> Dr. Washington had spoken to us in chapel that morning, and as always he had held me transfixed, the influence of his powerful personality lingering all day. I picked up his book, *Up from Slavery* by Booker T. Washington, read the faded cover, worn from much thumbing. This was the first book I had ever owned, and it had been an inspiration to me for some years now.[11]

Washington's views on race, personal autonomy and responsibility reflected a belief that individual merit and worth, not race, were the final determinants of success. As such, Washington articulated the position that race, whether perceived as superior or inferior, could not permanently advance or withhold the progress of the individual.[12] Additionally, Washington challenged the Blacks of his time to earn respect by making themselves valuable and indispensable to their communities through action and innovation. Washington's teachings and challenges, coupled with his philosophy of self-reliance and self-determination, were foundational to Gaston's later business and life philosophies.

In one of Washington's addresses to the students at the Tuggle Institute he used the analogy of a bald-headed man with only one tuft of hair at the forehead to represent opportunity. When confronted with opportunity, he told the students, they "must quickly grab it, that single patch of hair, and hold on; for when the opportunity pass[es] there [is] nothing to grab."[13] Stirred by Washington's teaching on seizing opportunities, as well as excited by the presumably glamorous life of World War I soldiers in Paris and the prospects of saving fifteen dollars a month (a private's wages), Gaston left the Tuggle Institute with the equivalent of a tenth grade education to join the army. He was only eighteen but enlisted as a twenty-one-year-old. The army was still segregated at that time, and army officials asked Dr. Robert Moton, President of Tuskegee Institute, to address the Black soldiers in a predeparture ceremony before they left for Europe. During his speech to the soldiers, Moton admonished them to stay in their place. When Gaston recounted the story years later, he stated, "I was a follower of Booker T. Washington, and I took his advice, I stayed in my place."[14]

Gaston saw action in Europe during the war, was awarded a medal for valor beyond the call of duty, and experienced full social and racial acceptance for the first time from the local French people he met. Upon his discharge, Gaston returned to Birmingham where he and the other Black veterans soon realized the sharp disappointment of homecoming. Gaston and the others believed they had earned first-class citizenship through their contributions to the war effort. This was not the case and soon these veterans found themselves in the same racially segregated and economically oppressed social system they had left. Gaston was disheartened and in his discouragement he looked to the great Booker T. Washington for inspiration. Gaston found solace in Washington's triumph over slavery, poverty, and extreme hardships to achieve greatness; Gaston knew he too could find a way out and up.[15]

Unable to find a job in Birmingham, Gaston took a job as a laborer in a steel mill in Westfield, a mining town west of the city, where he earned $3.10 a day. The work was not only physically demanding, it was also a struggle psychologically; his dream of becoming economically successful was in constant battle with his present reality of mind-numbing physical fatigue brought about by his labor in the mill. Nonetheless, his work ethic and frugality were further refined as he toiled in the steel mills and sold box lunches and peanuts to supplement his pay. From his wages, Gaston saved most of his money and shrewdly loaned it at an interest rate of 25% to his co-workers who needed extra money for "dating."

It was during the early 1920s, while working in the mill, that various circumstances converged in such a way as to ignite Gaston's entrepreneurial skills. He had long had an intense desire to be rich—he called it the "disease"—but had not yet had the opportunity to do anything about it. When he noticed an unmet need in his community during this time, Gaston realized that he not only had the ability to help meet it but could also turn it into a good business opportunity for himself. He grabbed tightly to the bald-headed man's tuft of hair and in so doing was able to help others as well as himself.[16]

The unmet need Gaston identified was making provision for a proper and decent burial for Black members of the community. A proper funeral was of great importance in the Black community; perhaps it was because they had so little in life that providing a decent funeral was so highly valued.[17] Gaston noticed that many Blacks died without enough money to pay for their own funerals so the community, church members, or ministers met this need by raising the funds on a case-by-case basis. Additionally, Gaston observed that most of his co-workers would help defray the costs of the funerals by contributing money when preachers solicited donations to pay burial expenses for members of the community. These solicitations had degenerated into a vicious racket; some people were out collecting funeral money for people who were very much alive. Gaston proposed the idea of a burial society, where members paid dues on a weekly schedule and in return were guaranteed a decent funeral. Gaston discussed his plans with local community and church leaders and with their approval began the society. Each member would pay twenty-five cents per week for the head of the household and ten cents for each additional family member enrolled in the burial society.

Gaston received plenty of encouragement from community members, but few actually contributed to this novel plan. When the first society member died, there was only thirty dollars available to cover the cost of the hundred-dollar funeral. Gaston persuaded the funeral director to extend him credit and provide the funeral services for the society's member. This financial setback placed the longevity of the burial society in question. Fortunately, one local minister decided that he would no longer take up collections for funerals and sent his flock to Gaston. It was 1923. The burial society began to flourish, and soon Gaston hired commissioned agents to solicit new business and to enroll new members. Gaston was now well on his way to realizing his dream of becoming a businessman.[18]

Gaston's job in the steel mill ended, and he took another position in the coal mines near Birmingham while continuing to manage the Booker T. Washington Burial Society. As the society prospered, and with it Gaston's confidence, he began to think of other things beside his financial future. Gaston had long admired an old acquaintance who had left Demopolis and became a successful businessman and Black community leader in Mississippi, but in fact it was this man's daughter whom Gaston most admired. He called on his old friend, Abraham Lincoln Smith, and soon began courting the woman who would become his wife.

Gaston and Creola Smith were married in the early 1920s and returned to Birmingham where they devoted themselves exclusively to the management of the burial society. The business expanded throughout the Black community of Birmingham and soon became too big for Gaston to handle alone, so he recruited his father-in-law to join him in the enterprise. Through the combined efforts of Gaston and Smith the burial society became even more successful and was eventually incorporated as the Booker T. Washington Insurance Company. Later they purchased the mortuary that had provided funeral services for members of the burial society and renamed it Smith and Gaston Funeral Home. The Booker T. Washington Insurance Company became the source of capital for all of Gaston's other ventures, and it was the cornerstone of his empire. He parlayed the initial burial society into a seven-company, multimillion-dollar enterprise.

Gaston's business empire was built on a philosophy deeply influenced by Booker T. Washington: individual merit combined with hard work, thrift, ingenuity, and innovation were the keys to economic freedom, which, in turn, was the key to broader societal respect and success for Blacks. Gaston's success was founded on identifying and satisfying the needs of people. Holding true to this philosophy, Gaston was constantly on the lookout for opportunities to help others in the Black community to improve their lives. Whenever he identified an unmet need, he used his business acumen and access to capital to craft a plan to address it. Embedded in his work, actions, and business enterprises were the distant voices of his past— Washington, Tuggle, and Smith communicating to the Black community through Gaston their message and now his: liberation, advancement, and respectability are only achieved through economic self-sufficiency.

By 1939 Gaston's wife Creola had died and he had remarried. His second wife, Minnie, a school teacher and a graduate of Tuskegee Institute, was instrumental in Gaston's next business endeavor. As Gaston's enterprise grew, he had difficulty finding enough trained clerical help, so he recruited an instructor from Chicago to train his clerical staff in typing, shorthand, and related business skills. Soon the public was interested in this program, and eventually the Booker T. Washington Business College was born and Minnie served as its administrator. Gaston commented on the college that it " . . . was in the direct tradition of the great Booker T. Washington, who preached to our race [that] . . . in proportion as the Negro learned to produce what the other people wanted and must have, [in] that sure proportion would he be respected."[19] In the tradition of Tuskegee Institute, the college provided practical tools and skills training to young Black students. Meeting the need for skilled workers through the provision of educational programs solved Gaston's workforce problems and benefited other local businesses as well. In addition, this practical education provided a vehicle for ambitious youth, many of whom were hoping eventually to leave the south for other parts of the country, to gain marketable skills.

The college, under the capable direction of Minnie, educated more and more students each year and prepared workers for a number of venues, including clerical support personnel for the defense efforts of World War II. Mrs. Gaston guided the college through a series of accrediting and approval processes, including accreditation by the Accrediting Commission of Business Schools, and approvals by the U.S. Department of Education, Veterans Administration, and the Alabama Board of Education. Additionally, Mrs. Gaston testified before a U.S. Senate Sub-Committee on Education of the Committee on Labor and Public Welfare, where she advocated for financial aid for Black students in higher education.[20] The Gastons' commitment to education as a path of economic liberation and advancement reflected the influence of Booker T. Washington and the Tuskegee model as well as their lifelong commitment to community improvement through philanthropic support of educational institutions.

Gaston continued to grow and diversify his businesses to include, among other things, a construction company, a realty and investment company, a housing development, and a senior citizens' home. Like Booker T. Washington, Gaston was acutely aware of the problematic housing conditions and purchasing practices of Blacks. Both men were appalled at the substandard housing in which many of their contemporaries lived. They were further frustrated when they observed people who lacked basic necessities yet purchased, often on credit, frivolous items. For example, Washington recalled a visit to the cabin of a Black family of four who had only one dinner fork but a six hundred dollar organ that no one could play.[21] Likewise, it upset Gaston to see a Cadillac in front of a substandard rented apartment.[22] He believed that home ownership, along with responsible citizenship, economic security, and education for children were essential priorities for personal and racial success and empowerment.

A significant reason for the abysmal housing conditions for Blacks in Birmingham was the lending policies for home loans. Few Blacks could secure loans from White lending institutions, and when they did the interest rates were exorbitant. Gaston, therefore, started Citizen's Savings and Loan in 1957, a company developed to help make housing affordable for Blacks. In addition to providing funds for the construction of new homes, Citizen's Savings and Loan penetrated the barriers to mortgage financing in Birmingham, making it easier for Blacks to obtain financial assistance from other lending companies.[23]

Another example of Gaston's philanthropic business ventures was the A.G. Gaston Motel. Gaston was devoted to his African Methodist Episcopal (AME) Church and served it in a variety of capacities. One such position was as an official AME delegate to the World Ecumenical Conference in Oxford, England, in the early 1950s. While at the conference, he learned of plans to bring the National Sunday School and Baptist Training Union Congress of the National Baptist Convention to Birmingham for its 1954 meeting. Gaston knew his segregated city did not have the commercial accommodations for the numbers of Blacks who would attend such an event. Gaston feared housing difficulties could prevent Birmingham from hosting the convention. Upon his return to the United States, Gaston began work on a motel which opened in 1954 in time to receive members of the Baptist Convention. The motel was operated with open access to all and received many White guests. Birmingham had strict laws and practices related to segregation within facilities, so city government officials did not approve of the motel's practice of having clientele of both races. Nonetheless, the motel flourished and established a reputation of great service and cuisine. The motel would later play a significant role in the imminent Civil Right's Movement.[24]

Other examples of Gaston's philanthropic business activity abound, but these will suffice as illustrations. His phenomenal business and entrepreneurial skills earned him a host of awards, honors, and special recognitions. These included *Black Enterprise*'s Entrepreneur of the Century,[25] Alabama Academy of Honor,[26] and the Alabama Men's Hall of Fame.[27] He was called the "dean of business" by the national Black media and at one time had the distinction of being the richest Black man in America.[28] In addition to these awards and accolades, Gaston received six honorary degrees from various institutions of higher education including one in Liberia, West Africa.[29] He and his wife traveled extensively and were received by heads of state and royalty on numerous occasions. Gaston, like Booker T. Washington, had risen from humble beginnings in rural poverty to become a man of influence, entertained by royalty, and a guest of the president of the United States. In recounting an invitation from President John F. Kennedy to a formal state dinner for the king and queen of Afghanistan, Gaston summarized his life and philosophy: "If I, a Negro with little education and no influence, could progress from a Black Belt farm of Alabama to a seat at a White House dinner, then anybody could. Any American who did not build a purposeful, satisfying life for himself just didn't have it on the inside."[30] This statement reflects Gaston's philosophy of self-determination, refusal to be constrained by social and environmental conditions, and innate belief in the triumph of individual will and persistence over adversity.

GASTON AND THE CIVIL RIGHTS MOVEMENT

Northern industrial companies, led by U.S. Steel, built Birmingham after the Civil War, capitalizing on its vast natural resources and exploiting a limitless supply of cheap labor, both Black and White. The emergence of the Ku Klux Klan in the 1920s benefited the industrialists as their anti-Catholic and anti-Black hate messages thwarted union organization attempts and prevented solidarity among workers. In the midst of the Great Depression, the coal and steel barons installed "Bull" Connor in the city administration as Commissioner of Public Safety, where he remained in power for more than twenty-six years. Supported by industry leaders and utilizing the considerable power of his office, Connor was successful in opposing labor unions and in sabotaging the New Deal agenda in Birmingham with what was later described as a "fascist regime."[31] The elite of Birmingham wanted to maintain absolute segregation, and Connor was their puppet. He ruled the city with a militia-like police force, ultimately leading the city down a path of destruction and violence.[32] In his *Letter from Birmingham Jail*, Dr. Martin Luther King described his captive city as

> ... probably the most thoroughly segregated city in the United States. Its ugly record of brutality is widely known. Negroes have experienced grossly unjust treatment in the courts. There have been more unresolved bombings of Negro homes and churches in Birmingham than any other city in the nation. These are the hard brutal facts of the case. On the basis of these conditions, Negro leaders have sought to negotiate with the city fathers. But the latter consistently refuse to engage in good-faith negotiations.[33]

By the early 1960s, Birmingham's racial tension had reached a boiling point. George Wallace was governor of the state, "Bull" Connor was in power locally, and Martin Luther King, Jr. and local civil rights leaders were advocating an end to segregation. Protests and demonstrations by Blacks were met with force and violence. Images of Connor's use of fire hoses and police dogs against Blacks are indelibly imprinted on the minds of Americans and have come to symbolize the Civil Rights Movement.[34] During these turbulent times, Gaston was not an active public advocate for the Movement but instead worked quietly and deliberately to deconstruct the system. He supported the Movement though a variety of ways, including direct financial contributions, free accommodations in his motel for civil rights leaders, allowing the Southern Christian Leadership Conference the use of his motel as its headquarters, and bailing out Martin Luther King, Jr. and others from jail.

While the riots where going on in the streets of Birmingham in the early 1960s, Gaston represented the Black community in peace talks with the White leaders of the city. King had made four demands of the White negotiators: 1) desegregate all public facilities in department and variety stores, 2) give Blacks equal job opportunities, 3) drop all charges against the 2,500 Blacks who had been arrested as part of the demonstration, and 4) establish a bi-racial committee to develop a timeline for reopening the city parks and facilities that had been closed to avoid integration.[35] Gaston worked with his White contemporaries in the business community to effect the changes called for by King. They reached some level of agreement, but the power to effect real change ultimately rested with the segregationist politicians.

Birmingham went to war. The streets were battle zones filled with riots and violence. Churches, homes (including Gaston's) and the A.G. Gaston Motel were bombed by Whites. Not only was Gaston's property under attack by Whites, his character and reputation were under attack by Blacks. His persistent belief that the differences between the races should be settled at the conference table and not the streets, the fact that he advocated for a cooperative effort between the races in the name of brotherly love, and his provision of bail for King and other protesters were all perceived by some to weaken the Movement. Militant blacks called him an Uncle Tom, a label he shared with Booker T. Washington.[36]

The situation reached a peak on September 15, 1963, when the Sixteenth Street Baptist Church was bombed, killing four little girls and injuring seventeen other people. In recalling this incident, Gaston remembered that: "The Negroes went wild with revenge and the good people of the White community were stunned. The situation was critical."[37] On September 19, just three days after the bombing, Martin Luther King, Jr., A.G. Gaston, and other leaders of the Black community went to Washington, D.C., to meet with President John F. Kennedy to discuss the latest rash of violence that had brought Birmingham to its current state of anarchy.[38] Their mission was to identify ways to restore order in Birmingham, to gain support and protection for the Black community, and to call for discrimination audits on all government contacts with Birmingham-based businesses. The possibility of sending Federal troops and initiating martial law was also discussed.[39] Gaston argued against the use of Federal troops, fearing it would only escalate the situation. Instead, he advocated for bi-racial dialogue and conference activities as a non-violent course of action, all of which were later implemented in an effort to restore order and to bring peace to Birmingham.

Gaston's position on key issues of the Movement was clear: he advocated for racial equality and for full realization of the rights provided to all under the Constitution of the United States. It was with his views on how these rights should be acquired that some of the more militant of his race disagreed. Throughout the time of racial crisis in Birmingham, Gaston advanced the position that resolution of issues should be achieved through patient bi-racial dialogue founded on human dignity and respect for all as American citizens and sons of God. He often spoke to and wrote essays of encouragement and admonishment to the Black community. The central theme in these messages was the relationship between economic potential and civic responsibility. He believed that economic potential would equal civil rights advancement, stating that "a broke first-class man will find it very difficult to use his civil rights to the fullest; . . . only the prudent and wise use of his [the Negro's] earnings will solidify his gains in the field of civil and human rights."[40] His advocacy for fiscal responsibility, peaceful resolution to issues through open communication, and compromise made him, like Booker T. Washington, a target for criticism by those who favored an aggressive approach to gaining individual rights and freedom.

Through the efforts of many, peace gradually came to Birmingham. With it came the rise of integration and the end of segregation and the barriers that defined it. Black customers were no longer imprisoned behind the walls of segregation and restricted to shopping with Black merchants. With the advent of a free market economy, many Black-owned companies were not prepared to pursue White customers and even less prepared to compete for Black customers who now had access to the mainstream market. Many Black businesses could not withstand the market competition and ultimately closed. Gaston's business legacy however, remained successful, and in 1992, the Booker T. Washington Insurance Company and Citizens Federal Savings Bank, both founded by Gaston, were listed in *Black Enterprise's B.E. 100*.[41] The *B.E. 100* is the classification of the largest Black-owned industrial or service companies, auto dealerships, advertising agencies, banks, asset managers, and equity firms in the United States. In 2002 the Booker T. Washington Insurance Company—the oldest of all of Gaston's ventures—was still on the list.[42]

Gaston's Birmingham-based enterprise was a key factor in the transformation of the city and helped to change its image as a dirty steel mill town and a cesspool of segregation and hate. His various businesses contributed to the economic growth and development of the city and facilitated its diversification from a primarily industry-based economy to one that is multi-faceted. African Americans now run City Hall, and U.S. Steel has given way to the sixty-block University of Alabama at Birmingham Medical Center as the major employer. As Birmingham diversified so did Gaston Enterprises.

PHILANTHROPY AND A.G. GASTON

African Americans as a group are far more charitable than any other segment of the American population; it is estimated that Blacks donate more than 2.1% of their income to charity compared to Whites who donate 1.7%.[43] The history and current condition of Black America are enriched by the actions of many individuals who give of their time, talents, and money to help those in their communities and in the nation. Giving to benefit individuals and to strengthen families and communities is the hallmark of Black philanthropy. It has been a mechanism for survival, mutual assistance, and self-help. Black giving helped to start schools and churches and launched leaders and institutions that promoted and effected civil rights and social change. Black giving has supported community-based initiatives that strengthen and uplift communities.[44] Prior to 1960, Black philanthropy could be described as "philanthropy among friends"; most Black giving focused on aiding individuals in the immediate community. Most Black giving within communities was channeled through the efforts of churches, mutual aid societies, and collegiate organizations. Recipients of the aid provided by these organizations generally had some connection to the organization, either as a member or as a relative or friend of a member.[45] Until recently few Blacks had the wealth to make sizable donations to institutions or organizations, which also kept Black giving in the local community.[46]

Gaston's life and philanthropic practices closely paralleled these historic practices of community-based Black giving. He made generous philanthropic donations to his church, to mutual aid and community-based organizations, to various educational institutions, and to socio-political causes. He was National Treasurer of the African Methodist Episcopal Church, a benefactor to Tuskegee Institute and a member of its Board of Trustees. Gaston was a supporter of the YMCA and was instrumental in founding programs for African American youth. He organized the 11,000-member Smith and Gaston Kiddie Club in 1945 in an effort to reduce juvenile delinquency and sponsored the Gaston Statewide Spelling Bee for Black Students.

Gaston's observations of Black youth during the violent riots of the Civil Rights demonstrations disturbed and inspired him. He had a growing concern that young Black children did not have proper outlets for their energy, and if left to their own devices would get into trouble. This observation most likely rekindled the old admonition from his mother and grandmother not to "fall into bad company." Gaston committed himself to a project through which that admonition and its goal could be realized. In a fashion similar to Carrie Tuggle, Gaston enlisted a bi-racial coalition to support a Boys Club. He donated the building valued at $50,000 for the club and launched a campaign to raise $350,000 to equip and renovate it. The slogan for the campaign was "Help build boys . . . not mend men."[47] Birmingham responded with dollars. The A.G. Gaston Boys Club was perhaps the first tangible expression of the entire community working together. Most importantly, it communicated to the boys they lived in a community that cared about them.

While Gaston was a "traditional" philanthropist in many ways, these donations of money and foundings of organizations were not his greatest acts of philanthropy. In 1987, Gaston cured himself of "the disease" of wanting to be rich by virtually giving his vast empire to his employees. He created a stock option program for his various businesses and sold all of his stock to his employees. The combined value of his companies was estimated at 34 million dollars; he sold his empire for one-tenth its worth. This single act of giving was a manifestation of Gaston's life-long commitment to racial uplift through economic empowerment. This legendary philanthropist touched the lives and hearts of thousands and made the world and his community a better place because he was there.

NOTES

1. *In Memoriam: Dr. A.G. Gaston* (accessed 17 February 2003); available from http://www.ebonyfigures.comA-G-Gaston.htm.
2. *Arthur G. Gaston*, in *Biography Resource Center* [database online] (2001, accessed 15 February 2003), available from Gale Group, Inc. http://www.africanpubs.com/apps/bios/0047GastonArthur.asp.
3. Robert Johnson, *A. G. Gaston Tells How He Lived to Be 100 and Made Millions* in *LexisNexis* [database online] (1992), (accessed 12 February 2003), available from Reed Elsevier Inc. http://www.gsu:2055/university/document).
4. Arthur G. Gaston, *Green Power, The Successful Way of A.G. Gaston* (Birmingham: Southern University Press, 1968), 6.
5. Ibid.,1–11, 6, 7.
6. Ibid., 14, 16.
7. Ibid., 20.
8. *Alabama Women's Hall of Fame*, in [database online] Alabama 1979, (accessed 20 March 2003); available from, accession no. http://www.awhf.org/tuggle.html, 2.

9. *Knights of Pythias—The Pythian Story*, (accessed 21 March 2003), available from, accession no. http://www.pythias.org.

10. Gaston, *Green Power*, 22.

11. Ibid., 26.

12. Booker T. Washington, *Up from Slavery* (New York: Doubleday, Page & Company, 1902), 202.

13. Gaston, *Green Power*, 26.

14. H. Jackson, "True Grit," *Black Enterprise*, June 1992, 102.

15. Gaston, *Green Power*, 48.

16. Jackson, "True Grit," 12.

17. Gaston, *Green Power*, 52.

18. Johnson, "True Grit," 12.

19. Gaston, *Green Power*, 80.

20. Ibid., 141–142.

21. Washington, *Up from Slavery*, 113.

22. Gaston, *Green Power*, 90.

23. Ibid., 112–113.

24. Ibid., 97, 98, 110.

25. *Black Enterprise Achievement Awards* in *LexisNexis* [database online] (1992, accessed 12 February 2003), available from Reed Elsevier, accession no. http.//ezproxy.gsu.edu2055/uiiverse/document.

26. *A.G. Gaston*, in [database online] (1969), (accessed 12 Dec. 2002), available from, accession no. http://www.archive.state.al.us/famous/adadmey/a_gaston.html.

27. *Arthur George Gaston* in [database online] (1999), (accessed 8 Dec. 2002), available from, accession no. http.//www.samford.edu.group/amhf/id22_m.htm.

28. C. Adams, *A.G. Gaston—Millionaire* in *Birmingham.Net* [database online] (1993), (accessed 17 February 2003)—available from Birmingham, accession no. http.//bham.net/gaton/history.html.

29. *Dr. Gaston—Alabama's Foremost Businessman* in [database online] (2001, accessed 17 Feb 2003), available from, accession no. http.//www.blackseek.com/bh/2001/44_AGaston.htm.

30. Gaston, *Green Power*, 130.

31. Diane McWhorter, *Carry Me Home: Birmingham, Alabama: The Climatic Battle of the Civil Rights Revolution* (New York: Simon & Schuster, 2001), 127.

32. Jack Key, "Sixteenth Street Church Bombing Trial: Rebirth for Birmingham," 2001 [journal online], available from http://www.troikamagazine.com/feathures/new/feature-bombing.htm; Internet; accessed 17 February 2003.

33. Martin Luther King, *Letter from Birmingham Jail* in *Academic Search Premier* [database online] Great Neck Publishing, 1963 (accessed 19 March 2003), available from Essential Documents in American History, accession no. 9706192840, 2.

34. Alabama Department of Archives and History, *Alabama Moments in History* (Montgomery: Alabama Department of Archives and History, 2003).

35. "Freedom Now," *Time Magazine*, 17 May 1963 [journal on-line], available from htppp://www.cgi.cnn.com/ALLPOLITICS/1996; Internet; accessed 17 Feb. 2003.

36. Gaston, *Green Power*, 124–125.

37. Ibid., 134–135.

38. *King and Kennedy Discuss Birmingham: The Presidential Record Project* in [database online] (accessed 17 Feb 2003), available from, accession no. htppp://www.millerceter.virginia.edu/resources, 1–9.

39. Ibid., (1–9).

40. Gaston, *Green Power*, 126–127.

41. H. Jackson, "*B.E. 100s* Special Report—A Measure of Profits," *Black Enterprise*, 29 June 1992, 1.

42. *B.E. 100s—2002 Report* (2002, accessed 23 March 2003), available from *Black Enterprise*, accession no. http://www.blackenterprise.com/BE100Home.asp.

43. G. Curry, "Building a Better Foundation," *Black Enterprise*, 12 July 1990: 58.

44. Erika Hunt, *African American Philanthropy: A Legacy of Giving* (New York: 21st Century Foundation, 2001), 2.

45. Emmett Carson, "Black Giving in Minnesota," 3. Working Paper, Minnesota Foundation, Minneapolis, Minnesota.

46. Curry, "Building a Better Foundation," 59.

47. Gaston, *Green Power*, 155.

CHAPTER EIGHT

Not IN Vain

The Philanthropic Endeavors of C. Eric Lincoln

DARRYL HOLLOMAN

If I can help somebody,
As I travel along
If I can help somebody,
With a word or song
If I can stop somebody,
From doing wrong
My living shall not be in vain
Religious Hymn

As suggested by hymns such as the one above, the Black church is a center for self-help. It is often cited as the nucleus of African American fundraising and as the most effective fundraising mechanism for Blacks.[1] But is the Black church the only example of African American philanthropic expression? What contributions have African Americans made to the philanthropic process in other areas? According to the Council on Foundations, the word philanthropy is most often associated with a few wealthy White individuals.[2] Consequently, those who study the philanthropic aims of African Americans outside the Black church usually focus on them as passive recipients of others' philanthropy rather than examining their agency within the giving process. Most philanthropic research overlooks African Americans' efforts on their own behalf.[3] Many of the chapters in this volume correct that view by demonstrating the varied ways that African Americans have themselves acted as philanthropists, giving of their time, talent, and resources to help those in their communities and beyond. This chapter provides a corrective to the traditional view by examining the role of a particular African American man who was a lifelong beneficiary of others' philanthropy but was a far cry from the feeble, helpless stereotype of that characterization.

Minister, novelist, religious scholar, and professor, C. Eric Lincoln was in many ways a product of the philanthropic efforts of northern White missionaries. Fiercely intelligent and curious but having no access to public high school in his racially segregated town, Lincoln was able to further his education by attending Trinity in 1929, an all-Black private school founded by the American Missionary Association (AMA). Later in his life Lincoln credited his many successes in part to the educational foundation laid by his northern missionary teachers.[4] He graduated as valedictorian from Trinity in 1939, went on to earn five degrees, including a Ph.D. in social ethics from Boston University in 1960, and ended his professional career as Distinguished Professor of Religion and Culture at Duke University. As a professor Lincoln continued to benefit from philanthropic efforts. Throughout his academic career he obtained funding from various philanthropic foundations which enabled him to complete work of both high scholarly achievement and great practical help to society.

If not for the beneficence of White philanthropists, Lincoln might never have gone to high school and might therefore have struggled on in his life as one of countless uneducated Black men. Even after Lincoln became a faculty member, the continued support of philanthropic foundations enabled him to make a difference that might not have been otherwise possible. It is in these ways, then, that Lincoln could be seen as a product of northern White philanthropists. But thinking of his story only in this way dehumanizes him and the many others with a similar story, for it implies that he was mere material, inert and doomed to uselessness unless someone (a White someone) came along and shaped him. That Lincoln's life was changed by others' help is undeniable, and he often and publicly expressed his awareness of this and his gratitude to the AMA and other benefactors. Yet Lincoln was also instrumental in shaping himself. He positioned himself in such a way as to win the interest of others, produced valuable work that earned accolades and further support, and leveraged the gifts he received to help uplift others. Throughout Lincoln's academic career he used his skills as an educator and researcher to highlight the experiences of African Americans. Lincoln saw his scholarship as encouragement for African Americans to view themselves as active contributors to mainstream American society. In one example, Lincoln told a graduating college class, "You as Black Americans must insist upon participating in a significant way in decisions about yourselves, your future, and the critical issues of your existence."[5] Lincoln often spoke such words, and they are a reminder of his desire for African Americans' participation in the quest for their own uplift.

Through the use of archival material at the Atlanta University Center's Woodruff Library (The C. Eric Lincoln Papers), I will show how philanthropy was an integral part of the life of C. Eric Lincoln. Specifically, I will look at examples of philanthropy that Lincoln witnessed early in his life and show how these shaped his later philanthropic relationships. I will examine the funding that he received as a faculty member to show how philanthropic organizations had an impact on his research interests and how he was able to maintain independence in the face of outside pressure. Lastly, I will demonstrate his agency in successfully maneuvering through the philanthropic process to garner support for his research interests. While this chapter focuses on an individual, the story of one person helps us understand much more than his or her biography. Norman K. Denzin reminds us that "[e]xperiences occur within larger historical, institutional, and cultural arenas that surround a subject's life. . . ."[6] By examining the life of C. Eric Lincoln and its divergence from what has become the traditional view of African Americans and philanthropy, I hope to show that even when Blacks were on the receiving end of a philanthropic relationship, they were actively advocating for racial uplift.

AS I TRAVEL ALONG: THE EARLY YEARS OF C. ERIC LINCOLN

Charles Eric Lincoln was born July 23, 1924, in Athens, Alabama, a small farming town. Lincoln never knew his parents and was raised by his grandparents, Less Charles Lincoln and Mattie Sowell Lincoln.[7] Less Lincoln farmed three acres of land, and Mattie Lincoln worked as a laundress for the White residents of Athens. Even though both his grandparents were employed, Lincoln grew up "dirt poor."[8] In an interview in the Durham (NC) *Morning Herald* Lincoln described how he wore the "cast-off clothing" of the son of the family for whom his grandmother worked and how he himself labored for a local dairy where he delivered milk from 4:30–9:30 A.M. for fifty cents a week.[9] Lincoln commented that the "$5.25 we managed to eke out together, augmented by an additional thirty-five cents I got in the summertime for watering the flowers and mowing the lawn for another quality family, meant survival."[10]

Even as a young man, Lincoln understood the dynamics of race relations in his small segregated town. Lincoln's Deep South of the 1920s and 30s was a challenging place to live if you were ". . . a barefoot black boy . . . [who] lived in the middle of a cotton patch."[11] He recounted that one of the first lessons he learned about Jim Crow occurred during the summer when, at nine years old, he went to the county health office to be immunized:

> As I stood in a long line of children, waiting for my turn at the needle, I became aware that some of the boys and girls were not required to wait in line. These favored children, who were taken as soon as they came into the room, were all "white." I was vaguely aware, of course, that they were somehow different beyond the fact of their whiteness, for this uncanny, unexplained awareness is the first bitter fruit of acculturation. But I had, as yet[,] no appreciation of the deadly meaning of that difference. I had swum and fished and fought and filched and played with anybody who would play, white or black. What did it matter, if you could hit the ball and run the bases? As often as not my playmates and fellow adventurers had been white, for those were the children who owned the baseballs, the bicycles, the air rifles, and all the other toys and paraphernalia that enhanced the fun and adventure to which every boy seemed somehow entitled.[12]

Because his grandmother worked for a White family Lincoln was known by most White folks and felt at ease anywhere in the town. Consequently, Lincoln's response to what he perceived as an obvious oversight on the part of the clinic staff was to step forward with the newly arriving White children and extend his arm so that he could receive his shot. What happened after this attempt Lincoln described as his "first lesson in race relations." He was grabbed and flung brutally against the wall by a White nurse who said, "Boy, get back in line! Get all the way back there! All you niggers have to wait!" This was the first time that Lincoln had personally felt and understood the effects of racism, and though bruised from his encounter with the nurse, he recalled that "it was not my arm that [hurt;] it was my soul."[13]

As an adult Lincoln said of this experience, "How could I have known that this instance of tending two races at the same time in the same place was itself an extraordinary concession to expediency in protecting the town from some sort of epidemic?" Although he later appreciated that this was evidence of progress, however slight, the question of why "Black Americans were waiting" was a question that Lincoln would spend his entire academic career trying to answer. In a moment of reflection in a piece entitled, "All Niggers Have to Wait," he posed this answer: "That [the] why was presumed to be innate to my being. Ultimately, the answer was ensured in the color of my skin."[14]

Although Lincoln described the incident in the health clinic as his first personal lesson in segregation, Jim Crow also played an important role in shaping his primary and secondary education. The combination of poverty and segregation of the Deep South was instrumental in Lincoln's early introductions to philanthropists and their endeavors.

LIFE AT TRINITY SCHOOL:
LINCOLN'S INTRODUCTION TO PHILANTHROPY

In Lincoln's town Black and White students were not allowed to attend school together. There was not even a public high school for Blacks in Athens because it was expected that their education should end after the sixth grade, if not sooner.[15] Lincoln remembered that even Blacks' primary education was substandard because the elementary school for them closed about six months out of the year so that its students could be available to pick cotton. Lincoln recounted:

> The town in which I lived did not afford a public high school that black people could attend. There were two public high schools for white youngsters, but as far as the city fathers and the county administration was concerned, education for black children should not exceed the sixth grade, especially if higher education for blacks meant scaled-down appropriations for white schools. And of course, for black and white children to attend the same school was a notion beyond the possibility of conception in the Alabama of that era.[16]

As a result of these segregated environments Lincoln attended Trinity, a private school for Blacks that was established by the American Missionary Association. Lincoln began his primary education around the age of four. It was at Trinity that he was exposed to philanthropic efforts that would leave an imprint on his professional life as a faculty member.

While it is unclear how Lincoln arrived at Trinity, he credits his grandmother as the one who sparked his interest in education. Lincoln stated, "She insisted that whatever else happened, I had to go to school and I had to do well. On those one or two occasions when I played hooky, she reached behind the door and took out one of her switches. . . ."[17] Described as a serious, studious youngster who was writing poetry at the age of six, Lincoln's most viable option may have been Trinity.

Mary Frances Wells, a White army nurse, founded Trinity in 1865. The aims of the school were to train teachers to work in elementary schools, prepare young men and women to attend college, and to prepare its students to serve as productive citizens.[18] The faculty consisted of twelve teachers, and the school was situated on ten acres of land. A three-story brick building served as the main facility and housed most of the classrooms. Additional buildings included Wells's cottage, a two-story brick home for the teachers, and a small wood frame building used for manual training.

In 1887 Trinity graduated its first class, consisting of five students, and by 1928 the school recorded 235 students in thirteen grades.[19] One of the primary means of getting the necessary operating funds for the school came through Trinity's tuition. Students were expected to pay all tuition and fees on the first of each month, and no child could be registered until the payment of an entrance fee and one month's tuition was paid.[20] Students themselves were held responsible for these expenses, and the school catalog indicated that, "no credit [would] be extended unless all fees had been paid."[21] "Tuition at Trinity High School was twenty-seven dollars a year," Lincoln stated, "but since no one ever had twenty-seven dollars to pay in a lump sum, tuition was computed at three dollars a month. Even this was difficult to come by, so more than half of the student body were either working for the school or were on scholarships provided by New England philanthropy (the AMA)."[22] Primarily, the scholarships offered at Trinity were earned through some form of manual labor to the school. Lincoln was one student who benefited from this offer, which was extended by Trinity to its less fortunate members. Lincoln recalled, "I first started earning my tuition when I reached the third grade by hauling horse manure from my Grandpa's stable to spread on the school garden at fifteen cents per wheelbarrow load."[23] Such examples provide a keen insight into young Lincoln's early introduction to the importance of being self-reliant in furthering his own educational goals (and most likely the goals of the White Protestant missionaries).

In addition to tuition money and AMA appropriations for Trinity, northern philanthropists contributed a small but important amount to Trinity each year. Yet the most important philanthropic contributions from the north came not in the form of money but of personal sacrifice. Many people during this era traveled to the Deep South to serve as educators, some of them forsaking the possibility of marriage and family to dedicate themselves to this cause. Louise H. Allyn, Trinity's second principal, and possibly the school's most effective fundraiser, was such a person. She also became one of Lincoln's most important mentors.[24]

Allyn spent the first two or three years of her work at Trinity "teaching and getting the necessary supplies," working to establish the school on a firm foundation before attempting to add on to it. When Trinity was destroyed by a fire, Allyn was quoted as saying, "We shall have another Trinity" and quickly raised $1,000 to aid in replacing the burned building.[25] Eventually she increased the educational opportunities provided at Trinity by adding the eleventh and twelfth grades and a kindergarten as well as expanding the curriculum to include manual training, athletics, music, and domestic science. Additionally, in response to the state of Alabama's requirement that Trinity meet imposed state regulations, she raised sufficient funds to add more floor space, put in a library, and purchase books and equipment. Allyn's expertise as a fundraiser can perhaps best be seen when the AMA promised her $20,000, if she could raise an initial $7,000; Allyn raised the money in less than two years, a truly impressive feat in that time and place.[26]

Allyn served as principal of Trinity when Lincoln was a student and was an influential force in shaping his ideologies. Lincoln reminisced that, "Miss Louise Hurlbutt Allyn was a Connecticut Yankee, and a more noble Christian woman never sacrificed marriage and family for the cause of black education and uplift."[27] Further, Lincoln recalled that his early lessons in race relations were also provided by Allyn:

> She [Allyn] could counsel her bigger boys, as often she did when they were required to do an errand downtown to "avert the eyes lest they compromise the soul!" and they did, or at

least they tried, because they trusted this white Yankee who had cast her lot among them. Avert the eyes! It was not only the soul that was in danger of being compromised; survival itself was at stake.[28]

Such words in the segregated Deep South were a matter of survival for Black boys, who if caught looking inappropriately at a White woman could be jailed or killed.[29] Lincoln and Allyn's relationship extend far past his years at Trinity, and he wrote to her throughout her life to inform her of his latest accomplishments. In a symbolic gesture of her affection for him, Allyn bequeathed her personal papers to him after her death in 1951.[30]

By 1930, while Lincoln was still at Trinity, Allyn reported that the school was finding it harder to collect tuition and that about a third of its students were requesting jobs to help with their tuition payments.[31] In response, Allyn allowed the children to fill hollows, mend fences, clear dead wood, and sweep, duties that gave Trinity's janitor the opportunity to beautify the school by planting shrubs and hedges. Allyn wrote to the AMA that Trinity was helping "children to stay in school, who otherwise would have to stop."[32] Allyn and her willing students, Lincoln included, also sought financial opportunities outside the bounds of the school itself.[33] In response to Trinity's financial needs Lincoln's class picked cotton over a three-day period for a White farmer who lived on the outskirts of Athens. The schedule was divided into three sections, with three teachers helping each section. Allyn herself picked cotton every day alongside both her pupils and their teachers. The school worked a total of 546 hours, picked over four thousand pounds of cotton and earned twenty-five dollars. Allyn stated, "It was good for the soul to be helping in the world's work . . . , and at the same time we were helping the school."[34] The money, however, only covered a third of the bill for the football shoes that the school needed to purchase.

Lincoln graduated from Trinity in 1939, valedictorian of his class at the age of fourteen. Sadly, due partly to White southerners' call for the expansion of segregated public schools in the South and partly to dwindling funds from AMA, Trinity would close its doors fewer than three years after he graduated.[35] Lincoln lamented, "In 1942, a year after I quit Alabama for Chicago, the South's takeover program of Yankee-based Negro schools finally took over Trinity, and Camelot ceased to exist in north Alabama, just as it was being choked to death all across the South."[36] However, before Trinity closed its doors, Allyn, in addition to shaping Lincoln's ideologies, also taught him how closely philanthropy interfaced with education. This understanding of philanthropic influences on education may have prepared him once he began to establish his own personal relationships with philanthropic organizations as a professor.

THE PHILANTHROPIC SCHOLAR: LINCOLN'S ASSOCIATION
WITH PHILANTHROPIC FOUNDATIONS

In the early 1940s, Lincoln attended LeMoyne College based on the recommendation of a mentor, Jay Wright. Wright was Allyn's successor at Trinity High School. Lincoln recalled, "[Wright] was a singularly remarkable individual, deeply involved in teaching not only academics, but things such as self-confidence—how to do things well, not simply to do them."[37] Lincoln credited Wright with introducing him to philosophy and classical music. Consequently, in 1943 Lincoln enrolled in LeMoyne College until World War II interrupted his studies. After serving in the U.S. Navy, Lincoln returned to LeMoyne, where he received a Bachelor of Arts degree in 1947. In 1953 Lincoln earned both a Master of Arts from Fisk University in Nashville, Tennessee, and a Bachelor of Divinity from the University of Chicago. And in 1960, with the help of a Ford Foundation grant, Lincoln earned his Master of Education and Doctor of Philosophy degrees from Boston University.

Lincoln's career as a faculty member began in 1960 as an Assistant Professor of Religion and Philosophy at Clark College in Atlanta, Georgia. While at Clark he advanced rapidly to the rank of full Professor, and in 1965 he moved to Portland State College, where he served as Professor of Sociology for two years until he became Professor of Sociology and Religion at Union Theological Seminary in New York. In 1973, he took an administrative post as Chair in the Department of Religion at Fisk University in Tennessee. Lincoln ended his career at Duke University in North Carolina where he served as Professor of Religion from 1976 to 1993 and was named the William Ran Kenan, Jr. Distinguished Professor of Religion and Culture in 1991.

Lincoln's most noted scholarship centered on the religious experiences of Black Americans.[38] He launched his career as a religious scholar in 1961 with the publication of his dissertation, *Black Muslims in America*. His other books on religion included *The C. Eric Lincoln Series in Black Religion; The Black Church; The Black Experience in Religion;* and *Race, Religion, and the Continuing American Dilemma*. One of his most comprehensive works on religion was the book he co-authored with Lawrence Mamiya, *The Black Church in the African American Experience*. Published in 1990, the work was an extensive study that covered the seven major historically Black denominations.[39]

Other research teams, guided by Lincoln and Mamiya, worked on related issues such as the role of women in the Black church and changes in Black consciousness during the Civil Rights Movement of the 1960s.[40] Lincoln and Mamiya indicated that although "the fierce independence of Black ministers and churches were a primary obstacle to gathering their data," ultimately their study would "significantly contribute to filling the gaps in information on Black churches."[41] This attempt by Lincoln and Mamiya to reveal the contributions of the religious experience of Black Americans was seen as groundbreaking, and it was acknowledged as such by two American philanthropic organizations.[42]

THE LILLY ENDOWMENT AND THE FORD FOUNDATION

The Lilly Endowment, a private philanthropic foundation established in Indianapolis by members of the Lilly family through gifts of stock in their pharmaceutical business, was created to support the causes of religion, education, and community development, with a special focus placed on projects that benefited youth and promoted their leadership in education.[43] Consequently, in acknowledgment of Eli Lilly's belief that "values [are] quite simply the core of both men and institutions," the Lilly Endowment sought research endeavors that supported these values.[44] In the early 1980s the Lilly Endowment began to concentrate part of "its resources and attention on helping the core leaders of theological schools and black denominations" in an effort to help them better serve their institutions.[45]

The Ford Foundation was established by Henry Ford in 1936 with a mere $25,000. After the death of Ford in 1947, the foundation adopted a new focus on racial issues. According to a 1984 working paper, "[i]n the decades prior to 1966, the year in which the Ford Foundation launched a major program in the field of civil rights, repeated instances of racially motivated attacks against Blacks and their supporters roused the conscience of the nation. Many Americans were awakened for the first time to the ugly realities of poverty and racism."[46] In a 1966 speech to the National Urban League, McGeorge Bundy, president of Ford Foundation, acknowledged "the harsh realities of life in black America and announced the role the Foundation hoped to play in their remediation."[47] In his speech, Bundy commented:

> The position of the Ford Foundation on this point can be clearly stated. We believe that full equality for all American Negroes is now the most urgent domestic concern of this country. We will not attempt to work through any single chosen instrument or in any single field of activity. We think the familiar listing of jobs and education and housing is right, but not exhaustive. We shall do what we can to help these fields. But we would add four concerns— for leadership—for research—for communication—and for justice.[48]

As a result of such leadership the Ford Foundation set forth new goals for its grant-making activities. These goals included "strengthening the leadership and the programs of minority organizations; exploring ways to achieve better race relations; supporting policy-oriented research on race and poverty; promoting integration in housing; and increasing the availability of legal resources through support of litigating organizations and minority law students."[49]

It was against the backdrop of these two foundation initiatives that Lincoln not only developed his research agenda on the Black church but that he also established relationships with each of these philanthropic organizations that assisted in his promotion of that agenda.[50]

LINCOLN AND THE FOUNDATIONS

Although a recipient of foundation funds, Lincoln also built strong ties with them that at times reached beyond his being solely a beneficiary. Lincoln's relationship with Ford can be traced to 1970, when Lincoln received a grant from the Ford Foundation to assist him in revising and updating his book, *The Black Muslim in America*.[51] This initial relationship further evolved in 1971 when Lincoln sought funding for a coalition of American students to travel to Africa. Lincoln stated to Bryant George of the Ford Foundation, "Pursuant our brief conversation in the hallway at the Ford Foundation some weeks ago, I am herewith enclosing a preliminary brochure on our African programs for 1971. I have just returned from Ghana and from Nigeria where final contractual agreements were concluded, and our programs are officially set and ready to go . . . I very earnestly solicit your continued interest in the American Forum and what we are trying to accomplish for Americans who are interested in Africa and African studies."[52] Such correspondence, coupled with a letter to Samuel Du Bois Cook of the Ford Foundation—which stated that, "This is to express my sincere appreciation to you for your efforts and interest in my behalf regarding the research grant for which I applied recently . . . I look forward to having an opportunity to do a little fishing, etc at my place up the river"—revealed that Lincoln understood his presence within philanthropic organizations and was aware of how to maintain their continued support of his research interests.[53] By 1974, as Lincoln learned that funds were "in trouble" at Ford he began to make introductions with the Lilly Endowment.[54] What again seems apparent is that Lincoln understood the necessity of navigating philanthropic organizations in the promotion of his research agendas.

By 1977, after Lincoln had arrived at Duke, he secured a grant in the amount of $73,000 to fund his publication of the *Black Church in America*. And by 1978 Lilly again sought Lincoln's expertise by asking him to participate in an "Interdenominational Dialogue among Black Churches."[55] From 1978–1982, Lincoln was able to secure from the Lilly endowment a total of $388,250 for his research on Black churches, with the largest amount being granted in the amount of $170,100. Such examples show that Lincoln was not only keenly aware that Lilly would promote his interest but that Lilly could be a vehicle through which he could personally benefit by rendering his professional expertise and services.

By 1985 funds from Lilly began to dwindle due to a refocus of foundation priorities. Lincoln began to seek funds from other sources, but it is clear that his relationship with the Lilly Endowment remained strong and friendly. Upon hearing that Lincoln had won a grant from a new source, Lilly's senior vice president of Religion, Robert Wood Lynn, wrote him an encouraging note: "Congratulations! I rejoice in the good word from The Ford Foundation. This is another confirmation of the extraordinary importance of the work which you and your colleagues have set out to do. I am very grateful for your willingness to reach another foundation, since this gives us more ways to stretch out scarce resources for research across a broader spectrum."[56] In 1989 Lincoln was asked to serve on the Lilly Endowment Black Church Research Advisory Committee, showing the continued good relationship between the two parties. Consequently, Lincoln very skillfully maneuvered between the Lilly Endowment and the Ford Foundation when funds become too tight in either organization. And whereas he remained at Lilly for a significant time, once funding became uncertain at Lilly, Lincoln sought the opportunity to return to the Ford Foundation.

In a letter addressed to Lincoln from Lynn Walker, Deputy Director at the Ford Foundation, Walker wrote:

> I am sure that you are used to the kinds of laudatory remarks which I am writing this letter to convey to you. For in truth, persons of intellectual stature and talent such as yourself are a rarity and must surely provoke others to acknowledge these gifts often. . . . Throughout the balance of our trip, I know that the Trustees heard no one who spoke better and had more substance that [sic] you. I just felt so proud when you were talking. Indeed, after the panel, several trustees and our President remarked that they wished they could have had more time to listen just to you. You have a definite fan club here. [57]

As with Lilly, Lincoln and Mamiya's report detailed an outline of their research project. The report was more thorough than the one that had been submitted to Lilly because their project was near its completion. Included in the Ford Foundation proposal was an explanation of the funding provided by Lilly, which indicated that although expenditures were "conservative and closely monitored[,] inflation proved costly to the project."[58] The proposal included an in-depth request for funding from Ford that consisted of a salary and benefit replacements for Mamiya, a summer stipend for Lincoln, travel, consultations, and research assistants. The proposal requested funding in the amount of $154,675. Hence, by the time Lincoln begins his second relationship with the Ford Foundation, he appears to be apt at conveying his interest and needs to philanthropic organizations. So much so, that by 1988, Ford awarded him $155,000 to continue his Black church study.[59]

By the early 1990s funding for Lincoln and Mamiya's research reached its conclusion as their book headed to the publisher.[60] However, just as with Lilly, Lincoln was able to secure a financial relationship with Ford that reached beyond his being simply the recipient of their funds. In a letter to Lincoln, James J. Howard stated, "I am pleased to confirm the extension of your appointment as a Consultant to the Ford Foundation's Human Rights and Governances to serve on the Advisory Committee of the Black Church Program review."[61] Lincoln's appointment began on February 1, 1990, and ran until November 8, 1990.[62] Again, such turns of events regarding Lincoln's relationships with philanthropic organizations indicated that he not only possessed an understanding of the purposes of philanthropic organizations but that he was also keenly aware of how he could commandeer personal financial gain from these organizations in exchange for his expertise, experience, and knowledge. Hence, Lincoln's role as both beneficiary and consultant gave him an unusual relationship with these organizations.

HELPING OTHERS: LINCOLN'S PHILANTHROPIC LESSONS

A review of the life of C. Eric Lincoln reveals that his philanthropic endeavors reached beyond the traditional means of giving often associated with Black Americans. A study of Lincoln's life as a professor shows that he was aware of, and quite comfortable with, maneuvering within White philanthropic organizations. Through his relationship with Allyn early in his life he became more comfortable working within White circles than most African Americans. Lincoln possessed a thorough understanding of the White northeastern Protestant culture that permeated corporate foundations. He understood the purposes of philanthropic organizations and how these organizations could best serve to promote his research interests. In addition, Lincoln understood his unique position within the philanthropic process, and he successfully navigated between philanthropic groups to ensure that he maintained their support for his research interest on the Black church.

An analysis of Lincoln's philanthropic relationships allows for a closer inspection of the role that he assumed as a Black faculty member within these organizations. This shows his agency as he was able to not only support their causes but also to ensure their promotion of his own research agendas. Lastly, an examination of Lincoln's life shows how he used his philanthropic connections to fulfill his own personal visions of "helping Black Americans travel along" in their quest towards their social and racial uplift.

NOTES

1. Alicia Byrd, ed., *Philanthropy and the Black Church* (Washington, D.C.: Council on Foundations, 1990); E. Franklin Frazier, *The Negro Church in America* (New York: Schocken Books, 1963); C. Eric Lincoln, *The Black Church since Frazier* (New York: Schocken Books, 1974); Calvin Pressley, "Financial Contributions for the Kingdom for the Elect: Giving Patterns in the Black Church," *New Directions for Philanthropic Fundraising* (spring 1995): 91–100.

2. Council on Foundations, "Cultures of Caring: Philanthropy in Diverse American Communities," (Washington, D.C., 1997): 7.

3. Cheryl Hall Russell and Robert H. Kasberg, *African American Traditions of Giving and Serving: A Midwest Perspective* (Indianapolis: Indiana Center on Philanthropy, 1997); Bradford Smith, Sylvia Shue, Jennifer Lisa Vest, and Joseph Villarreal, *Philanthropy in Communities of Color* (Bloomington: Indiana University Press, 1999).

4. C. Eric Lincoln to Louise H. Allyn, n.d. (hereafter referred to as Lincoln). Atlanta University Center Woodruff Library. Box 1, Folder 18.

5. C. Eric Lincoln Commencement Address to the LeMoyne-Owen Graduating Class, 1971, Atlanta University Center (AUC) Woodruff Library, folder 1, box 1.

6. Norman K. Denzin, *Interpretive Interactionism* (Newbury Park: Sage Publications, 1989).

7. Jack Adams, "C. Eric Lincoln from Poverty to Scholarship," Durham (NC) *Morning Herald*, Sunday, March 9, 1980, Section D, Lincoln Papers, folder 17, box 1.

8. Jack Adams, "C. Eric Lincoln from Poverty to Scholarship," Durham (NC) *Morning Herald*, Sunday, March 9, 1980, Section D, Lincoln Papers, folder 17, box 1.

9. Jack Adams, "C. Eric Lincoln from Poverty to Scholarship," Durham (NC) *Morning Herald*, Sunday, March 9, 1980, Section D, Lincoln Papers, folder 17, box 1.

10. C. Eric Lincoln, *Coming Through the Fire: Surviving Race and Place in America* (Durham: Duke University Press, 1996), 55.

11. Jack Adams, "C. Eric Lincoln from Poverty to Scholarship," Durham (NC) *Morning Herald*, Sunday, March 9, 1980, Section D, Lincoln Papers, folder 17, box 1.

12. C. Eric Lincoln, " All Niggers Have to Wait: A Child's First Lesson in Jim Crow," *The Journal of Blacks in Higher Education* 11 (spring 1996) 60.

13. Lincoln, "All Niggers Have to Wait," 60.

14. Lincoln, "All Niggers Have to Wait," 60.

15. Davia Odell, "C. Eric Lincoln," *Aeolus*, 1980, Lincoln Papers, folder 6, box 75.

16. C. Eric Lincoln, *Coming Through the Fire: Surviving Race and Place in America* (Durham: Duke University Press, 1996).

17. *The Athens News Courier*, Sunday, July 14, 1991, Lincoln Papers, folder 2, box 257, Folder 2.

18. "Trinity High School Catalog 1927–28," Lincoln Papers, folder 1, box, 1.

19. Lincoln graduated from Trinity in 1939 at the age of fourteen and was a student at Trinity in 1929.

20. "Trinity High School Catalog 1927–28," Lincoln Papers, folder 1, box 1.

21. "Trinity Catalog," Lincoln Papers, 1927–28 Catalog, folder 1, box 1.

22. Lincoln, *Coming Through the Fire*, 1996, p. 21.

23. Lincoln, *Coming Through the Fire*, 1996, p. 28.

24. This financial summary was drafted by Irving Gaylord, the AMA treasurer for the school year 1920–1921, Lincoln Papers, folder 1, box 1.

25. Synopsis by W.J. Turrentine, Lincoln Papers, folder 1, box 1.

26. Synopsis, Lincoln Papers, folder 1, box 1.

27. Lincoln, *Coming Through the Fire*, 1996, 28.

28. Lincoln, *Coming Through the Fire*, 1996, 29.

29. Lincoln, *Coming Through the Fire*, 1996, 29.

30. Ruth R. Beebe to C. Eric Lincoln, February 1951, Lincoln Papers, folder 1, box 1.

31. Louise Allyn to Dear Friends, 31 October 1930, Lincoln Papers, folder 1, box 1.

32. Louise Allyn to Dear Friends, 31 October 1930, Lincoln Papers, folder 1, box 1.

33. Louise Allyn to Dear Friends, 31 October 1930, Lincoln Papers, folder 1, box 1.

34. Louise Allyn to Dear Friends, 31 October 1930, Lincoln Papers, folder 1, box 1.

35. C. Eric Lincoln, "The Relevance of Education for Black Americans," *Journal of Negro Education* 38 (summer, 1969) 3.

36. Lincoln, *Coming Through the Fire*, 58.

37. *The Athens News Courier*, 14 July 1991, Lincoln Papers, folder 2, box 257.

38. Joan Oleck, "Lessons Along the Avenue," *Duke Perspectives*, 74 (July-August) 1988, Lincoln Papers, folder 17, box 1.

39. C. Eric Lincoln and Lawrence H. Mamiya, *The Black Church in the African American Experience*, (Durham: Duke University Press, 1990). Lincoln stated that his interest in studying the Black church grew out of the fact that, "Major scholars [of] religion [had] slighted black churches despite their great impact. I wanted to generate reliable information." In 1978 Lincoln began gathering data on the seven major Black denominations while Mamiya worked on surveying 2,200 Black churches. The seven denominations were: African Methodist Episcopal (A.M.E.) Church; the African Methodist Episcopal Zion (A.M.E.Z.) Church; the Christian Methodist Episcopal (C.M.E.) Church; the National Baptist Convention, U.S.A., Incorporated (NBC); the National Baptist Convention of America, Unincorporated (NBCA); the Progressive National Baptist Convention (PNBC) and the Church of God in Christ (COGIC).

40. Mamiya, "The Sociological Field Survey of Black Churches," v.d., Lincoln Papers, folder 3, box 252.

41. Lincoln and Mamiya, *Lilly Report*, Lincoln Papers, folder 3, box 252.

42. Robert Wood Lynn to C. Eric Lincoln, 14 December 1977, Lincoln Papers, folder 2, box 252.

43. Lilly Endowment, Inc., "Annual Report 1985," folder 3, box 251.

44. Lilly Endowment, Inc., "Annual Report 1985," folder 3, box 251.

45. Lilly Endowment, Inc., "Annual Report 1985," folder 3, box 251.

46. The Ford Foundation, "Civil Rights, Social Justice and Black America," January 1984, Lincoln Papers, folder 2, box 248.

47. The Ford Foundation, "Civil Rights, Social Justice and Black America," January 1984, Lincoln Papers, folder 2, box 248.

48. The Ford Foundation, "Civil Rights, Social Justice and Black America," January 1984, Lincoln Papers, folder 2, box 248, 6.

49. The Ford Foundation, "Civil Rights, Social Justice and Black America," January 1984, Lincoln Papers, folder 2, box 248, 7.

50. The Ford Foundation, "Civil Rights, Social Justice and Black America," January 1984, Lincoln Papers, folder 2, box 248, 7.

51. C. Eric Lincoln to William P. Gormbley, 6 August 1970, Lincoln Papers, folder 4, box 45.

52. C. Eric Lincoln to William P. Gormbley, 6 August 1970, Lincoln papers, folder 4, box 45.

53. C. Eric Lincoln to Samuel Du Bois Cook, 6 August 1970, Lincoln papers, folder 4, box 45.

54. C. Eric Lincoln to Benjamin F. Payton, 26 September 1974, Lincoln Papers, folder 3, box 248.

55. Jacqui Burton to C. Eric Lincoln, 24 May 1978, Lincoln Papers, folder 1, box 252.

56. Robert Lynn Wood to C. Eric Lincoln (25 October 1985), Lincoln Papers, folder 5, box 252.

57. Lynn Walker to C. Eric Lincoln, 14 October 1987, Lincoln Papers, folder 6, box 248.

58. 1985 Proposal to the Ford Foundation for Support in the Completion of a Research Project on the Black Church, Lincoln Papers, folder 5, box 248.

59. Lynn Walker to C. Eric Lincoln, 7 November 1988; Duke University Standard Revenue/ Expense Report with Budget; Lincoln Papers, folder 5, box 248.

60. C. Eric Lincoln to Lynn Walker (7 November 1988), Lincoln Papers, folder 5, box 249.

61. James J. Howard to C. Eric Lincoln, 29 August 1990, Lincoln Papers, folder 4, box 45.

62. James J. Howard to C. Eric Lincoln, 8 February 1990, Lincoln Papers, folder 5, box 45.

CHAPTER NINE

Howard Thurman

A Life Journey for Service, Religion, and Philanthropy

MARK GILES

Active giving in the African American experience must be understood in the context of the socio-historical reality that blacks, due to state-sponsored segregation and racism, were forced to rely on their own collective will and actions to survive and advance. Whether it is the phenomenon of extended family, who facilitated the care for abandoned, estranged, or orphaned children or the care of the elderly, blood kin or not, black families and the black community have largely survived and advanced through their own efforts. Raymond Gavins noted that, "Denied equal citizenship and excluded from politics, blacks turned to their own churches, schools, lodges, burial and secret societies for a meaningful existence."[1] These acts of giving and approaches to survival in racially hostile environments were successful because of an ethic of mutual care and sharing of resources that has long characterized the African American experience. This phenomenon reflects the individual and collective agency that sustained and strengthened black communities throughout their history and continues to do so today. Included in that tradition are the black clergy who, through their professional commitment to provide religious leadership, gave emotional and spiritual comfort to others, often collecting and allocating money, food, and clothing to their congregations and community members. Following in this legacy was the African American theologian Howard Thurman (1900–1981). Although not a household name, Thurman was a highly influential preacher, mentor, and educator for over sixty years, and in 1954 *Life*

Magazine recognized him as one of America's twelve most influential clergymen of the twentieth century.[2]

By its very nature the vocation of a minister is philanthropic, for a minister's calling is to care for others, seek to improve their welfare, and advance higher ideals in the broader society. Furthermore, the history of the black church in America is a history of community and social action on behalf of African Americans.[3] Yet Howard Thurman's philanthropy was exceptional and deliberate, and not simply the inevitable accompaniment of his profession. Although Howard Thurman established a philanthropic organization in the 1960s, this chapter will focus on the early years of his educational journey as a way to understand his template for helping others, his spiritual outlook as a means to understand why he preached and how he influenced others religiously, and how he used personal funds and brokered gifts from others for the use of needy black students. Particular attention is also given to the notion of agency, a concept central to and inherent in the African American experience and in the black church's historical spirit of self-determination.

COLLECTIVE AGENCY IN THE BLACK EXPERIENCE

I define agency as the self-determined action of an individual or group supported primarily by their own self-reliance, to make the change they feel is necessary to achieve a desired result. The notion of self-help, uplift, and commitment to find solutions to problems within the black community by black people and for black people finds its foundation in slavery and extends through to the twenty-first century. The sense of agency is found in the self-determined act of a poor farmer giving a hog or donating his labor to the founding efforts of an early black school or college.[4] It is found in the legacy of slaves who possessed rudimentary reading skills and risked a beating or worse to share what they knew with other slaves. It is understood as the commitment of ex-slaves who pooled resources to establish the foundations of their communities (churches, schools, etc.) and made sure their children not only valued education but doggedly pursued it regardless of the hardships associated with its attainment. In addition, the spirit of collective agency is found in the Herculean efforts of the black families and professionals who challenged the ingrained social custom of Jim Crow in the pursuit of desegregating schools in the *Brown v. Board of Education* case and making the promise of democracy a reality for black Americans.

The concept of self-agency and self-reliance within the black community, whether instinctive or conscious, is one of the essential elements of why and how blacks survived and achieved individual and collective gains in America during and after slavery. According to Rodney M. Jackson,

... philanthropy has been an integral part of African American history since the 1700s. It was then that African Americans, most of whom were slaves living in the South, began to form the mutual aid and benefit societies that, along with the Black Church, would form the backbone of self-help within the black community.[5]

This powerful spirit of agency permeates the narrative of the black experience in America. It is an indelible part of the collective character of blacks in the struggle to overcome racial, political, and economic oppression. The examples of the founding of schools, churches, and social and political organizations are all clear examples of the spirit of agency, the do-for-self attitude that was born from both the racism and segregation of America, and deeply rooted connection based on common experience. A paraphrased reference to biblical scripture illustrates this point and is one that is common in the black community: God helps those who help themselves. Emmett D. Carson noted, "Historically, black philanthropy has been a survival mechanism through which African American people have directed their money, time, and goods to lift up and advance the myriad interests of African American people."[6]

Thurman's life-long commitment was to help other blacks improve their lot in life. This sense of commitment was forged from his upbringing in his home community in Florida, from the family values that were instilled and reinforced in his home, church, schools, and spiritual intuition. He spoke to wide audiences about the need to challenge race- and faith-based prejudices and the need to understand and respond spiritually to timeless issues such as what it means to be human. For example, the Civil Rights Movement of the 1950s and 1960s brought about many social changes, yet the deeper philosophical issues that leaders like Martin Luther King, Jr. asked the nation and the world to consider and act upon are still unanswered and largely unresolved. Thurman believed that non-violence would eventually help people love one another and that this love ethic would lead to the change of the human soul that would steer people away from the undesirable and common behaviors of hate, segregation, and violence. Timeless issues are those that are bigger than an immediate social concern; they are both spiritual and practical and are the types of questions that prophets, theologians, and philosophers ask and wrestle with.

Philanthropy should be understood in terms broader than mere monetary donation; it includes religious experience, community service, mentoring, and other "gifts" that cannot be measured financially.[7] Notions of philanthropy can expand beyond institutional dynamics and encompass personal intentions and actions. Understanding philanthropy in this way helps illustrate how a life lived at the confluence of religion, education, and service can be an exemplar and model of love-for-others in action. Largely influenced by people like Mary McLeod Bethune and Mordecai Johnson, the longtime president of Howard University, as well as by advice received from Dr. George Cross while a student at Rochester Theological Seminary, Thurman devoted his life to the "timeless issues" of the human soul. In remembering Mrs. Bethune, whose funeral service he preached in 1955, Thurman wrote, " . . . the inner strength and authority of Mrs. Bethune [. . .] gave boys like me a view of possibilities to be realized in some distant future."[8] These individuals shaped Thurman's life, thought, ministry, and his influence on others.

A JOURNEY TOWARDS SERVICE

Thurman lived and breathed the African American experience. His maternal grandmother lived the early years of her life in slavery and passed on to Thurman a strong sense of faith and the essence of what past experiences meant to her and to other blacks. Thurman was raised knowing first-hand what it meant to live in a segregated and racist society and learned to navigate and make meaning of the world around him at an early age. He learned to view segregation and racism as part of the world but not the determining factor in how he viewed himself in the world. Racism was an external reality, not an internal matrix for self-knowledge and identity. He absorbed life lessons from his community to gain penetrating insights into the human soul and the psyche of segregation and how it shaped and affected others. For example, as a young boy, Thurman worked small jobs around Daytona to earn spending money and to contribute to the household income. During one of these jobs he had a peculiar incident with a young white girl whose family he knew and for whom he often worked. The incident had a significant influence on him and helped to shape his future thinking on interracial social conditions in America. While Thurman was raking leaves, the family's young daughter wanted to play by kicking the neatly stacked piles that Thurman had gathered. After repeatedly asking her to stop and under a threat of being reported to her father, she took a straight pin from her garment and stuck him sharply in the hand. He drew his hand back in pain, and the little girl exclaimed, "Oh, Howard, that didn't hurt you! You can't feel!"[9] For Thurman, this incident would prove to be a point of reference for future intellectual and spiritual investigation and critical analysis of racial prejudice, segregation, and racism in America and within the human spirit. Thurman eventually provided an analysis of the young girl's thinking as she had been taught by her family and her environment and how the limitations of segregation create conditions of inhumanity:

> In other words, I was not human, nor was I a creature capable of feeling pain. . . . [I]t indicates the social and psychological climate in which it would be possible for a little girl to grow up in a Christian family with such a spontaneous attitude toward other human beings. Segregation guarantees such inhumaneness and throws wide the door for a complete range of socially irresponsible behavior.[10]

Thurman devoted the majority of his career to serving as a religious leader and faculty member in higher education. Consistent with the African American historical tradition of self-agency,[11] Thurman's sense of identity and responsibility to help other blacks was developed from his family and his childhood community. As the grandson of ex-slaves in a close-knit black community in Florida where the church was the center of most social, economic, and educational activities, he was instilled with a strong sense of self and a deeply abiding commitment to receiving an education in order to serve and help other blacks. James D. Anderson's history of the education of blacks in the South is an illustration of this powerful and self-determined movement for education. Anderson noted,

> The values of self-help and self-determination underlay the ex-slaves' educational movement. To be sure, they accepted support from northern missionary societies, the Freedman's Bureau, and some southern whites, but their own action—class self-activity informed by an ethic of mutuality—was the primary force that brought schools to the children of freed men and women.[12]

Thurman's commitment to and emphasis on community shaped most of his activities, including his preaching, teaching, and commitment to others. Walter Fluker, a leading scholar on Howard Thurman, claimed that "Thurman's quest for community was the central category of his life and thought."[13] Regarding his cultural ideology and identity, Thurman stated, "My roots are deep in the throbbing reality of the Negro idiom and from it I draw a full measure of inspiration and vitality. I know that a man must be at home somewhere before he can feel at home everywhere."[14] His career and notions of giving reflected a firm grounding in the African American experience.

In the late 1920s, Thurman began to emerge as a national black leader while working at Morehouse and Spelman Colleges as Professor and Campus Minister. From 1932–1944, he served as Dean of Chapel and Professor of Religion at Howard University. After leaving Howard University in 1944, Thurman and his family moved to San Francisco where he co-founded and led the Church for the Fellowship of All Peoples. Fellowship Church was founded as an interfaith and interracial ministry. It was both an answer and challenge to the racial segregation in American Christianity and American society. The social and religious experiment known as Fellowship Church had somewhat mixed results. It was successful in the sense that it operated for many years, touched and changed the lives of many people of diverse faith traditions. It led to several members becoming believers in the social and spiritual change advocated by Thurman, and they remained staunch supporters, even to the extent of contributing to the Thurman Educational Trust and serving on its board of directors. It did not, however, spark a religious revolution of interracial and interfaith worship. Few people in 2004 will readily know about

Fellowship Church and its work between the mid-1940s and 1970s. By the early 1950s, Thurman was eager for a new challenge and longed to return to higher education, in part because of his growing frustration with some organizational dynamics surrounding Fellowship Church and in part due to his desire for new intellectual and spiritual pursuits. Finally, he was presented a unique opportunity by Harold Case, president of Boston University.

In 1953 Thurman returned to higher education, serving as Dean of Chapel and Professor of Theology at Boston University until 1965. Until the mid-nineteenth century, the role of providing guidance for the spiritual life of colleges and universities rested with the presidents, who were often men of the cloth. As this practice waned many colleges and universities created separate positions with the sole responsibility of guiding the spiritual life of the campus and students.[15] Campus Minister and Dean of Chapel were positions that reflected this newer practice. Both positions were responsible for organizing campus-based religious worship services and working with students. The dean's title symbolized additional duties, such as managing budgets and supervising chapel support staff and had a direct reporting line to the president. Clearly, a dean's title represents a high profile and senior-level position at any educational institution. When Thurman joined the faculty and senior administrative staff of Boston University as Dean of the Chapel in the fall semester of 1953, he became the first person to break the color line of senior-level administrative positions at predominately white institutions of higher learning. Throughout his educational career Thurman was afforded the respect of a senior-level campus leader and had direct access to other high-ranking administrators and faculty members.

A well-respected African American Baptist minister and intellectual, Thurman was also an unheralded agent of social change who believed in the possibility of genuine spiritual development, national and international social justice, and interracial and interfaith harmony. He maintained a life-long commitment to the ethical and moral principles of philanthropy and served as a mentor and spiritual guide to many 1950s and 1960s Civil Rights leaders, including James Farmer, Martin Luther King, Jr., and Whitney Young. Thurman lived as a "spiritual philanthropist" in a broad sense: his gifts to others included time as well as money and were aimed at meeting the spiritual, social, and financial needs of individuals in his community and around the country.

As a member of a generation of professional black leaders who clearly understood the primary need to rely upon themselves for the changes they sought and to link arms with others of goodwill, Thurman's service bridged many racial and religious differences. He was motivated by Jesus' social gospel to help those who are poor and marginalized, applying practical techniques to get resources where they were needed most. Thurman lived a life of social service and believed there to be no essential difference between giving time, energy, spiritual guidance, or money to those in need. He never sought fame and was content to remain in the background on many of the national and international projects and initiatives in which he played a critical role. Because of his philanthropy, he made a unique contribution to and significant difference in the lives of countless American citizens.

EARLY COMMITMENT TO EDUCATIONAL EXCELLENCE AND HELPING OTHERS

As a boy in Daytona, Florida, Howard Thurman proved to be a bright and eager student. He excelled in elementary school and became the first Negro child from Daytona to attend school past the seventh grade and earn a high school diploma. The story is worth telling.

Thurman's elementary school principal, Professor Howard, believed that young Thurman had exceptional promise and could challenge and break an insidious educational barrier long established under Florida's Jim Crow laws which limited access to high school for black Floridians. Professor Howard tutored Thurman on the eighth grade curriculum and, when he felt the young scholar was ready, petitioned the white superintendent for permission to administer the eighth grade exam. The superintendent, suspicious about the request, insisted on administering the test personally. Thurman passed with excellent marks.

With this accomplishment, Thurman became an educational trailblazer in Daytona, but an obvious problem remained. Daytona did not have a black high school. In fact, there were only two public high schools for blacks in the entire state of Florida in the 1910s. Thurman had earned the qualifications to get into high school but lacked a local school to attend. Although public black high schools were scarce, private schools—many operated by black churches—were not. The closest school of this type was in nearby Jacksonville, Florida, where, fortunately, the Thurman family had cousins who were willing to provide young Howard with lodging. Thurman, with his family's blessing, applied to and was accepted at Jacksonville Baptist Academy. The year was 1915.

Because of his academic abilities, Jacksonville Baptist Academy offered him a scholarship to cover tuition expenses, but the Thurman family lacked the resources to provide their emerging scholar with new clothes, sturdy luggage, or sufficient funds for traveling and living. Thurman borrowed an old trunk from a neighbor to transport his belongings, which was in such bad shape it was without a lock or handles. He had to use a piece of rope to tie it securely. After saying goodbye to his family, he made his way alone to the train station. Thurman only had enough funds for his train fare and thought he could keep the trunk with him as he traveled. He soon found, however, that the condition of his trunk (no handles) required that it be sent as freight. This would cost more than Thurman had and he instantly felt defeated. As he sat crying, a tall black man wearing overalls and a denim conductor's cap approached and asked him what he was crying for. Upon hearing Thurman's story, the stranger reached into his pocket and paid the freight for the trunk, intimating that if Thurman was trying to get out of town to get an education, this was a small price to pay. Thurman had never seen the man before, nor ever would again, yet his act of philanthropy changed Thurman's life, by both enabling him to continue his education and modeling the kind of service to others that would become a hallmark of Thurman's professional career.

While traveling to Jacksonville by train, Thurman, overcome with humility and gratitude and a clear sense of his humble station in life, promised God two things: (1) that after he got an education and begun to earn a living, he would care for his mother; and (2) that each year of his life he would save money to give to students trying to get an education. This promise was born out of his sense of duty and indebtedness to the sacrifice and struggle of his grandparents, parents, and the community that nurtured his growth and development. The essence of his philanthropic spirit grew within that context. Thurman clearly understood that his opportunity and success were due, in large measure, to those who had paved his way, and that he had a responsibility to give back to future generations so they too might have opportunities to get an education.

This genuine commitment to giving and service, made when he was 15 years old, set the tone for his future life as a philanthropist. Thurman's four years of high school at Jacksonville Baptist Academy challenged him; he worked hard and excelled in his studies. The Thurman family was a close-knit unit. After his father Solomon's death when he was eight years old, he had a burning need to stay close to his maternal grandmother, mother and two sisters. While in high school, the time away from his family and home community proved difficult, especially when his older sister, Henrietta, died of typhoid fever during his sophomore year. In part, this tragedy moved him toward a career in the ministry.

Thurman graduated at the top of his class in Jacksonville and earned a scholarship to Morehouse College. While still a high school student, Thurman had an opportunity to hear a brilliant young black preacher deliver a sermon. After the sermon, they engaged in conversation and later exchanged correspondence. The preacher was Mordecai Johnson, who simply and frankly advised Thurman to prepare himself for a life of service. This advice later helped him pick a college. Choosing Morehouse College was simple; according to the policy of the time, any of the top black students from Baptist-sponsored high schools could receive scholarships to a black Baptist college. In addition, he would learn to become a man of honor and distinction under the leadership and tutelage of Morehouse president,

John Hope. The sense of mission and service to others was ingrained in Morehouse students of that era. Thurman wrote:

> I was profoundly affected by the sense of mission the college inculcated in us. We understood that our job was to learn so that we could go back into our communities and teach others. Many of the students were going into the ministry; many were the sons of ministers, which accounted in some measure for the missionary spirit of the place. But over and above this, we were always inspired to keep alive our responsibility to the many, many others who had not been fortunate enough to go to college.[16]

He proved to be a superior student and graduated at the top of the Morehouse class of 1923, a class that boasted several prominent future black leaders, such as James M. Nabrit, Jr., and Martin Luther King, Sr. With his mind set on becoming a Baptist minister, he attended Rochester Theological Seminary from 1923–26. Again, Thurman finished at the top of the class.

While the freight fare from the unknown man at the train station helped launch Thurman's educational career, he worked hard to make sure he could stay in school. Each summer he returned to Daytona to earn money for the following school year. In the summer after his first year at Jacksonville Baptist Academy he worked as a shoeshine boy, and as he worked he would often take note of the large homes belonging to wealthy white people on the other side of the Halifax River. One of those winter homes belonged to James N. Gamble of the Proctor and Gamble Company. Knowing that Mr. Gamble's monetary giving addressed some of the social needs of Daytona's black community and that Gamble contributed to the Daytona Educational and Industrial Training School, founded by Mary McLeod Bethune, Thurman boldly decided to write a letter to ask for his financial assistance. In doing so he practiced the philosophy he would later preach, namely, that people must work hard for themselves but that sometimes even those who do will need help from others.

While pondering what to say in the letter and how he might get Gamble's address, a white woman asked Thurman to mail some letters for her. Coincidentally, one of the letters was addressed to Mr. James Gamble in Cincinnati, Ohio. Taking advantage of this good fortune, Thurman sent his letter to Gamble and soon after received a favorable reply. Gamble agreed to help and sent Thurman five dollars each month throughout his high school and college years. Thurman and Gamble corresponded regularly during those years, and their relationship ultimately benefited Thurman far beyond the modest monthly stipend.

ESTABLISHING RELATIONSHIPS WITH WHITE PHILANTHROPISTS

During Thurman's junior year at Morehouse College he represented the student body at the national meeting of the Colored Men's Division of the YMCA in

Cincinnati. Several of the major players in American philanthropy were present: Jesse Moreland, senior secretary of the YMCA; Julius Rosenwald, owner of Sears Roebuck and a strong supporter of Negro education through the famous Rosenwald schools; John R. Mott, a leading figure in the YMCA organization, an internationally known Christian leader, and recipient of the 1946 Nobel Peace Prize; and James N. Gamble. Thurman interacted with all of these men at the conference, hearing them speak and engaging them in conversation. He left a favorable impression on several of them, such as Moreland and Mott, which led to his long-time affiliation with the YMCA. These two men were influential on an international level and often invited Thurman to serve the mission of the Y in multiple capacities. This particular association led to Thurman serving on the YMCA's national speaker's circuit and being invited to lead a goodwill pilgrimage to India in the early 1930s.

This conference proved beneficial in many ways. In addition to giving Thurman an opportunity to meet and begin a professional relationship with several white philanthropists, he finally met Mr. Gamble. According to Thurman, they enjoyed a pleasant visit including a chauffeured limousine tour of the city and dinner at a restaurant overlooking the city. Throughout their time together Gamble referred to him as "Mr. Thurman." This was significant to Thurman because he was unaccustomed to that level of respect and deference from a white man. When it was time to go their separate ways, Mr. Gamble exited the car at his office building in downtown Cincinnati and instructed the chauffeur to drive Thurman back to the YMCA. With Gamble out of the car and the young black man still seated in the back of the limousine, the chauffeur told Thurman to sit up front. Thurman immediately understood that the white chauffeur did not want to be seen driving a black man in the back seat as a lone passenger. Thurman refused, remained in the back seat, and contemplated his future as a leader and champion for social justice.[17]

Thurman carried himself with a quiet dignity that signaled his confidence, perceptiveness, and intellect. He was a thoughtful man, who never spoke without thinking and found ways to connect with those around him in non-threatening ways. Thurman intentionally tried to associate with broad-minded people who were in positions of influence and who felt improvements in racial relations were desirable and possible. Because Thurman was a Christian minister, he moved in religious circles where some interracial interaction occurred on a regular basis. Many of these whites were often willing to invest time and resources to affecting social change. Through his associations with men like Gamble and Mott, doors of opportunity opened for him that otherwise might not have, and he in turn was able to open doors for others. Further, these personal relationships strengthened his faith in the possibilities of improved interracial relationships. The Howard Thurman archives contain hundreds of pages of correspondence between Thurman and leading national and international figures in religious and educational circles, revealing a network of connections that was both broad and deep. These documents reveal connections that spanned most of the twentieth century and illuminated how Thurman was influenced by and had influence on many civic, religious, and educational leaders. Throughout his professional experiences in the 1920s and 1930s, Thurman kept the promise he made on the train to Jacksonville. In the mid-1940s, his monetary giving began to include brokering gifts from others.

NEGOTIATING THE GIVING OF OTHERS

From his youthful pledge to save money to help others get an education, Thurman moved toward serving as a conduit for financial philanthropy. By the mid-1940s, Thurman had established a national reputation as a preacher and lecturer. He was in constant demand to speak at colleges, churches, and YMCA- and YWCA-sponsored events. Thurman traveled a great deal. This enabled him to spread his messages of inward spiritual development and social and racial justice and earned him the respect of many good-willed people. Many whites who heard him speak felt moved to help Negro people and their causes, particularly educational institutions. With an engaging personality, intellectually stimulating messages and sermons, and a mild, solemn speaking style, Thurman engendered high levels of trust and spiritual commitment from a wide spectrum of people. He often received letters from people who heard him speak at their college or in their hometowns and felt moved to offer financial help to fight the social and racial inequities embedded in American culture. This type of influence is difficult to measure but hard to ignore. One such person was Annie Herkner from Philadelphia, who had heard Thurman speak at the Unitarian church in the Germantown neighborhood.

In a handwritten letter dated April 17, 1946, she requested information from Thurman on some "colored schools" where she might make a gift upon her passing.[18] Thurman replied and suggested several institutions worthy of such a legacy: Palmer Memorial Institute, Morehouse College, and Howard University. Besides these institutions as recipients of Herkner's generosity, Thurman suggested that he serve as the custodian of her gift. Thurman noted that several of his friends contributed to a fund he maintained for helping needy Negro students. Clearly, Thurman's entrée into economic philanthropic initiatives and his intent to give to others in a practical as well as a spiritual manner merged into the fabric of his professional practice. His agency in giving and facilitating the giving of others manifested itself over the course of his long career in higher education.

Another measure of his giving is illustrated in his mentorship of black leaders. Through his dedication he provided guidance to many civil rights leaders, from Whitney Young, Bayard Rustin, and Martin Luther King, Jr., to Vernon Jordan,

Barbara Jordan, and Jesse Jackson. Thurman's mentorship was both formal, through his teaching and relationship with students during his years at Morehouse and Spelman Colleges and Howard and Boston Universities, and informal through his conversations with those seeking his wisdom and advice. Jackson considered Thurman as a "Jackie Robinson of the academic world" and plainly acknowledged the tremendous impact Thurman had on him and many others:

> Dr. Thurman was a teacher of teachers, a leader of leaders, a preacher of preachers. No small wonder, then, that Martin Luther King, Jr., Whitney Young, Samuel Proctor, Vernon Jordan, Otis Moss, and I sat at his feet, for we knew it was a blessing to give this prophet a glass of water or to touch the hem of his garment. . . . [19]

SPIRITUALITY AS A GUIDING FORCE

Thurman's definition and understanding of spirituality was centered on the inward journey of human beings to find not only the essence of their belief in God but also to find themselves and their true humanity. The titles of many of his books, such as *Deep Is the Hunger, The Inward Journey,* and *The Centering Moment,* reveal the thinking of a man who was focused on addressing questions of basic human existence in a world that is often cold, harsh, and without love. Thurman grounded much of his thinking on the "love ethic" found in the teachings of Jesus.[20] The notion of loving those who hate, despise, and would do you harm is an ideal that is extremely difficult to accomplish. Yet it was exactly this level of love that Jesus recommended and practiced. He loved his own people although they rejected him and questioned his motives; he found love for the Romans under whose oppression he and other marginalized people lived, and he loved other groups, who were also oppressed by the Romans but who might have had little use for Hebrews. In this same vein, Thurman believed that blacks could love whites despite of the oppressive nature of segregation and that whites could love black people despite the legacy of racism, white supremacy, and hate that permeated the fabric of American life. Martin Luther King, Jr. would adopt this love ethic perspective in his belief and practice of nonviolence as the only acceptable approach to social change. Refusing to adhere to narrow interpretations of the Bible or a blanket rejection of the legitimacy of other faith traditions, Thurman sought to link his belief and training in Christian doctrine with an awareness of the inherent value of other belief systems.

One example of Thurman's life-long pursuit of an in-depth spiritual meaning and the willingness to expand beyond his own religious training was when he studied for six months with the Quaker theologian and mystic, Rufus Jones. A professor at Haverford College, Jones provided Thurman with an opportunity to search inwardly for a greater understanding of God and how to address the condition of the human soul.[21] This experience greatly influenced Thurman's thinking and strengthened his resolve to continue to search for ways to create community among all people. He developed his firm belief and understanding of the power of the inner life while studying with Jones, and this became a central element of his personal spirituality and his theology. Thurman was sincere in his search for spiritual common ground about notions of God regardless of faith traditions, nature, and humankind. His work in higher education and teaching to others reflected his belief in the potential of education combined with personal spiritual growth to lift the soul and develop higher principles for those who seek knowledge and a better life.

CONCLUSION

Thurman understood the complexities of racial identity politics and the major obstacles it created in establishing common ground in American life. During Thurman's ministry and service in higher education, he confronted many spiritual and secular issues, such as the development of the individual human spirit and intellect, the strengths and limitations of Christianity, being black in America, American race relations, and ways to create and promote concepts of ethical leadership and community. His service at Howard University and Boston University, in particular, illustrated his commitment to teaching and providing spiritual guidance to college students, knowing full well that his influence would shape, in some way, their future lives. Thurman's willingness to tirelessly travel across the country to preach and deliver lectures was another means of influencing countless numbers of people, both black and white. By spreading his message of the importance of inner spiritual development, his vision of interracial understanding and reconciliation, and his perceptive challenging of the social norms and limitations of American religious life, Thurman separated himself from many of his peers to become a sage-like figure who possessed a unique understanding of and instinct for changing the individual life in order to change society and the world. These spiritual, intellectual, and moral explorations formed the landscape of his life's work, which remains deeply important yet largely unknown to the public. The narrative of the black experience in America is inextricably linked to Thurman's life story. The lessons he learned in his youth, his strong sense of pride and self-reliance, the power of faith and spirituality, the indisputable value of education and the pursuit of excellence, and the virtue of giving back to his family, community, and society, all establish Howard Thurman as a model of black philanthropy. This sense of collective agency and philanthropy as a survival and perseverance strategy connects Thurman to the legacy of black leaders who dedicated their lives to helping other blacks and the wider society.

Through his vocation Howard Thurman dedicated his life to helping other people. The conscious choice to become a minister and educator was a practical way to serve others and pursue his own need for spiritual and intellectual growth. Perhaps it was his way of returning a blessing he received as a young boy. Remembering the stranger who helped him pay his train fare, Thurman returned that gesture of kindness to countless others in many ways throughout his long and fruitful life. One only needs to read the biography or autobiography of any number of black leaders of the nineteenth or early twentieth century to discover the common themes of philanthropy, agency, and an unwavering commitment to serving the collective uplift of other blacks they might never know personally. It is in this tradition of unselfish giving and commitment to making a way out of no way that is also a part of Thurman's legacy.

NOTES

1. Raymond Gavins, *The Perils and Prospect of Southern Black Leadership: Gordon Blaine Hancock, 1884–1970* (Durham: Duke University Press, 1977), 5.
2. Matthew Allen, "Howard Thurman: Paradoxical Savior," *Journal of Negro History* 77 (spring 1992): 84–96.
3. Albert J. Raboteau, *Slave Religion: The Invisible Institution in the Antebellum South* (New York: Oxford University Press, 1980); Hans A. Baer and Merrill Singer, *African American Religion in the Twentieth Century: Varieties of Protest and Accommodation* (Knoxville: University of Tennessee, 1992).
4. Carter Julian Savage, "Cultural Capital and African American Agency: The Economic Struggle for Effective Education for African Americans in Franklin, Tennessee, 1890–1967," *Journal of African American History* 87 (spring 2002): 206-236. The author begins the article with a story about an ex-slave farmer in Tuskegee, Alabama, who attended a meeting called by Booker T. Washington in the early 1880s as he tried to raise funds from local blacks to start Tuskegee Institute. The farmer, lacking money to give and compelled by a love for his race and a sincere hope for the prosperity of future generations, offered to donate one of his two hogs to help Washington establish Tuskegee Institute.
5. Rodney M. Jackson, "Strengthening African American Philanthropy Fund Raising," in *At the Crossroads: The Proceedings of the First National Conference on Black Philanthropy*, ed. Rodney M. Jackson (Oakton, VA: The Corporation for Philanthropy, Inc., 1998), 142.
6. Emmett D. Carson, "African American Philanthropy at the Crossroads," in *At the Crossroads: The Proceedings of the First National Conference on Black Philanthropy*, ed. R. M. Jackson (Oakton, VA: The Corporation for Philanthropy, Inc., 1998), 2
7. Lawrence J. Friedman and Mark D. McGarvie, eds., *Charity, Philanthropy, and Civility in American History* (New York: Cambridge University Press, 2003). Friedman and McGarvie describe philanthropy in broad terms and include the statement, "In our view, the giver's intent becomes an acid test to distinguish who is and who is not a philanthropist," 2.
8. Howard Thurman, *With Head and Heart: The Autobiography of Howard Thurman* (New York: Harcourt Brace & Company, 1979), 23.
9. Ibid., 12.
10. Howard Thurman, *The Luminous Darkness: A Personal Interpretation of the Anatomy of Segregation and the Ground of Hope.* (New York: Harper & Row, 1965), 8.

11. James D. Anderson, *The Education of Blacks in the South, 1860–1935* (Chapel Hill: the University of North Carolina Press, 1988); John Hope Franklin and August Meier, eds., *Black Leaders of the Twentieth Century* (Chicago: University of Illinois Press, 1982); Samuel DeWitt Proctor, *The Substance of Things Hoped for: A Memoir of African American Faith* (Valley Forge, PA: Judson Press, 1995); Lea E. Williams, *Servants of the People: The 1960s Legacy of African American Leadership* (New York: St. Martin's Griffin, 1998).

12. Anderson, *The Education of Blacks in the South*, 5.

13. Walter Fluker, *They Looked for a City: A Comparative Analysis of the Ideal of Community in the Thought of Howard Thurman and Martin Luther King, Jr.* (Lanham: University of America Press, 1989), 37.

14. Thurman, *The Luminous Darkness*, x.

15. Conrad Cherry, Betty A. DeBerg, and Amanda Porterfield, *Religion on Campus* (Chapel Hill: The University of North Carolina Press, 2001); Frederick Rudolph, *The American College & University: A History* (Athens: The University of Georgia Press, 1990).

16. Thurman, *With Head and Heart*, 35.

17. Thurman, *With Head and Heart*.

18. The Howard Thurman Collection in the Mugar Memorial Library at Boston University contains many letters of this type that substantiates Thurman's role as a broker for the giving of others.

19. George Makechnie, *Howard Thurman: His Enduring Dream* (Boston: The Howard Thurman Center, Boston University, 1988), 81.

20. Howard Thurman, *Jesus and the Disinherited* (Boston: Beacon Press, 1976).

21. Throughout his life, Thurman pursued relationships and learning opportunities with other religious thinkers and leaders. One example is his independent study with Rufus Jones; another is visiting with Mohandas Gandhi in a 1935 trip to India. Thurman provides detailed descriptions of both experiences in his autobiography.

CHAPTER TEN

Quiet Grace, Clothed Spirit

Oseola McCarty and the Benevolence of a Gift

MARCI M. MIDDLETON

The year 1995 was marked by such national newsmaking events as the first all-female crew winning the America's Cup race; Bonnie Blair skating to a new woman's record in the 500 meter; the Mississippi House of Representatives ratifying the Thirteenth Amendment (almost 130 years after it was written); Shannon Faulkner becoming the first woman to attend a previously all-male public military college; and the bombing of the Federal building in Oklahoma City. These events all garnered national media attention and were important stories for days and even weeks. As is typical, the everyday activities of individuals helping one another within their communities barely registered in the national mind that year. Yet such philanthropic activities—actions expressing love and care for fellow human beings—continued without interruption. This was the year when the activities of one individual, Oseola McCarty, inspired the nation to rekindle the embers of giving and realize the spirit of philanthropy.

In July 1995, Oseola McCarty, a simple laundress for over seventy-five years, donated $150,000 to the University of Southern Mississippi. This chapter will provide a historical analysis of McCarty's gift and will offer an examination of the factors that led to the donation, particularly McCarty's reasons for choosing the University of Southern Mississippi as the recipient of her donation. In addition, the chapter will focus on McCarty's contributions to the community, her views on financial stewardship, and the importance she placed on establishing and maintaining long-term relationships. Given Oseola's extreme self-denial, it would be easy to pass her actions off as an anomaly: an act of an eccentric and one not likely to be repeated by others. In fact, Oseola's actions are the product of a philanthropic spirit present in the African American community that has the potential to be tapped and nurtured.

Philanthropy is an integral part of society in general and is of particular importance to the African American community. Throughout their history Americans of African descent have provided resources, even when scarce, to assist community members and organizations dedicated to racial uplift. The merging and redistribution of wealth and resources is often facilitated by church and civic-related agencies in addition to individual efforts. Philanthropy, as defined for this chapter, pertains to gifts of funds, time, or property used to address immediate needs or provide access and opportunities to others as a means of remediating and absolving the inequities of the past and the dismal circumstances of the present. Philanthropy is also presented as an everyday behavior because the spirit of giving and helping others is simply considered a way of life or, rather, what one is "supposed to do" in the African American community. Such selfless acts of generosity, benevolence, and trust are commonplace among Blacks and are extended inward to immediate family members and outward to those in the broader community.[1]

According to a University of Southern Mississippi press release, the 87-year-old McCarty wanted to "help somebody's child go to college, someone who would appreciate it and learn."[2] McCarty, a laundress for three generations of White families in Hattiesburg, Mississippi, saved monies from her earnings over the course of her lifetime. Her gift exemplifies King Davis's postulation that "social, economic, and political control and power over the environment and institutions in the community strongly correlate with Black philanthropy."[3] The inspiration behind McCarty's gift was magnified by her lack of discretionary income coupled with personal experiences involving educational and economic barriers—barriers that were eclipsed by the triumph of the human spirit. According to Brian O'Connell's book *America's Voluntary Spirit*, "the ultimate mark of dignity will be the use of more time, and more resources on voluntary service."[4] This use of existing resources is tied to the values placed on freedom and the ability to positively impact on institutions directly by appealing to human needs.

The early years of the twentieth century were turbulent for Mississippians, particularly African Americans. The tenant system, lumber, and sawmills were the economic drivers of a state that had previously relied on cotton, sharecropping, family labor, and slavery. The 1907 boll weevil invasion that destroyed cotton increased Mississippi's reliance on lumber as its greatest resource. The state's available income was low, and the amount spent on education ranked at the bottom of the country. State-provided facilities for education were poor, and the state practiced a strictly segregated system of education. Governor James Vardaman, in his 1903 campaign for re-election, preached racist hate and proposed that many Black schools close because there was no value in educating African Americans. The governor's campaign of hatred was heightened by the recognition given to such persons as Booker T. Washington by former president Theodore Roosevelt. Vardaman felt that honoring Washington by letting him dine at the White House was a slap in the face of American Whites. This southern governor's administration lasted until the time of Oseola McCarty's birth.

Born in 1908 in D'Lo, Mississippi to Lucy McCarty, by age 5 Oseola was living in Hattiesburg with her grandmother Julia and her aunt Evelyn. Lucy McCarty and her husband (Oseola's stepfather) moved to Chicago to find better job opportunities. They had no family ties in the northern city and therefore placed Oseola with family members in the south rather than with strangers in the north.

Oseola McCarty followed her grandmother into the laundering business, learning how to wash clothes and make soap. According to Evelyn Coleman's portrayal of life in Hattiesburg and the early years of Oseola McCarty, the following is a vivid description of young Oseola's introduction to the principles of work and laundering:

> Sometimes Ola [Oseola] stopped playing to watch her grandmother drop clothes into the big black iron wash pot. She watched the fire spark underneath it. The clothes boiled and bubbled inside this pot that had been in the family for many years. Next, her grandmother took a long stick and moved the steaming clothes from the wash pot to metal washtubs. Ola scrubbed clothes along the ridges of a metal scrubboard [sic]. When the clothes were clean, she dipped them into a tub of clear water and then squeezed them for a second rinsing. The clothes were wrung tightly by hand and placed on line to dry. Oseola also watched her grandmother make lye soap in a wash pot by witnessing the use of leftover cooking grease as one ingredient in the process. As the grease boiled, crystals of red lye were added. Then the mixture boiled and was stirred until it was smooth and thick. The soap was placed in a square pan to cool and cut into bars.[5]

Laundering was a physically grueling, lengthy, and menial chore. In Faye Dudden's description of washing from diaries of nineteenth-century house servants, we see a similar glimpse of the hard work and physical effort involved in becoming a laundress, including the difficulties borne by the laborer to save money and subsist on such work:

> . . . The entry 'washed' in Phebe Eastman's diary meant that she had done a laundry, a major daylong effort that began with stoking large fires to heat the water. Using hard well water complicated the task: one woman recalled that she had to spend half of every washday softening the water by adding lye, boiling, stirring, and skimming. Hauling water, hand-wringing wet clothes, and lifting and carrying tubs to empty them made washing hard physical labor. . . .[6]

As the family worked together to maintain the household, McCarty's involvement in the business evolved from delivery person to participant and producer of outcomes associated with the labor of cleaning clothes. After Oseola's stepfather died in a drowning accident, her mother moved back to Hattiesburg where a strong work ethic and the value of saving were part of a daily regimen for the family's livelihood. The entire family worked to sustain the home and daily existence.

Oseola stopped attending elementary school to care for her sick aunt while her grandmother supported the family. As Aunt Evelyn recuperated Oseola returned to school. At this point she had not progressed with her other classmates and was behind a few grades. She still had to help at home with the laundry. The long days began with an early start and ended late, leaving few hours for study and school. Illness in the family and an obligation to care for her aunt thwarted McCarty's plans to return to school after sixth grade. She became a laundress full time. "From about 1920 to 1935, Black washerwomen in Mississippi made from fifty cents to one dollar and fifty cents per bundle. Some clients put as many clothes as possible in one bundle."[7] It was during these early days of doing laundry that McCarty opened her first account at a Hattiesburg bank.

Church attendance was a key aspect of the McCarty household. Oseola and her grandmother walked to Friendship Baptist Church to worship each Sunday. They read the Bible aloud to one another, and Oseola was baptized as a teenager in the church pond. McCarty's grandmother and aunt faced increased illnesses as they aged. While in the hospital attending to family members, McCarty admired the nurses and their uniforms and described them as uniformed angels because of the care they provided to those in need. She aspired to become a nurse and regretted the fact that she had not returned to school earlier. During this period, McCarty studied with a local beautician until she received her license as a hairdresser. Upon completing her license, she started beautician services for neighboring clients in her home. Facing the first of a series of deaths in the family, in particular the loss of her grandmother in 1944, McCarty assumed ultimate responsibility for the laundering business.

With the loss of her mother in 1964 and the death of her aunt in 1967, McCarty remained self-sufficient by providing laundry services to White members of the community and beautification services to African Americans in her neighborhood. The tiny home in which she resided was a gift of property from her Uncle John who had worked at the Hercules Powder Company in Hattiesburg. As McCarty's savings grew to a sizable amount, bank personnel advised her to conservatively place portions of her money into CDs and mutual fund accounts. Living frugally, she never owned a vehicle, usually walked or used public transportation, and by 1996 had only recently purchased an air conditioner. In addition, she was able to charge far more for her labor than previously, earning $5.00 to $20.00 for each bundle of laundry.

As McCarty's savings grew, her health began to wane. Nancy Odom and Ellen Vinzant, two employees of Trustmark Bank, became concerned about McCarty's personal welfare and often discussed her future and health. These women attended to McCarty's personal interests upon the deaths of her immediate family members. Odom explained "We both talked with her about her fund and what [would happen] to her if something happened. . . . She knew she needed someone to take care of her."[8] It was at this point that McCarty became interested in providing funds to the University of Southern Mississippi because she relished the chance to become a social change agent by providing opportunities to others that had not been available to her.

The University of Southern Mississippi was located in an area that was the "hub of four major railroads."[9] Administrators of the institution designed a public educational experience that was both practical and professional with a focus on equipping teachers for the public schools. The first matriculates were a minimum of 15 years old, and the academic prerequisite was satisfactory completion of the common school course.[10] The University of Southern Mississippi was an institution that Oseola would never have been allowed to attend due to the racial discrimination during her lifetime.

The discussion of the gift to the University of Southern Mississippi had its beginnings with a dialogue between McCarty and Paul Laughlin, Trustmark Bank's assistant vice president and trust officer. The idea was then discussed with Jimmy Frank McKenzie, one of McCarty's clients and her personal attorney. As McCarty determined to whom her estate and wealth would be given, the bank personnel used analogies of dimes divided between charities to make sure that any final decisions were solely McCarty's and not the will of Trustmark Bank or her personal attorney. In the end, McCarty decided that her accumulated savings, $150,000, would be donated to the University of Southern Mississippi. The gift was the result of savings from her lifetime earnings and the appropriation of property from deceased relatives. According to historian Marybeth Gasman, McCarty was a deeply religious person who "gave 10 percent of her assets to her church." Gasman also notes that Oseola believed that education and religion should be the focal point of one's life.[11] Smith et al. in *Philanthropy in Communities of Color*, characterize African American philanthropy as addressing "reciprocity, fair play, equality, and graciousness."[12] McCarty epitomized this, as a University of Southern Mississippi news release that quoted her demonstrated: "I just want the scholarship to go to some child who needs it, to whoever is not able to help their children. . . . I'm too old to get an education, but they can."[13]

McCarty's expression of philanthropy also speaks to her role as a caregiver to several individuals within the community. Her gift was a means for her to vicariously realize a dream of becoming a nurse through the educational aspirations and accomplishments of others. The gift that keeps on giving was bestowed in the form of a scholarship to Stephanie Bullock, the University of Southern Mississippi's first recipient of the Oseola McCarty Scholarship. In addition to the gift, a sense of community was perpetuated with a heightened awareness of kinship. According to *Southern Miss News* Bullock's mother, Leedrester Bullock, exclaimed, "I feel like she's got another grandmother . . . this is the kind of thing your family does for you."[14] According to the University of Southern Mississippi, the tuition scholarship gives "priority consideration to those deserving African American students who clearly demonstrate financial need."[15] Interestingly, Bullock indicated in an interview that she was worried about how her family would afford college. In a reflection on the circumstances leading to the awarding of the scholarship, Bullock said, "I told my parents that I don't like growing up because there's too much to worry about."[16] Bullock's concern is indicative of the lack of opportunities for young people who are unable to realize their educational aspirations due to limited financial resources.

In response to her donation, McCarty received several gifts of art, pictures, honorary diplomas, and special recognitions. In her typical humble style, she, in turn, gave them to the university. McCarty explained, "I love 'em all, but I just don't have room for them. I gave 'em to the school."[17] McCarty further explained that there were no small or large rewards but rather that she was proud of all of them. Suffering from arthritis, McCarty retired in 1994 at age 86. Upon donating the gift, she received an honorary degree from Harvard University, an Award in 1996 from *Essence* magazine, the Presidential Citizens Medal from President Clinton, several other awards, and the first honorary degree in the history of the University of Southern Mississippi on May 15, 1998. The University of Southern Mississippi indicated that McCarty showed quiet grace in the wake of the excitement surrounding her gift to the institution. Institutional press records show that this was the single largest gift given to the institution by one individual. McCarty's gift sparked additional contributions and a private fundraising campaign to match the donation. According to *Southern Miss News*, "contributions began pouring in from scattered locations across the nation to the USM Foundation, which administers the scholarship fund, and more than $65,000 had been raised as of mid-September 1995."[18] Had the spirit of social change evident in the culture permeated to the state's college-level educational system? Oseola McCarty's gift is particularly interesting when one notes the unflattering history of the University of Southern Mississippi in the early 1970s:

The university had a racist past that was symbolized by the school's mascot. Sexism pervaded the college community such that a professor could be fired for having a baby or missing a day of work due to the pregnancy. Professors suffered cuts by serving as delegates to the Democratic Party National Convention and the administration censored the student newspaper.[19]

Although such recollections were part of the University of Southern Mississippi's past, the institution itself and others in the state became change agents for the future. McCarty's gift to the University of Southern Mississippi inspired others to promote social change, give to the institution, and provide access to opportunities for students who did not have the necessary financial resources. Through her donation to one of the city's leading institutions, McCarty was emboldened to interact with the community at one level as that of domestic employee to a select few, to another level as liberator and care-giver to many. McCarty's concerns were given voice by the fact that the resultant scholarship was awarded to students in her name. In addition, McCarty's philanthropic action was highly publicized within the local community and through the university's fund-raising, alumni, and student literature. In a memorable statement at the time of the announcement, she said, "I can't do everything, but I can do something to help somebody."[20] McCarty's act of philanthropy was only matched by her grace. To many, her gift represented more than mere financial assistance but rather a demonstration that the world was filled with persons who were altruistic in their giving. McCarty's philanthropic action, although unexpectedly large, is indicative of the kind of giving that is prevalent in many African American communities—selfless acts that further the race.

NOTES

1. Emmett Carson, *A Hand Up* (Washington, D.C.: The Joint Center for Political and Economic Studies, 1993).

2. Sharon Wertz, "Oseola McCarty donates $150,000 to USM." Hattiesburg (MS) *Southern Miss News*, July 1995.

3. King E. Davis, *Fundraising in the Black Community: History, Feasibility and Conflict* (Metuchen: The Scarecrow Press, Inc., 1980), 124.

4. Brian O'Connell, ed., *America's Voluntary Spirit: A Book of Readings* (New York: The Foundation Center, 1983), 284.

5. Evelyn Coleman, *The Riches of Oseola McCarty* (New York: Albert Whitman & Company, 1998), 12.

6. Faye Dudden, *Serving Women: Household Service in Nineteenth-Century America* (Middletown: Wesleyan University Press), 106.

7. Coleman, *The Riches of Oseola McCarty*, 22.

8. Wertz, "Oseola McCarty Donates $150,000 to USM."
9. Chester Morgan, *Dearly Bought, Deeply Treasured: The University of Southern Mississippi, 1912–1987* (Jackson: The University Press of Mississippi, 1987), 5.
10. Morgan, *Dearly Bought, Deeply Treasured*, 16.
11. Marybeth Gasman, "Oseola McCarty, Laundress and Traditional African American Philanthropist," in Robert T. Grimm, ed., *Notable American Philanthropists* (Westport, CT: Greenwood Publishing Group, 2002).
12. Bradford Smith, Sylvia Shue, Jennifer Lisa Vest, and Joseph Villarreal, *Philanthropy in Communities of Color* (Indianapolis: Indiana University Press, 1999), 36.
13. Wertz, "Oseola McCarty Donates $150,000 to USM."
14. Wertz, "Oseola McCarty Donates $150,000 to USM."
15. Sharon Wertz, "Stephanie Bullock Receives 1st McCarty Scholarship," Hattiesburg (MS) *Southern Miss News*, August 1995.
16. Wertz, "Stephanie Bullock Receives 1st McCarty Scholarship."
17. Sharon Wertz, "Oseola McCarty's Gift Keeps Right on Giving: A One-year Review of Miss McCarty's Activities," Hattiesburg (MS) *Southern Miss News*, July 1996.
18. Wertz, "Stephanie Bullock Receives 1st McCarty Scholarship."
19. Monte Piliawsky, *Exit 13: Oppression and Racism in Academia* (Boston: South End Press, 1982), xi.
20. Wertz, "Oseola McCarty Donates $150,000 to USM."

CHAPTER ELEVEN

A Gift OF Art

Jacob Lawrence as Philanthropist

EDWARD M. EPSTEIN

I've always been interested in history, but they never taught Negro history in the public schools ... I don't see how a history of the United States can be written without honestly including the Negro.

—JACOB LAWRENCE[1]

Art is either plagiarism or revolution.

—PAUL GAUGUIN[2]

Throughout history, artists have longed to know that their work has an impact on the world around them. In former times, society furnished the artist with a neat framework in which this could take place. During the European Renaissance, for example, artists typically worked for the church—ensuring a certain role, audience, and content for the work of art. In the modern era, however, the function of art became disconnected from the society around it. It became fashionable to speak of the artist as one who toiled alone in the studio, waiting for a chance to inspire a yet-undefined mass of viewers. And it was given to the artist to eke out a role for him- or herself: to bridge the gaps between cultural heritage, economic resources, and audience.[3] One artist who did this very nicely was Jacob Lawrence. A Black man living in a White-dominated world, Lawrence found a role that was unique to the racially charged atmosphere of his time. He availed himself of the tools of western modernism in order to provide a window into the society and culture from which he came—showing in a highly individual and sometimes humorous way its history, hopes, fears, and flaws.

The idea of the socially conscious artist is a specifically modern one and one which grew out of nineteenth-century debates about the role of art. It is the type of role proposed by French writer and social critic Pierre Joseph Proudhon, who said that the aim of art is "to improve us, help us and save us." Throughout his life, Proudhon associated himself with painters of ordinary life like Gustave Courbet and advocated a type of realism in which "man will become his own mirror, and he will learn how to contemplate his soul through studying his true countenance."[4] Lawrence, whose work mirrored the history and struggles of African Americans (along with those of all of humanity), is often described as a socially conscious artist.

Philanthropy is frequently defined as the giving of monetary gifts, but recent scholarship on the topic has expanded this definition to include many forms of service to a community. Thus, a person of modest means who gives of his or her time and talent might also be considered a philanthropist. Jacob Lawrence was just such a person. He gave in conventional ways (i.e., donations of time and money to civil rights causes), but in a certain sense his entire oeuvre, with its broad social impact, was also a contribution to society. At the end of his life he established a foundation to continue this work—to educate the public about his art and to promote the work of other African American artists.

The question raised by this chapter, then, is in what sense is an artist also a philanthropist? Can philanthropy be used as a model to describe the work of an artist like Jacob Lawrence—a politically active individual in his art and life? From modest beginnings, this African American painter and printmaker went on to produce a body of work that was innovative in style but also gave us a new picture of the lives of African Americans. In the process, Lawrence contributed to the support system for Black artists in America. In particular, he worked to push aside notions of cultural inferiority that kept Blacks from contributing to mainstream American life. Along the way, Lawrence made some contributions, such as donating limited edition prints of his work to help non-profit causes, which fit traditional notions of philanthropy. But more broadly, this chapter asserts that the things Lawrence 'gave' on a regular basis—as a part of his everyday work life—can also be considered bequests to the world.

LAWRENCE'S PATH TO ARTISTIC ACCOMPLISHMENT

Born in Atlantic City, New Jersey, in 1917, Jacob Lawrence followed an unlikely path toward a career in art. After his parents separated, he spent several years living in foster homes. When he moved back to his mother's house in Harlem in 1930 he had his first real exposure to art. While his mother struggled to make ends meet

during the Depression, Lawrence found an early outlet for his creativity in community art classes run by Charles Alston at the Utopia Children's House in Harlem.
These classes aided greatly in the artist's development and, more importantly,
introduced him to individuals who would play a pivotal role in his early career.
Alston's studio at 306 W. 141st street was known as a meeting place for artists and
cultural luminaries from the Harlem Renaissance, including painter Aaron Douglas,
writer Langston Hughes, and sculptor Augusta Savage.[5]

Both Douglas and Savage would have a profound effect on the young artist's
work. As a painter, Aaron Douglas had pioneered a heroic style of painting that
fused elements of cubism and African sculpture. Described as a "pioneering
Africanist," by Harlem Renaissance activist Alain Locke, Douglas often depicted
traditional religious subjects like the crucifixion and Noah's Ark, but his use of
African-looking figures as the main characters of the stories gave the works a
uniquely Black focus.[6] He also created murals at the 135th Street Library illustrating Blacks' journey to America. Although Lawrence's work would differ in style from
Douglas's, the latter's paintings clearly furnished a precedent for the younger artist,
who would also use the flat, hard-edged shapes of modernist painting to depict
aspects of Black history and show the world from a Black point of view.

Augusta Savage, on the other hand, was a key figure in art education in Harlem
at that time, having opened the Savage Studio of Arts and Crafts in 1932 and the
Uptown Art Lab in 1937. It was in Savage's classes that Lawrence became acquaint-
ed with his future wife, Gwendolyn Knight.[7] Savage took a keen interest in the
young artist, twice escorting him to the Works Progress Administration (WPA)
headquarters to help him gain a commission in the Federal Arts Project.[8] During
the time he was taking Savage's classes (1936–1937), Lawrence created a number
of works that highlighted the social problems plaguing that neighborhood. These
paintings of street scenes, nightlife, and the squalid interiors of Harlem tenements
provided a more candid and unapologetic view than idealized portraits of Black life
painted by the artists of the Harlem Renaissance, including his instructors, Savage
and Alston.

Lawrence completed only two years of high school, dropping out in 1934 and
thereby ending his mother's hopes that he become a postal worker.[9] Instead, he managed to further his education in other ways. As he developed his skills as a painter
in workshops conducted by Alston and Savage, Lawrence became an avid reader,
visiting the nearby 135th Street (later Schomburg) branch of the New York Public
Library. There he perused books on African American history, and was particularly captivated by such Black liberators as Harriet Tubman and Toussaint L'Overture.
Lawrence was also influenced by the teachings of "Professor" Seifert, a carpenter-
turned-lecturer who made frequent speeches about Black history at the library. These
gifts of inspiration from various mentors and role models ignited the artist's life-

long interest in creating an art that was focused on Black history and Black experience.[10]

In time, Lawrence would receive material gifts as well. While learning art from these various mentors and teachers during the 1930s, Lawrence had always supported himself with odd jobs such as delivering papers, working in a laundry and a print shop, and building a dam for the Civilian Conservation Corps.[11] These jobs might have easily distracted him on his march toward becoming a professional artist. Help finally came in 1938, however, when Augusta Savage's efforts paid off, and he was awarded an easel painting commission from the Federal Arts Project. The pay was not spectacular, yet the $23.86 Lawrence earned every week covered the cost of materials and allowed him to rent a corner of Charles Alston's studio at 306 W. 141st Street. Above all, The WPA's Federal Arts Project introduced him to some of the most well-known artists of the time and thereby contributed to the education of an artist who had no opportunity to learn in an academy of art. According to Lawrence, "[This] was my education. I had no college education. . . . They [the WPA artists] used to talk about what was going on in the world. Oh, not only about art, but everything."[12]

Lawrence completed 18 months in the WPA artist's project after which he became the beneficiary of another significant philanthropic source. The Rosenwald Fund, founded by Sears Roebuck tycoon Julius Rosenwald, gave generously to Black education in the south and supported numerous Black scholars and artists. Lawrence was awarded a Rosenwald fellowship in 1940 for the purpose of creating *The Migration of the Negro,* a series of paintings on the early twentieth-century exodus of Blacks from the rural South to the urban North. He used the funds to rent space in a studio building on 125th street that was also home to artist Romare Bearden and writer Claude McKay.[13] Bearden was close in age to Lawrence, and the two had previously shared information on technical issues. But it was Claude McKay in particular who had a strong influence on the young painter. The Jamaican-born poet, novelist, and journalist was known for his defiant verse on Black struggles, essays on Blacks and socialism, and novels that candidly described the lives of ordinary African Americans.[14] Lawrence recalled:

> Claude McKay was a mentor. He was an older man, and I always appreciate him because he spoke to me like a peer. I have a book of his that he inscribed for me, *A Long Way Home.* I think he appreciated me because he was a nationalist, from Jamaica, and I was dealing with this kind of content.[15]

It was not just the nationalistic content that the two had in common. McKay and Lawrence shared an unflinching gaze: both McKay's writing and Lawrence's painting showed the realities of Black life un-softened by the idealism of the Harlem Renaissance.

It was during this time period—the late 1930s and early 1940s—that Lawrence painted some of his most significant works.[16] Bringing together various influences, including his Harlem Renaissance artistic mentors and the reading he did at the 135th Street Library, he completed series depicting the lives of Toussaint L'Overture, Frederick Douglass and Harriet Tubman. He also began work on what was to be his most famous series, the aforementioned *Migration of the Negro*. In it, ordinary Black Americans were the heroes. The paintings showed their hurried flight from Jim Crow oppressors by train, their hard work in Northern factories, and their encounter with the squalid conditions of the cities.

Thus an unlikely set of circumstances led to the flowering of one of America's greatest artistic talents. Growing up in economically troubled times and with the disadvantage of being Black in a still openly racist society, Lawrence might easily have been satisfied with the stable career in the post office that his mother had envisioned for him. But because of the beneficence of others—including teachers, artistic mentors, and in the case of the WPA, the federal government—he was able to choose the financially less certain path of the artist.[17] A critical factor in Lawrence's early growth, of course, was the artistic community that existed in Harlem during the 1930s. The friendships he developed with other artists at that time would last a lifetime, and it is likely that the nurturing he received from them shaped his views about teaching, mentoring, and the role of art in society.

INTO THE MAINSTREAM

During the 1940s new support systems would emerge for Lawrence's work. One breakthrough occurred when Harlem Renaissance proponent Alain Locke brought Lawrence's work to the attention of the well-known White dealer Edith Halpert.[18] As part of a plan to feature Black artists at mainstream venues, Halpert offered to show the artist's work at her Downtown Gallery. In joining this important New York institution, Lawrence became part of a vibrant group of artists that included Ben Shahn, Julian Levi, and Jack Levine.[19] Significantly, the gallery provided a venue for the display of the *Migration* series, which was eventually made the subject of a feature article in *Fortune* magazine. As a result of the publicity it earned from the Downtown gallery showing, this work was later acquired jointly by the Museum of Modern Art (MOMA) and the Phillips Collection.[20]

It is not surprising that the *Migration of the Negro* had great appeal for Black audiences and the Harlem milieu in particular. During an era when segregation was still firmly in place—when Hollywood relegated Black characters to the service quarters, and most textbooks ignored the accomplishments of African Americans— Black viewers thirsted for art that placed their heroes in the foreground. The need for a Black-focused art was not lost on Lawrence, who complained about the absence of Blacks from most history curricula. But for him the point was not just to learn about the past, but to spark change in the present. As he commented in 1940,

> I didn't [paint] just as a historical thing, but because I believe these things tie up with the Negro today. We don't have a physical slavery, but an economic slavery. If these people, who were so much worse off than the people today, could conquer their slavery, we can certainly do the same thing.[21]

Most likely, the artist had absorbed the lessons of Black Nationalism that were part of the time and place where he matured. The "New Negro" of Alain Locke's famous 1924 essay—one who would stand up to oppression and celebrate the accomplishments of his people—was very much on the minds of those who educated Lawrence.[22] Claude McKay especially, who worked side by side with Lawrence, must have impressed the young artist with his leftist-oriented writings that described the lives and struggles of ordinary African Americans. Beginning in the 1940s, Lawrence contributed directly to Black racial struggles, producing politically charged illustrations. In 1948, for example, he created an intense series of drawings for poet Langston Hughes' volume, *One Way Ticket,* which told of the oppression of Blacks under Jim Crow. He also illustrated a pair of *New Republic* articles on racial injustice in 1947 and 1948.[23]

But more often than not, Lawrence was simply reflecting his own experience as a Black person living in the United States. As he said, "any experience that evolves because of your ethnic background, and especially pertaining to the Negro . . . [adds] another kind of dimension to the work."[24] This direct reflection of lived experience is very consistent with the type of realism championed by Pierre Proudhon, which called for the representation of life: "In order to improve us, it [art] must first of all know us and in order to know us, it must see us as we are and not in some fantastic, reflected image which is no longer us."[25]

Given the subject matter of his paintings, then, it is easy to place Lawrence in the role of the socially conscious artist. Yet Lawrence's art was appreciated quite broadly, and often by those who had little interest in the "social" artist. Lawrence himself always resisted such a role, years later declining an invitation by President Carter to be honored along with nine other artists whose work had protested race discrimination. "I never use the term "protest" in connection with my paintings. They just deal with the social scene . . . they're how I feel about things."[26] Thus, Lawrence was wary of being labeled a propagandist and drew a distinction between art that merely reflected social conditions and that which promoted a particular political agenda.

As mentioned, Lawrence received critical support from the Museum of Modern Art, whose collections by and large reflected a different attitude about the purpose of art than the one expressed by Proudhon. MOMA tended to favor the type of "high modern" art made by abstractionists like Vassily Kandinsky and Kasmir Malevich (and later the abstract expressionists like Jackson Pollock and Mark Rothko), who embraced a kind of spiritual detachment in their work.[27] Another nineteenth-century critic, Charles Baudelaire, heralded this view with his ideas of "art for art's sake." For Baudelaire, true creativity resided in the imagination, and it was the artist's job to detach him/herself from the world: "I consider it useless and tedious to represent what *exists*, because nothing that *exists* satisfies me. Nature is ugly, and I prefer the monsters of my fancy to what is positively trivial."[28] Baudelaire could be quite contemptuous of the public and had little use for art that was connected to current social upheaval.

How, then, did Lawrence come to be appreciated in such wide circles—eventually earning the praise of both the NAACP and White establishment critics such as Hilton Kramer of the *New York Times?*[29] How did an institution like MOMA, whose collections had focused on the formalist language of abstraction, come to appreciate the universal appeal of his work? While they were certainly 'Black-focused,' Jacob Lawrence's paintings and prints were never narrow and propagandistic. As mentioned, his early works cast day-to-day life in Harlem not in the idealized mold of the previous generation but showed its blemishes—gambling, street crime, etc.[30] His migration series, too, showed the darker side of the Black exodus from the rural south: squalid, overcrowded conditions and class conflict between well-established Northern Blacks and their poorer Southern brothers and sisters.

Moreover, Lawrence's stylistic influences were quite broad. Through his training at the Harlem workshops, a stint at the American Artist's Workshop starting in 1937, and frequent trips to the downtown museums, Lawrence had been exposed to a vast spectrum of the art of his time. He counted among his influences the Mexican muralists and Polish realist Kathe Kollwitz; American modernists Arthur Dove and John Marin; European masters Giotto and Goya; as well as Harlem Renaissance pioneers such as Aaron Douglas and Augusta Savage.[31] With the interest in color, shape and pattern that is evident in his work, it is not surprising that Lawrence was invited by Josef Albers to teach at the cutting-edge Black Mountain College in 1946. Later, he would count the famous Bauhaus teacher as one of his influences as well, on his teaching as much as his painting.[32]

Furthermore, the subject of much of his work was not Black history in particular, but the world at large as seen through the eyes of a Black man. While serving on a Coast Guard ship during the Second World War, for example, Lawrence produced a set of works depicting life on the ship and the hardships of battle. After a bout of depression in 1950, Lawrence voluntarily checked in to Hillside Hospital in Queens, where he painted a very compelling series on the lives of the psychiatric patients there. In both cases, most of his subjects are White—but the style is the same as in the *Migration* series: attention to abstract shapes, rhythmic and lyrical use of color. His later work would tackle themes ranging from work (carpentry, sewing, theatre, libraries) to the tragedy of Hiroshima. Even his political illustrations owe as much to an expressive, realist tradition (encompassing such artists as Goya, Kathe Kollwitz and the Mexican Muralists) as they do to the Black-centered ideas they show. Thus, Lawrence might best be described as a humanist—an African American who reflected the tenor of his times, who looked closely at the world and depicted it with all of its blemishes but also with a sense of humor. On presenting the Spingarn medal to Lawrence at an NAACP award presentation in 1970, Bayard Rustin commented,

> I do not want to imply that the Negro artist should resemble in any way the social artist. The very concept of a social artist, an artist whose objective is to sell a cause or to sell a political party or even to sell capitalized Negroes, is a vulgarity and would be a misunderstanding of the nature of art and of the Negro struggle.[33]

Lawrence's contribution to racial uplift came more through the status of his work within the larger art world than through any specific messages contained within his paintings. The path that Lawrence took—raising the status of the Blacks through cultural accomplishments—was one that had been hewn years earlier by Lawrence's Harlem Renaissance mentors. The wider recognition gained by these artists and writers paved the way for an artist like Lawrence to be appreciated by MOMA and the *New York Times* as much as his African American audiences. With Lawrence's ascendancy, art that was unapologetically Black entered the inner sanctum of the avant-garde.

LATER CONTRIBUTIONS: ART AND ACTIVISM

By the 1960s, Lawrence had become part of the art establishment. His work had been purchased for MOMA's permanent collection, he had been featured in national magazines and he had received widespread critical acclaim. Just as he had been nurtured by a previous generation of African American artists and activists, Lawrence felt it important to contribute to the work of the next generation. When asked how his work related to the Civil Rights Movement that was then in progress, Lawrence had this to say:

> I think you can relate in any number of ways, and the individual artist has to solve it in his own way. He may participate through the content of his work, or by donating a piece that

has no specifically relevant content. I know that we all relate to the civil rights movement, and we all make contributions.[34]

In keeping with this idea, Lawrence continued to make art about Black struggles but also began to donate art to raise funds for Black organizations. These included the Schomburg Center for Research in Black Culture, the Northside Center for Child Development, the Amistad Research Center in New Orleans, and the NAACP Legal Defense Fund.[35] An example of Lawrence's politically relevant work from this time was his first solo exhibition at the Terry Dintenfass Gallery in New York. Held during the climax of the civil rights era struggles in 1963, this show included a series of works that dealt directly with the subjects of racism and protest. Among them was *Ordeal of Alice,* which, in a composition reminiscent of St. Sebastian paintings from the European masters, showed a young Black schoolgirl set upon by a crowd—pierced by arrow-like barbs that embody the racial taunts of the hideous figures behind her. Clearly, this image referred to the school desegregation struggles that were happening at the time. Another important piece was the poster image Lawrence created to publicize the show, *Two Rebels.* This work depicted a pair of African American protesters being carried off by baton-wielding policemen. Yet the majority of the works in the show were not about Civil Rights but everyday life experience—themes such as street scenes with children, libraries, and entertainment. In a sense, Lawrence's decision to include overtly political images in the show was all the more bold, given the fact that the exhibition was not specifically political—it was intended to appeal to a broad audience.

Lawrence made another important gesture when he visited Nigeria, once alone in 1963 and with his wife in 1964. During the latter trip, he created a series of marketplace scenes that documented the lives of ordinary Africans. Though the works had no overt political content, it was significant that he made his visits at a time when many African countries were just gaining their independence from the European colonial powers. As such, he was subjected to humiliating treatment by the U.S. State Department, which placed him under surveillance and often inhibited his passage. Apparently, the government could not decide whether his actions were subversive or helpful to Cold War aims. Going, as he did, with the American Society of African Culture (a group whose goal was to foster exchange between Africans and members of the African Diaspora)—suggested a certain sympathy with a Black Nationalist or pan-African agenda. Although this position was considered to be subversive by some in the U.S. government, Lawrence's trips were probably as helpful to U.S. foreign relations as they were to Black consciousness. The artist exhibited his *Migration of the Negro* series twice, once in Lagos and once in Ibadan. He also gave weekly workshops for Nigerian artists at the American Society of African Culture's center. This was exactly the type of cultural exchange that helped to promote the U.S. system over that of the Soviets. In the end, the State Department actually invited Lawrence to exhibit his work in its auditorium.[36]

Throughout the 1960s and into the 1970s, Lawrence continued to make works on the subject of civil rights and Black struggles for freedom. For example, he created a series of illustrations in 1967 for a children's book on Harriet Tubman—a new take on his earlier cycle from the 1930s. While some found these tame compared to other Black "protest art" from that time, the publisher of the book found at least one of the panels too troubling to print.[37] Based on a 1968 painting *Wounded Man*, which depicted a Black man with a gash on his abdomen (posed in the manner of Christ on the cross), Lawrence created a cover illustration for a 1969 issue of *Freedomways*, a magazine of the Methodist Student Movement. He also created illustrations of well-known civil rights leaders for *Time* magazine covers (e.g., Lieutenant Ojukwu of Biafra in 1968, Jesse Jackson in 1970, and Stokely Carmichael in an issue that was never published).[38] Lawrence returned once more to the civil rights theme in 1975 with his print entitled *Confrontation at the Bridge*, depicting Black protesters' encounter with police on the Edmond Pettus Bridge in Selma, Alabama.[39]

Also at this time, Lawrence formed the Rainbow Art Coalition along with artists Romare Bearden, Willem de Kooning, and Bill Caldwell. Begun in 1976, this organization was committed to nurturing the work of young printmakers and focused in particular on minority artists.[40] An organization like this one can be linked in its purpose to the types of community art programs in which Lawrence first received training in Harlem: a place that developed the talents of those who might ordinarily be overlooked.

Like the literary and artistic figures who preceded him in the Harlem Renaissance, Jacob Lawrence must have had a sense of his place in history—as a Black American who was fulfilling the role set forth by Alain Locke in the "New Negro":

> He now becomes a conscious contributor and lays aside the status of a beneficiary and ward for that of a collaborator and participant in American Civilization. The great social gain in this is the releasing of our talented group from the arid fields of controversy and debate to the productive fields of creative expression. The especially cultural recognition they win should in turn prove the key to any revaluation of the Negro which must precede or accompany further betterment of race relationships.[41]

That he thought extensively about his role and the effect that his art had is apparent from many of his public statements. On receiving the Spingarn Medal in 1970, for example, Lawrence acknowledged his debt to the community: "If I have achieved a degree of success as a creative artist, it is mainly due to the black experience, which is our heritage—an experience that gives inspiration, motivation, and stimulation.

We do not forget . . . that encouragement which came from the black community."[42] While the need to give thanks expressed here could easily be attributed to
acceptance-speech rhetoric, with Lawrence the notion of indebtedness to previous
generations was genuine and came out in other contexts as well. When asked, during the 1960s, how he felt about political art and, in particular, the pressure exert-
ed by his students to take a radical stance, Lawrence had this to say:

> What I found is that you could accept the health of this rebellion intellectually, but emo-
> tionally you couldn't. You want to tell these people, "Look, I've been through some things,
> too, and so have the people before my generation, and they're the ones who made it possi-
> ble for you to have this kind of protest."[43]

In exhorting young Blacks to "cool off" in this way, Lawrence revealed something
important about his thinking not just as an artist, but as a human being and member of the Black community: that he was truly aware of how much others had contributed their talents and hard work to him, and how much he had benefited from
it. This is consistent with the logic of philanthropy: each generation is expected to
give back to its community in order to honor the gifts given by the previous one.
The notion of "giving back" is particularly strong among African Americans, whose
earliest and most important philanthropies were founded on the notion of self-help.
These included mutual aid societies, in which newly-freed slaves received help
from those who already enjoyed their freedom, and the Black church, which was created as an alternative to White churches that were hostile to Black worshippers.[44]

CONCLUSION: ART AS BEQUEST

Art endures when it offers cultural significance beyond mere wall adornment.
What then, is the role of the artist in creating that significance? Is the artist a social
protester, holding up a mirror to society's ills, or a hermit, acquiring a transcendent
vision by withdrawing from society? Another way to think about the artist's role is
by comparing it to that of a philanthropist. The philanthropist is one who, given
many gifts (and especially those of the material sort), chooses to give back to the
community in which he or she was nurtured. Giving back requires a certain social
engagement. Artists play the role of philanthropists when, on a limited basis, they
open their ears and eyes to the concerns of the community around them—its pas-
sions, anxieties, and the sweep of its past. Having absorbed this information, they
can then utilize the full range of their talents to reflect what they see—hopefully
in the form of imaginative and personal works of art. As a young man, Jacob
Lawrence certainly did absorb the lessons of his community, observing the sights
and sounds of Harlem, the exhortations of its most renowned voices (Claude

McKay, Alain Locke, etc), and the stories of its past (the Underground Railroad, the great migration). By allowing society to influence the direction of his work, Lawrence came close to Proudhon's vision, as paraphrased by art historian Moshe Barasch: "Precisely because the painting or statue has such a great power of incitement, it is society as a whole, and not the individual, even if he is the artist, that must determine the subjects or uses of art." But there is a caveat here. Artists who follow this path risk becoming "popular artists," "social artists," or even "illustrators"—individuals who are tied to the time and place in which they live, whose audience is limited to those who have a direct knowledge of and concern for the subject matter they depict. Jacob Lawrence recognized this; in the end, it was by adhering to an original and personal vision, one that drew on the broadest range of influences and subjects, that he was able to avoid this pitfall. That Jacob Lawrence was able to pull this off—to reflect on the concerns of his day without making work that was clichéd or didactic—is a tribute to his genius. He was a socially conscious artist without a social agenda.

Of course, Jacob Lawrence was a philanthropist in the more conventional sense as well. In addition to the contributions of time and resources to the Black community that he made during his lifetime, he specified (along with his wife Gwendolyn) that a charitable foundation be created from his estate, committed to informing the public about his life's work and that of other African American artists. Among the goals of this foundation were to create a website that hosted a visual archive of Lawrence's oeuvre and provided educational materials that assist in classroom instruction on his art. Significantly, the philanthropic activities of the Jacob and Gwendolyn Lawrence foundation run parallel to those of Lawrence's own work: contributing to "American, and particularly African American art."[45] The idea that an artist works to make a contribution is a striking one given recent debates about his or her role in society. Modern society has suggested opposing roles for the artist: provocateur or revolutionary on the one hand; maker of rare, yet saleable commodities on the other. Neither of these poles is entirely satisfying. Artist as philanthropist, however (the role embodied by Jacob Lawrence's life), represents a middle point on this continuum. In this paradigm, the artist creates objects that have material value, but with the goal of leaving behind a legacy, not simply accumulating wealth. For those who wish to view art as something more than a commodity (as do many in contemporary art circles), viewing it as a bequest is a compelling alternative.

NOTES

1. Quoted in the Jacob Lawrence Foundation website, www.jacoblawrence.org, accessed 2 December 2002.

2. Quoted in James Huneker, *Pathos of Distance. A Book of a Thousand and One Moments* (New York: Charles Scribner's Sons, 1913), 128.

3. Suzi Gablick, *Has Modernism Failed?* (New York: Thames & Hudson, 1984), 30.

4. Pierre Joseph Proudhon, quoted in Moshe Barasch, *Modern Theories of Art* (New York: New York University Press, 1990), 1:333.

5. Leslie King-Hammond, "Inside-outside, Uptown-downtown: Jacob Lawrence and the Aesthetic Ethos of the Harlem Working-class Community," in Peter Nesbett and Michelle DuBois, eds., *Over the Line: The Art and Life of Jacob Lawrence* (Seattle: University of Washington Press, 2001), 68–73; Ellen Haskins Wheat, *Jacob Lawrence, American Painter*, 28–31.

6. David Driskell, "The Flowering of the Harlem Renaissance: The Art of Aaron Douglas, Meta Warrick Fuller, Palmer Hayden, and William H. Johnson," in Charles Miers, ed., *Harlem Renaissance: Art of Black America* (New York: Harry Abrams, 1994).

7. King-Hammond, "Inside-outside, Uptown-downtown," 70–71.

8. As part of the Roosevelt administration's Depression-era employment programs, the WPA gave commissions to numerous artists to create easel-sized or mural paintings. The WPA roster was a "who's who" of mid-twentieth century American artists and included Mark Rothko, Ben Shahn, Louise Nevelson, Stuart Davis and Jackson Pollock, among others.

9. Elizabeth Hutton Turner, "The Education of Jacob Lawrence," in Nesbett and DuBois, eds., *Over the Line: The Art and Life of Jacob Lawrence*, 99–100.

10. King-Hammond, "Inside-outside, Uptown-downtown," 77–78; Wheat, *Jacob Lawrence, American Painter*, 35–36.

11. Wheat, *Jacob Lawrence, American Painter*, 30–32.

12. Wheat, *Jacob Lawrence, American Painter*, 44.

13. Wheat, *Jacob Lawrence, American Painter*, 59.

14. For examples of McKay's writing, see the poems "If We Must Die" (1919) and "The Lynching" (1920); the essay "Soviet Russia and the Negro" (1923); and the novel *Home to Harlem* (1928).

15. Quoted in Wheat, *Jacob Lawrence, American Painter*, 59.

16. King-Hammond, "Inside-outside, Uptown-downtown," 70–73; Wheat, *Jacob Lawrence, American Painter*, 28–31.

17. Wheat, *Jacob Lawrence, American Painter*, 29.

18. A key figure of the Harlem Renaissance, Alain Locke (1886–1954) provided an intellectual blueprint for the emergence of a new and distinctive African American culture. These ideas appear prominently in his essay "The New Negro" (featured in the seminal collection of essays of the same name) which told of the appearance of a more assertive generation of Black Americans—young people who are aware of their history and celebrate it through visual art, music, and literature.

19. Carroll Greene, "Oral History Interview with Jacob Lawrence" (Washington, DC: Archives of American Art, Smithsonian Institution, 26 October 1968), 14; Wheat, *Jacob Lawrence, American Painter*, 63. Ben Shahn (1898–1969) was a pioneering American realist whose drawings and photographs highlighted the lives of people on the street. Julian Levi (1900–1982) and Jack Levine (1915) were two another highly acclaimed realists.

20. Greene, "Oral History Interview with Jacob Lawrence," 18.

21. Quoted in Patricia Hills, "Jacob Lawrence's Expressive Cubism," in Wheat, *Jacob Lawrence, American Painter*, 16.

22. Wheat, *Jacob Lawrence, American Painter*.

23. Wheat, *Jacob Lawrence, American Painter*, 74–76.

24. Greene, "Oral History Interview with Jacob Lawrence," 18.

25. Pierre Joseph Proudhon, quoted in Barasch, *Modern Theories of Art,* 333. Proudhon was an advocate of art based on observed experience rather than that which was fabricated in the studio. In much academic art from nineteenth-century France, artists chose to represent mythology or idealized pastoral scenes and ignore the world around them.

26. Wheat, *Jacob Lawrence, American Painter,* 114.

27. Gablick, *Has Modernism Failed?* 22.

28. Charles Baudelaire, quoted in Barasch, *Modern Theories of Art,* 369.

29. Wheat, *Jacob Lawrence, American Painter,* 146.

30. Greene, "Oral History Interview with Jacob Lawrence," 18–19.

31. Wheat, *Jacob Lawrence, American Painter,* 38; Greene, "Oral History Interview with Jacob Lawrence," 15.

32. Greene, "Oral History Interview with Jacob Lawrence," 16–17. The Bauhaus was a school of art founded in Germany in 1919. It embraced abstract art and a unified approach to design in which form followed function. Although the Bauhaus had a social agenda (unifying craft with modern industrial production, putting thoughtful design within the reach of the average worker), the spiritual detachment and focus on abstraction advocated by its teachers (including Vassily Kandinsky, Josef Albers, and others) precluded direct reference to social concerns. The Bauhaus continued until 1933, when the Nazis disbanded it, and many of its faculty (including Albers) fled to the United States. Black Mountain College in North Carolina, also an experimental school of art, operated in the late 1940s and early 1950s, and included many Bauhaus expatriates in its faculty.

33. Bayard Rustin, "The role of the artist in the freedom struggle," *Crisis* 77, no. 7 (August-September, 1970).

34. Patricia Hills, "Jacob Lawrence's Paintings During the Protest Years of the 1960s," in Nesbett and DuBois (Eds.), *Over the Line: The Art and Life of Jacob Lawrence,* 182.

35. Personal correspondence with Peter Nesbett, Executive Director, Jacob and Gwendolyn Lawrence Foundation, 14 November, 2002.

36. Hills, "Jacob Lawrence's Paintings," 182–3.

37. Hills, "Jacob Lawrence's Paintings," 187.

38. Wheat, *Jacob Lawrence, American Painter,* 141.

39. Hills, "Jacob Lawrence's Paintings," 187.

40. Jacob Lawrence Foundation Website, www.jacoblawrence.org, accessed 2 December, 2002.

41. Alain Locke, "The New Negro," in Alain Locke, ed., *The New Negro* (New York: Albert & Charles Boni, 1925), 15.

42. Quoted in Paul J. Karlstrom, "Jacob Lawrence: Modernism, Race and Community," in Nesbett and DuBois, eds., *Over the Line: The Art and Life of Jacob Lawrence,* 229; Text appears in *Crisis* magazine, vol. 77, no. 7 (August-September 1970): 266–7.

43. Wheat, *Jacob Lawrence, American Painter,* 113.

44. Marybeth Gasman and Sibby Anderson-Thompkins, *Fund Raising from Black College Alumni: Successful Strategies for Supporting Alma Mater* (New York: CASE Publications, 2003), 14–16.

45. Jacob and Gwendolyn Lawrence Foundation website, www.jacoblawrence.org, accessed 2 December, 2002; Peter Nesbett, foreword, in Nesbett and DuBois, Eds., *Over the Line: The Art and Life of Jacob Lawrence,* 7.

Bibliography and Suggested Reading List

"A Changing Palette. The Nation's Minority Population Is Reshaping the Nonprofit Landscape." *The Chronicle of Philanthropy* (January 10, 2002): 4–57.

Abbe, Ann M. "The Roots of Minority Giving. Understand the Philanthropic Traditions of Different Cultures to Solicit Them More Effectively." *Case Currents* (July/August 2000).

Allen, I. H. "A Comparative Study of Alumni Attitudes Toward Their Alma Mater at Selected Small Black Church-Related Colleges in Texas." Ph.D. diss., Kansas State University, 1981.

Anderson, James D. *The Education of Blacks in the South, 1860–1935.* Chapel Hill: University of North Carolina Press, 1988.

Anderson, Eric, and Alfred A. Moss, Jr. *Dangerous Donations: Northern Philanthropy and Southern Black Education, 1902–1930.* Columbia: University of Missouri Press, 1999.

Anft, Michael. "Nonprofit Leaders Urged to Seek Greater Support from Black Donors." *The Chronicle of Philanthropy* (May 31, 2001): 12–14.

Arnove, Robert F. ed. *Philanthropy and Cultural Imperialism: The Foundations at Home and Abroad.* Bloomington: Indiana University Press, 1980.

Baer, Hans A., and Merrill Singer. *African-American Religion in the Twentieth Century: Varieties of Protest and Accommodation.* Knoxville: University of Tennessee, 1992.

Barrett, Gregory T. "Institutional Culture, Life-cycle Issues and Other Factors: Issues That Selected Alumnae Who are Actively Involved in Spelman College Self-Report as Being Influential in Their Giving Decisions." *The CASE International Journal of Educational Advancement.* 2, no. 3 (2002): 259–279.

Beito, David T. "Mutual Aid, State Welfare, and Organized Charity: Fraternal Societies and the 'Deserving', 'Undeserving' Poor, 1900–1930." *Journal of Policy History.* 5, no. 4 (1993): 419–434.

Berry, Mary Francis. "Twentieth-Century Black Women in Education," *Journal of Negro Education.* 52, no. 3 (summer 1982): 288–300.

Boyce, S. M. "Fund Raising and Marketing Effectiveness at Historically Black Colleges and Universities." Ph.D. diss., State University of New York at Albany, 1992.

Browne, Robert S. "Developing Black Foundations: An Economic Response to Black Community Needs." *Black Scholar.* 9, no. 4 (1977): 25–28.

Burbridge, Lynn C. *Status of African Americans in Grantmaking Institutions.* Indianapolis: Center on Philanthropy, 1995.

Burnett, Alice Green. "Among Friends or Strangers?" *Philanthropy Matters.* 11, no. 2 (Fall 2001): 3–5.

———. "Giving Strength. Understanding Philanthropy in the Black Community," *Philanthropy Matters* 2, no. 1 (2001): 4–6.

———. "The Privilege to Ask: A Handbook for African American Fund-Raising Professionals. Atlanta: Interdenominational Theological Center, 2000.

Byrd, Alicia, ed. *Philanthropy and the Black Church.* Washington, D.C.: Council on Foundations, 1990.

Carlton-LaNey, Iris, Jill Hamilton, Dorothy Ruiz, and Sandra Alexander. "'Sitting with the Sick': African American Women's Philanthropy." *Affilia.* 16, no. 4 (winter 2001): 447–466.

Carson, Emmett D. *A Charitable Appeals Fact Book: How Black and White Americans Respond to Different Types of Fund-Raising Effort.* Washington, D.C.: Joint Center for Political Studies, 1989.

———. *A Hand Up: Black Philanthropy and Self-Help in America.* Washington, D.C.: Joint Center for Political and Economic Studies Press, 1993.

———. "Black Philanthropy: Shaping Tomorrow's Nonprofit Sector." *The NSFRE Journal.* (summer 1989): 23–31.

———. "Despite Long History, Black Philanthropy Gets Little Credit as 'Self-Help' Tool," *Focus* 15, no. 6: 3, 4, (June 1987): 76.

———. "Black Volunteers as Givers and Fundraisers." *Center for the Study of Philanthropy, Working Papers.* Graduate School and University Center, City University of New York, 1990.

———. "The Charitable Activities of Black Americans: A Portrait of Self-Help?" *Review of Black Political Economy.* 15, no. 2 (winter 1987): 100–111.

Collier-Thomas, Bettye. "The Impact of Black Women in Education: An Historical Overview." *Journal of Negro Education.* 51, no. 3 (1982): 173–180.

Collison, Michele. "The Changing Face of Philanthropy." *Black Issues in Higher Education.* 17, no. 7 (May 2000): 18–23.

Conley, Dalton. "The Racial Wealth Gap: Origins and Implications for Philanthropy in the African American Community." *Nonprofit and Voluntary Sector Quarterly.* 29 (December 2000): 530–540.

Council on Foundations. *Cultures of Caring: Philanthropy in Diverse American Communities.* Washington, DC: Council on Foundations, 1999.

Davis, King. *Fundraising in the Black Community: History, Feasibility, and Conflict.* Lanham, MD: Scarecrow Press, 1975.

Dillon, Patricia. "Clubwomen and Civic Activism: Willie Lowry and Tampa's Club Movement." *Florida Historical Quarterly.* 77, no. 4 (1999): 429–444.

Dozier, Richard Kevin. "Tuskegee: Booker T. Washington's Contribution to the Education of Black Architects." Ph.D. diss., University of Michigan, 1990.

Duran, Lisa. "Caring for Each Other: Philanthropy in Communities of Color." *Grassroots Fundraising Journal.* 20 (September-October 2001): 4–7.

Edmondson, Vickie Cox, and Archie Carroll. "Giving Back: An Examination of the Philanthropic Motivations, Orientations and Activities of Large Black-Owned Businesses." *Journal of Business Ethics.* 19, no. 2 (1999): 171–179.

Evans, Jeanette H. "A Study of the Attitudes of the Alumni of Historically Black Colleges and Universities Towards Financial Giving to Their Alma Maters." Ph.D. diss., Morgan State University, 1987.

Fairfax, Jean E. "Black Philanthropy: Its Heritage and Its Future." *New Directions for Philanthropic Fundraising.* 8 (summer 1995): 9–21.

Fisher, Mark A. "Developing Diversity." *CASE Currents* (April 1992) www.case.org/currents.

Fleming, Jacqueline. *Blacks in College.* San Francisco: Jossey-Bass, 1984.

Forum of Regional Associations of Grantmakers. "Baltimore Giving Project: African American Segment Research Findings." www.rag.org/promote/abagreport.html (2000).

Franklin, V. P. *Black Self-Determination: A History of African American Resistance.* New York: Lawrence Hill Books, 1992.

Frazier, E. Franklin. *Black Bourgeoisie.* New York: Free Press Paperbacks, Simon and Schuster, 1977.

———. *The Negro Church in America.* New York: Schocken Books, 1963.

Fluker, Walter. *They Looked for a City: A Comparative Analysis of the Ideal of Community in the Thought of Howard Thurman and Martin Luther King, Jr.* Lanham, MD: University of America Press, 1989.

Garibaldi, Antoine, ed. *Black Colleges and Universities: Challenges for the Future.* New York: Praeger, 1984.

Garrow, David. *Philanthropy and the Civil Rights Movement.* New York: Center for the Study of Philanthropy, 1987.

Gasman, Marybeth. "Charles S. Johnson and Johnnetta Cole: Successful Role Models for Fundraising at Historically Black Colleges and Universities." *The CASE International Journal of Educational Advancement.* 1, no. 3 (2001).

———. "Convincing Words: Fundraising Language Used by the United Negro College Fund in the Aftermath of the *Brown* Decision." *History of Education Quarterly.* 44, no. 1 (winter 2004).

———. "Sisters in Service: African American Sororities and the Philanthropic Support of Education." In *Women, Philanthropy, and Education,* edited by Andrea Walton (Bloomington: Indiana University Press, 2005).

———. "An Untapped Resource: Bringing African Americans into the College and University Giving Process." *The CASE International Journal of Educational Advancement* 2, no. 3 (2002): 280–292.

———. "W. E. B. Du Bois and Charles S. Johnson: Opposing Views on Philanthropic Support for Black Higher Education." *History of Education Quarterly.* 42, no. 4 (winter 2002).

———. "A Word for Every Occasion: Appeals by John D. Rockefeller, Jr. to White Donors on Behalf of the United Negro College Fund." *History of Higher Education Annual.* (2002).

Gasman, Marybeth, and Sibby Anderson-Thompkins. *Fund-Raising from Black College Alumni: Successful Strategies for Supporting Alma Mater.* Washington, D.C.: CASE Publications, 2003.

Gaston, Arthur G. *Green Power, The Successful Way of A.G. Gaston.* Birmingham: Southern University Press, 1968.

Gatewood, William B. *Aristocrats of Color: the Black Elite, 1925–1960.* Bloomington: Indiana University Press, 1990.

Goodson, Martia G., ed. *Chronicles of Faith: The Autobiography of Frederick D. Patterson.* Tuscaloosa, Alabama: The University of Alabama Press, 1991.

Gordon, Beverly. *Bazaars and Fair Ladies. The History of the American Fundraising Fair.* Knoxville: The University of Tennessee Press, 1998.

Graham, Lawrence Otis. *Our Kind of People: Inside America's Black Upper Class.* New York: HarperPerennial, 2000.

Griffin, Farah Jasmine. "'A Layin' on of Hands,': Organizational Efforts Among Black American Women, 1790–1930." *Sage: A Scholarly Journal on Black Women,* Supplement, (1988): 23–29.

Gumbs, Juliet. "African American Donors: An Untapped Resource." *Connections* 9 (winter 1998): 4–5.

Hall, Holly. "Black Giving Comes into Its Own." *Chronicle of Philanthropy*. 6 March 1997.

———. "When Black Donors Give, Many Feel Obligation to Help Other African Americans." *Chronicle on Philanthropy* 6 March1997.

Hall-Russell, Cheryl. *Rising to the Call: Evolving Philanthropic Trends in the African American Megachurch*. Indianapolis: Center on Philanthropy, 1999.

Hall-Russell, Cheryl, and Robert H. Kasberg. *African American Traditions of Giving and Serving: A Midwest Perspective*. Indianapolis: Indiana University Center on Philanthropy, 1997.

Harlan, Louis. *Booker T. Washington: The Wizard of Tuskegee*. New York: Oxford University Press, 1983.

———. "The Secret Life of Booker T. Washington." *The Journal of Southern History*. 37, no. 3 (1971): 393–416.

Height, Dorothy. *Open Wide the Freedom Gates*. New York: Public Affairs, 2003.

Henry, Tanu T. "Black Philanthropy," *Africana.com*, www.africana.com.

Higginbotham, Evelyn Brooks. *Righteous Discontent: The Women's Movement in the Black Baptist Church 1880–1920*. Cambridge: Harvard University Press, 1993.

Hine, Darlene Clark. *Hine Sight: Black Women and the Re-Construction of American History*. New York: Carlton Publishing, 1994.

Hine, Darlene Clark, Elsa Barkley Brown, and Rosalyn Terborg-Penn, eds., *Black Women in America: An Historical Encyclopedia: Volume I, A-L*. Indianapolis: Indiana University Press, 1993.

Hine, Darlene Clark, and Kathleen Thompson. *A Shining Thread of Hope: The History of Black Women in America*. New York: Broadway Books, 1998.

Holloman, Darryl, Marybeth Gasman, and Sibby Anderson-Thompkins. "Motivations for Philanthropic Giving in the African American Church: Implications for Black College Fundraising." *Journal of Research on Christian Education*. 12, no. 2 (fall 2003).

Hunt, Erika. *African American Philanthropy: A Legacy of Giving*. New York: 21st Century Foundation, 2001.

Hunter, Catrelia S., and Enid B. Jones. "A Study of the Relationship Between Alumni Giving and Selected Characteristics of Alumni Donors of Livingstone College, NC." *Journal of Black Studies* 29, no. 4 (March 1999): 523–540.

Institute of Church Administration and Management. "A Study on the Financing of the Historically Black Church." Lilly Foundation, Indianapolis, Indiana, 1998.

Jackson, Philip. "Black Charity in Progressive Era Chicago." *Social Service Review*. 52, no. 3 (1978): 400–417.

Jackson, Rodney, ed. *At the Crossroads: The Proceedings of the First National Conference on Black Philanthropy*. Oakton, Virginia: The Corporation for Philanthropy, Inc, 1998.

Jackson, Tysus. "Young African Americans: A New Generation of Giving Behavior." *International Journal of Nonprofit and Voluntary Sector Marketing*. 6 (September 2001): 243–253.

Jacobs, Claude F. "Benevolent Societies of New Orleans Blacks during the Late Nineteenth and Early Twentieth Centuries." *Louisiana History*. 29, no. 1 (1988): 21–33.

Jeavons, Thomas H. *Cultivating a Critical Compassion: Nurturing the Roots of Philanthropy*. Indianapolis: Center on Philanthropy, 1994.

Jones, Jacqueline. *Labor of Love, Labor of Sorrow*. New York: Vintage Books, 1995.

Joseph, James A. *Remaking America. How the Benevolent Traditions of Many Cultures Are Transforming Our National Life*. San Francisco: Jossey-Bass Publishers, 1995.

Leatherman, Courtney. "Black Colleges Step up Efforts to Win Alumni Gifts," *The Chronicle of Higher Education*. 25 October 1989.

Levine, Daniel. "Immigrant/Ethnic Mutual Aid Societies, 1880–1920: A Proposal for a Typology." *Essays on Philanthropy.* No. 18, Indiana University Center on Philanthropy, Indianapolis, Indiana, 1995.

Lincoln, Eric C. "All Niggers Have to Wait: A Child's First Lesson in Jim Crow." *The Journal of Blacks in Higher Education.* 11 (spring 1996).

———. *The Black Church since Frazier.* New York: Schocken Books, 1974.

———. *Coming Through the Fire: Surviving Race and Place in America.* Durham: Duke University Press, 1996.

Lincoln, Eric C., and Lawrence H. Mamiya. *The Black Church in the African American Experience.* North Carolina: Duke University Press, 1990.

Lomax, Pamela E. "Diversity Now!" *CASE Currents* (November/December 2000), www.case.org/currents.

Makechnie, George. *Howard Thurman: His Enduring Dream.* Boston: The Howard Thurman Center, Boston University, 1988.

Mehegan, Sean. "Black Colleges Find Diversity a Fundraising Challenge." *NonProfit Times* 8, no. 1 (October 1994).

Mjagkij, Nina, ed. *Organizing Black America: An Encyclopedia of African American Associations.* New York: Garland Publishing, Inc., 2001.

"Minority Homeowners Give More to Charity than Whites, Study Finds." *The Chronicle of Philanthropy.* 10 January 2002.

Musick, Marc A., John Wilson, and William B. Bynum, Jr. "Race and Formal Volunteering: The Differential Effects of Class and Religion." *Social Forces* 78, no. 4 (June 2000): 1539–1570.

Orosz, Joel, and Ricardo Millett. *Emerging Philanthropy in Communities of Color: A Report on Current Trends.* Battlecreek, Michigan: W.K. Kellogg Foundation, 1998.

Owens, Darryl, Sherry Owens, and Marilyn McCraven. "Giving Back." *Black Voice Quarterly* (2002): 21–22.

Parker, Marjorie. *A History of the Links, Incorporated.* Washington, D.C.: Links, Incorporated, 1982.

Pettey, Janice Gow. *Cultivating Diversity in Fundraising.* New York: Wiley & Sons, 2002.

Pollard, William L. *A Study of Black Self Help.* San Francisco: R and E Research Associates, 1978.

Pressley, Calvin. "Financial Contributions for the Kingdom for the Elect: Giving Patterns in the Black Church." *New Directions for Philanthropic Fundraising* (spring 1995): 91–100.

Rogers, Pier C., ed. "Philanthropy in Communities of Color: Traditions and Challenges." *ARNOVA Occasional Paper Series.* 1, no. 1 (2001).

Ross, Lawrence C. Jr. *The Divine Nine. The History of the African American Fraternities and Sororities.* New York: Kensington Publishing, 2000.

Rury, John. "Philanthropy, Self Help, and Social Control: The New York Manumission Society and Free Blacks, 1785–1810." *Phylon.* 46, no. 3 (1985): 231–241.

Scanlan, Joanne. *Cultures of Caring: Philanthropy in Diverse American Communities.* , D.C.: Council on Foundations, 1999.

Scott, Emmett J., and L. Stowe. *Booker T. Washington: Builder of a Civilization.* New York: Doubleday, Page & Company, 1918.

Scott, Lekita V. "A Description of Successful Fund-raising Units at Public Historically Black Colleges and Universities." Ph.D. diss., The Florida State University, 2001.

Scott, Spencer I. "Black Philanthropy in America." *Association of Fundraising Professionals.* 17 October 2002. www.afpnet.org.

Smith, Bradford, Sylvia Shue, Jennifer Lisa Vest, and Joseph Villarreal. *Philanthropy in Communities of Color.* Bloomington: Indiana University Press, 1999.

Stanfield, Stanfield. *Philanthropy and Jim Crow in American Social Science*. Westport, CT: Greenwood Press, 1985.

Sterling, Dorothy, ed. *We Are Your Sisters. Black Women in the Nineteenth Century*. New York: W.W. Norton & Company, 1984.

Ward, Andrew. *Dark Midnight When I Rise: The Story of the Jubilee Singers, Who Introduced the Word to the Music of Black America*. New York: Farrar, Straus and Giroux, 2000.

Washington, Booker T. *The Story of My Life and Work*. Atlanta: J.L. Nichols & Company, 1901.

———. *Up from Slavery*. New York: Doubleday, Page & Company, 1902.

Wenglinsky, Harold H. "The Educational Justification of Historically Black Colleges and Universities: A Policy Response to the U.S. Supreme Court." *Educational Evaluation and Policy Analysis*. 18, no. 1 (spring 1996): 91–103.

Wesley, Charles H. *The History of Alpha Phi Alpha: A Development in College Life*. Washington, D.C.: Howard University Press, 1957.

White, Deborah Gray. *Too Heavy a Load: Black Women in Defense of Themselves, 1894–1994*. New York: Norton & Company, 1999.

Williams, J. "Factors Related to Fund-raising Outcomes at United Negro College Fund Member Institutions." Ph.D. diss., University of Maryland, College Park, 1992.

Winters, Mary-Frances. "Reflections on Endowment Building in the African American Community." In *Cultures of Caring. Philanthropy in Diverse American Communities*. Washington, D.C.: Council on Foundation, 1999.

Contributors

Jayne Beilke—Dr. Beilke is an associate professor in the department of educational studies at Ball State University. Her research interests focus on African American education and philanthropy.

Michael Bieze—Michael Bieze recently received his Ph.D. in educational policy studies from Georgia State University. His dissertation examined Booker T. Washington's development of separate media identities for different audiences. He has been an art history consultant for Educational Testing and the College Board for many years in the Advanced Placement program. He teaches art history and studio art at Marist School in Atlanta where he is the fine arts department chair.

Fred H. Downs—Mr. Downs holds a bachelor's degree in nursing from Jacksonville State University in Jacksonville, Alabama, and a master's degree from the University of Alabama at Birmingham. He is currently a Ph.D. student in educational policy studies at Georgia State University. Additionally, Mr. Downs is an adjunct faculty member at the Rollins School of Pubic Health of Emory University, Atlanta, Georgia.

Noah D. Drezner—Mr. Drezner is a Ph.D. student at the University of Pennsylvania Graduate School of Education. His research focuses on philanthropy within higher education. Mr. Drezner decided to pursue graduate education after beginning his career as a development officer at his undergraduate alma mater.

Noah is an alumnus of the University of Rochester and University of Pennsylvania.

Edward M. Epstein—An artist and educator, Mr. Epstein lives in Philadelphia. He received his art degree from Yale and Indiana University. Mr. Epstein contributes regularly to *Art Papers* magazine and has authored numerous scholarly articles pertaining to the intersection of visual art and African American higher education. He has taught at Spelman College, Georgia Tech, Indiana University, and San Antonio College. Mr. Epstein currently runs an artist residency program designed to provide a new creative outlet to people living in his West Philadelphia neighborhood.

Marybeth Gasman—Dr. Gasman is an assistant professor in the Graduate School of Education at the University of Pennsylvania. She received her Ph.D. from Indiana University in higher education in 2000. In addition to numerous articles in scholarly journals, she is author of *Charles S. Johnson. Leadership behind the Veil in the Age of Jim Crow* (with Patrick J. Gilpin) and *Fund Raising from Black College Alumni: Successful Strategies for Supporting Alma Mater* (with Sibby Anderson-Thompkins).

Mark S. Giles—Dr. Giles earned his Ph.D. in higher education administration from Indiana University and serves as director of programs in the Office of Diversity, Equity, and Global Initiatives with the Association of American Colleges and Universities.

Nia Woods Haydel—Ms. Haydel is a Ph.D. candidate in the department of educational policy studies (higher education) and assistant director of student life and leadership for intercultural relations at Georgia State University. Her research interests include access and equity in higher education, the role of community-university partnerships, and the various elements of social justice. Ms. Haydel has published in the *Journal of Excellence in College Teaching*.

Darryl Holloman—Mr. Holloman is a Ph.D. student in educational policy studies at Georgia State University. He also serves as an assistant dean in the College of Arts and Sciences at Rutgers University. Mr. Holloman's research interests include African American history and African American male experiences as faculty and students.

Kijua Sanders-McMurtry—Ms. Sanders-McMurtry is a Ph.D. candidate in the department of educational policy studies with a concentration in higher education. She is an adjunct faculty member at Georgia State University and the Atlanta Technical College. Her research interests include African American philanthropy, African American history, and women's studies.

Marci Middleton—Ms. Middleton serves as the academic coordinator for program review at the University of Georgia Board of Regents. She is also a Ph.D. student in the educational policy studies department at Georgia State University.

Ms. Middleton's research interests include finance and policy issues related to higher education.

Jeffrey Mullins—Dr. Mullins was educated at Reed College and the Johns Hopkins University and is an assistant professor in the history department at St. Cloud State University. He has held fellowships from the Spencer, Pew, and Mellon Foundations and research appointments at Emory University's Center for Humanistic Inquiry and at the history of science department of the University of Oklahoma. Dr. Mullins is currently completing a book that uses a cross-racial murder trial to explore issues of racial identity, social reform, and human nature in antebellum America. In addition to this, Mullins is investigating African American engagements with nineteenth-century reform movements, particularly the American Colonization Society.

Katherine V. Sedgwick—Ms. Sedgwick is a Ph.D. student at the University of Pennsylvania. Her research interests include the history of higher education, in particular, pluralism, educational mission, and small liberal arts colleges. Ms. Sedgwick has published in the *Teacher and Teacher Education Journal*.

Index